D1539876

THE LAND OF MILK AND HONEY

a cooking book
an epicurean tour
of Israel

with
a history of foods in the Holy Land

THE LAND OF MILK
AND HONEY

a cooking book
an epicurean tour
of Israel

with
a history of foods in the Holy Land

by
Norton Locke

shley Publishing Co., Inc.
Fort Lauderdale, Florida 33319

THE LAND OF MILK AND HONEY.
Copyright ©1992 by Norton Locke.

Library of Congress CIP Number:90–40784
ISBN:0–87949–343–7

ASHLEY PUBLISHING COMPANY INC./Publishers
Fort Lauderdale, Florida 33319–3307

Printed In The United States of America
First Edition

Library of Congress Cataloging in Publication Data:

LOCKE, NORTON.
  The land of milk and honey : a cooking book : an epicurean tour of Israel : with a history of foods in the Holy Land / by Norton Locke.
    p.   cm.
  Includes bibliographical references and index.
  ISBN 0–87949–343–7
  1. Cookery, Israeli. 2. Cookery—Israel—history.
  I. Title.
  TX724.L59   90–40784
  641.595694—dc20   CIP

Dedication

To Peggy Jane Locke, my wife, who has been my support and motivation throughout our life together. The creation of this book is a result of that support.

Acknowledgements

Special thanks and appreciation are due to a number of people whose support of this project, and faith in the completion, played a major role in making it a reality. I gratefully acknowledge the assistance of the following:

A. The artist, Cantor Bruce Siegel, Milwaukee, for capturing the spirit of the theme and developing these works of beauty.

B. Alexandria Locke Shuval, a graduate of Bar-Ilan University, Tel-Aviv, Israel, for assistance in gathering and testing Israeli recipes.

C. Jonina L. Arazi, Givat Shmuel, Israel, for assistance in testing Middle Eastern recipes.

D. The Shvili family of Givitayim, Israel, for assistance in identifying herbs and spices of Israel, as well as Yemen foods.

E. Ziv Davis, M.D. and his wife Jackie, formerly of Tel-Aviv now of Chicago, who whet my appetite for Israeli cooking, and the spirit of the land.

F. Brother Herman Zaccarelli, Director H.R.I. Institute, Purdue University, who gave unselfishly of his time and efforts in my behalf, and allowed me the luxury of his thoughts.

G. Ira Hirschmann & Staff for performing the monumental task associated with the first cut and the reorganization of the work.

H. Rabbi Charles Shalman, Oklahoma City, who examined the work for clarity and correct Hebrew.

I. Rabbi David Nelson, Detroit (Oak Park), who believed in my concept and gave me tremendous support.

J. Kenneth Schrupp, Shawnee, who supplied moral support when I needed it.

I wish to express special thanks to those very great

friends who supported this project in the most unique fashion and gave of their time as well as fiscal support. These were the ones who showed extra enthusiasm, excitement and belief in the Land of Milk and Honey, a cooking book. Without these people this work would have died-a-borning. I thank them for their support:

1. Pat and Larry Bloomer, Oklahoma City, Oklahoma
2. The Goihl Family: John H., Mary Ann, Denise, Diane, David, Shakopee, Minnesota
3. Judy and Kenn Schrupp, Shawnee, Oklahoma
4. Harriett Marcus Locke, Rancho Bernado, California
5. Irma M. Cragun, Brainerd, Minnesota

Table of Contents

THE LAND OF MILK AND HONEY

a cooking book
an epicurean tour
of Israel

with
a history of foods in the Holy Land

Prologue

THE LAND OF MILK AND HONEY

"THE HERITAGE"

Canaan the land of the Israelites was an agricultural paradise. Agriculture was the spearhead of its economy; wheat & barley in the valleys, fruit trees of many kinds on the hills, animals grazing on the lower lands, tropical fruits and vegetables as well as herbs and spices in the Jordan Valley. (Deuteronomy 8:7,8,9,10) "Vines, and fig trees, and pomegranates, olive, and honey." Indeed, "a land which the Lord Thy God careth for."

Food preparations was basic, utensils were few. Jars for grain storage, crocks for water and cookery. Pottery bowls and saucers. Gourds for serving. Metal of iron and brass for pots used in cooking. Knives of flint or copper. Stone mills for grinding. Isaiah 7:14, 15 talks of "curds, bread and figs for food." Donkeys and oxen to pull the plow. Grain hand sewn and poked with a stick. The pace of the day was slow and life was simple.

Food and its preparation can be called a cornerstone of the Israelites. The full fabric has yet to be woven, but certainly the crosspollenization of the Sumerians, Akkadians, Sumers, Assyrians, Egyptians, Elams, Agadeans, Amorites, Babylonians, Hittites, Urartu, Scyths, Kassites, Anatolians, Greeks, Romans, all played a strong role in the creations of the foods of the Bible. Each of these people added spice, an herb, a cut of meat, a method of preparation, a grain, so that the flow of cuisine development created what today is known as Jewish or Middle Eastern food.

As trade developed so did the food. Yam (Potatoes of

11

Africa) made their way into Egypt, Canaan and Mycenaen (Greek) diets. Rome talks of the sweet potato.

The Indus Valley civilization fed cotton, barley, spice, gold and silver into Mesopotamia and Eastern Mediterranea.

And so we have it, the foods of the Land of Milk and Honey.

Introduction

Rabbi David Nelson
Congregation Beth Shalom
Oak Park, Michigan 48231

Rarely does a book faithfully deliver the promise of its title - but "The Land of Milk And Honey — A Cooking Book", (A taste of our Heritage), is that rare exception. Norton Locke has prepared a magnificent blend of historic and traditional Jewish cooking along with contemporary-mealtime delights to satisfy even the most demanding of appetites.

As a rabbi, I attempt to bring into the life of my congregants an awareness of the spiritual and cultural traditions of Judaism. It was surely a fact that the culinary customs and traditions of our people are of great significance in our lives. Norton Locke has captured that culinary tradition in his beautifully rendered work.

In the Talmudic tractate of YOMAH, 74b, we are advised: "If you have a fine meal, enjoy it in a good light." With the availability of this fine new cookbook, it will be possible to enjoy and savor many fine meals. By following its many varied and intriguing suggestions we are able to do what the Kabbalistic word, for ZOHAR, counsels: "Consider your table as a table before the lord: chew well and hurry not."

This volume could be well used by Jew or non-Jew alike. All that is required is a desire to taste and appreciate the rich culinary delights of the Judaic tradition. I know that this book will enrich the field of Jewish homemaking for all.

— Rabbi David A. Nelson

Hebrews carrying grapes
Jerusalem Seal

In The Beginning

History indicates that the first domesticated sheep were in the Iraq/Iran area in the period 9000/8000 B.C.E. at the site of the Zawi Chemi Shanidar. Wild goats and other small animals as well as wheat and barley fell into the overlapping domestication program. It is fairly safe to say that woman, in her role of seed gatherer, was responsible for the domestication of crops and animal. Man was the hunter and traveler and would not have had the time nor the notion as to seed selection, storage and planting. Beidha south of Jerico was reported as another site of domestication, as was Jerno in Kurdistan. Deh Luran (Dehloran) in Iran, was a major local for wheat culture and the development of the mutant hexapoloid wheat. Flax was the secondary crop of the same area.

In the period 5000 B.C.E./4000 B.C.E. great strides of development were taking place. Copper smelting, tool and bowl manufacturing, domesticating of animals for hitching to plow and sledge. With the invention of the wheel large loads could be moved over long distances with great ease. The development of the sail meant larger ships could be built and loads of merchandise could be transported around the then known world. Now excess crops and production could be sold and moved in commerce.

In Eridu, 4000 B.C.E./3500 B.C.E., man learned to work together in the construction and upkeep of the irrigation systems for the collective farms and the draining of the swamps. This was the first true example of community living, the start of towns.

Migrants of the farms from Mesopotamian fields were responsible for the introduction of plant and animal husbandry to western Europe. From here the information moved east and west into all lands.

THE LAND OF MILK AND HONEY

The Yangshao period of north China saw the growth of rice. These crops found their way into the Mid East via the trade routes of Arabia.

As the community of Eridu expanded it became necessary to grow more food on the farms, so it was also necessary to expand the irrigation system. As Eridu expanded, the population moved northward and founded a new city, Uruk. The need for houses created the craft of carpentry and metal smithing. Soon weavers and musicians were added to the fabric of the crafts, and community grew. Next came the towns of Ur, Lagash and Nippur. Cities and the city state were upon us.

With the complexity of managing large farms, and the evolution of trade, sales, and construction, written communication was the next natural step in development and stability of culture.

The plow (3000 B.C.E.) changed the entire scope of farming and allowed a complex form of agriculture to develop. Copper and iron plowshares (400 B.C.E.) simplified and improved farming methods. These same methods can be seen in the region today. Colters, plow cutters (10 B.C.E.) introduced by the Romans again changed the methods of farming and the field of cultivation.

A wall painting in the tomb of the Theban acropolis (15th century B.C.) during the reign of Thutmose IV, shows a detailed farming scene, wheat harvest in progress; cutting, binding and tabulation of yield. In the background of the painting can be seen the olive harvest.

Archeological digs have uncovered flint sickles, grindstones, mortars, and hoelike tools, as well as stone axes, testifying to the farming skills of the Natufians of Palestine/Canaan. These finds are similar to those of Honan and Kansu in China, as well as those of the Indus Civilization.

It is hard to remember when we look at the sand and deserts of today that this land was filled with forests and agriculture 3000 years ago.

A. Grissim — Grain

Wheat (Hittah) and Barley (Se'orah) had their domestic beginnings in the Zagros Mountains of Iran and Iraq, the Taurus mountains of Turkey and the Galilean uplands of Israel as well as in Phoenicia (Lebanon). Each area took wild Emmer and Einkorn grass and selected the best seed for planting. Dating indicates true farming of these grains date back some 8,000 years ago. The major produce produced was a flat bread of ground grains and water, cooked on a hot rock or flat stones by the fire. The Egyptians of the 5th dynasty (2600 B.C.E.) developed the beehive oven as well as selective leavened bread, followed soon after with the invention of the sieve. The sieve allowed a social distinction in bread, white bread for the kings and princes, and dark meal bread for the lower classes. Mureybat in Syria shows historic evidence of emmer milling and chaff crushing mills (Quarms).

B. Bread

Bread of the Bible (Exodus 29:2) speaks of the best bread, that of the semolina. Other Bible references do not specify bread as to it being barley, wheat, wheat semolina, rye, beans or any of the other milled items. We can assume that Solomon's ovens baked all types. "Bread of the first fruits" must have been (II Kings 4:42) of barley since it ripens and is harvested before wheat. II Kings 7:1, 16, 17, 18 also talks of bread (cakes) baked on hot stones. We can assume the cakes in the spring and early summer were barley cakes and late summer and fall were wheat cakes.

Early bread was flat bread and hard pancake made of barley flour, sesame seed flour and crushed onion, mixed with water and baked. This bread is still made and eaten in Iraq today.

The Israelites made a sour dough bread. The sour dough was a leaven. Later the yeast in the leaven was isolated and true yeast rising bread was the result. Now it was possible to make varying sizes and shapes of breads, not just the common flat bread. Flat breads, without leaven, were called MATZOT and those breads with leaven were called HAMETZ. Each of the various shaped breads had a specific name and use (Exodus 29:23,32) some for general use and others for consecration.

Bread (LEHEM) is a major part of the Festival of SHAVUOT: HAG HA-KATZIR, the festival of the grain harvest, celebrates the beginning of the barley harvest, it is the story of spring turning into summer. Symbolically, two loaves of fresh bread, made of newly harvested grain were taken to the Temple as an offering to God. The holiday is also celebrating the giving of the Torah to the Jewish people at Mt. Sinai. It could be called the birthday of the Jewish people.

Up to 70 C.E. the holiday was primarily a harvest festival. However, with the destruction of the Temple, the holiday changed to the celebration of the giving of the Torah. The major foods of the festival are BIKKURIM, the new fruits: grapes, figs, pomegranates, olive (oil), honey, wheat and barley. Dairy foods, including cheeses, creams, pies and cakes are usually eaten.

In Egypt the bread of the poor was made from Papyrus reeds and the bulrushes and sometimes even crushed lotus plants. It was reported by Herodotus, that this bread was good... but not as good as the Pharaoh's bakers made when mixing their dough with almonds, sweet herbs, honey, or fruits and spices.

Kikkar (Exodus 29:23) is the flat round loaf of the peasant that was baked on a stone next to the fire. This bread is still found today in any Arab market (fatteh). The kikkar is talked of in Ezekial 4:12. The bread is cooked in an oven and covered with the embers of the fire. Small wonder that "Ugah" of the bible was baked with "choice" fuel, rather than the dung fuel of the peasant.

"The Lord declared; I will grant you this new grain, —" Joel 2:18.

#1
Genesis Bread
"Rock Bread"

2 cups Barley flour
1 cup Sesame seed flour
1 cup Onion, grated
1 1/2 cups Water
1 tsp. Salt

Mix all together into thick past. Pat into balls. Press flat.
Put on dry griddle. Brown and turn. Brown and eat. This
must be eaten while warm. Can be toped with bean paste or
garlic spread.

In the ruins of Capernaum (Kefar Nahum) can be found
today the fully operational remains of a basalt flour mill that
produced the fine flour for the best breads and a huge oil-
press from the pre-Herod period.

"Eat thy bread with joy" (Ecclesiastes 9:7). It was during
the early Jewish period that panary fermentation was developed in the bread making procedures. This method was soon
adapted by the Greeks and Egyptians, and the race was on to
bake the lightest and largest breads and rolls.

Rakik, a thinner version of Ugah has come down to
modern times as the wafer or tea biscuit. Hubs, the Ugah of
Yemen, is baked today plastered on the side wall of the oven
as it was (Isaiah 44:19) 3000 years ago.

The gift of bread and "foods" was often offered as a sign of
friendship and of religious observance. "Forget not to show
love to strangers, for thereby some have entertained angels."
Abigail, wife of Nabal, (I Samuel 25:18) showed kindness to
the soldiers of David. "Then Abigail made haste, and took 200
loaves (of bread), and two skins of wine, and five sheep, and
five measurers of parched corn, and a hundred clusters of
raisins, and two hundred cakes of figs," and brought them to
David's camp. Ziba in II Samuel 16:1,2,3, did a similar act of

love by supplying bread, wine and raisins to the hungry. It should be noted that withholding bread from the poor or hungry was a sin (Job 22:7).

A bread of great strength building character was the austerity loaf, the Fitch Bread, "Take though also unto thee wheat, barley, and beans, and lentils, and millet, and fitches, and put them in one bowl, and make thee bread thereof." O.T. This bread was used during famine or siege as a major life support food.

#2
Fitch Bread

2 cups Hard Wheat Flour
1 cup Barley Flour
$^1/_4$ cup Beans, Ground smooth (Use limas or horse beans)
$^1/_4$ cup Lentils, ground smooth
$^1/_2$ cup Millet
$^1/_2$ cup Fitch
2 Eggs, beaten
2 cups Water
3 Tbsp. Oil
2 Tbsp. Honey
$^3/_4$ cup Beer

Mix all ingredients together, blend well. Turn out on floured surface and knead well for ten minutes. Cover with moist cloth and let rise one hour. Punch down and knead for five minutes. Form into a round loaf 7" at the bottom. Place on a sheet pan, cover and let rise one hour. Bake at 350 for 45 minutes. Don't expect this to be a high rising bread.

This loaf was a flat dense loaf very high in nutrition if not high in appearance. Of all the breads made, leavened was the desired loaf in all of the countries of the "Fertile Crescent". It was softer, looked better and most important ate easier due to the injection of air through the yeast actions process.

C. Beer

The Egyptians used beer as a leaven, as did the Iberians and Gauls. It didn't take long for the entire area to find out that beer produced a lighter bread. This leaven was easy to acquire since beer was a major drink when grapes were not available. Beer was made of Barley and water. In Egypt beer was the major beverage as water was mostly unpotable and and unreliable source of intake liquid. The national food of this period was roast goose and beer. Today in both Israel and Egypt goose is a very popular food item and is cooked on most holidays and festivals.

According to the ancients, beer (Bira) was the reason that Dionysus fled from Mesopotamia and returned to Greece. It is reported that it was because of local addiction to barley ale that "he fled the poor influence." Records indicate that up to 40 percent of the Sumerian grain crop went into beer production.

In Sumer the temple workmen were issued a daily ration of beer. The local breweries produced eight different types of beer from barley, and made three types of beer from mixed grains. Other beers and ale were made from wheat. Some of the beers were spiced and had the flavors of herbs.

The Egyptian breweries made many spiced beer (Haq); some very strong and others quite mild. They also produced a series of beer breads. In the period circa 1750 B.C.E., the Hammurabi code talks of ale houses and their overpriced weak beer.

D. "CAKES"

Under Cyrus of Persia, 539 B.C.E., the people of Israel were allowed to return home. They brought with them many new dishes to add to their native ones. These new dishes included many sweet cakes and cookies. An Egyptian painting of 1175 B.C.E. shows the court bakery of Rameses III at Thebes. Here can be seen many kinds of cakes and breads, some baked and some fried. Of great interest are the cakes in the shape of animals which the poor people would buy to be used when they would sacrifice. Animal breads were used as a surrogate when the people could not afford the real animal.

The Greek writer Aristophanes talks of the variety of baked goods (400 B.C.E.), some for Festivals and some for daily use. One such bread was the fritter called Encris, which was buckweat flour, olive oil and honey. A fried cake, Dispyrus, was cooked then dipped in wine and eaten warm. Obolios were fried between two pieces of hot iron, these were the ancestors of today's waffles. They were called "Iron Cakes" (Ugiyot - Vaflim).

The Romans made "Dulciarius" — confections like a flat cheese cake. These cakes were found in all seaport towns in Egypt, Israel, Jordan and Greece. The Roman bakers belonged to a Pastillarium — trade union. While the Romans were developing their "fancy" bakery procedures, the Chinese were developing their rice flour baking with the development of rice fritters and soya flour cakes filled with sugar and rose preserves, and some with bean paste and others with meat. The Chinese baked goods found their way into the mideast via the Arabian trade routes.

Honey Cake was probably the first sweet cake produced in all of the lands. Made in various shapes and sizes, it was for sacrifice as well as home use. Some of the Honey Cakes were flavoured with Anice and some with Cinnamon. Honey Cake held well so it was often taken on long journeys via land or sea.

Many interesting items were developed for sea use. Piscot was one of those items. Piscot was wheaten bread, sliced and dried, used as ship biscuits served with fruit compote. This item most probably developed into "Biscoct" and later "Bisquit" or Hard Tack.

In 1 Kings 19:6, Elijah ate "a cake baked on hot stones, and a cruse of water." Pie Baking can be traced to the early Greeks where it quickly spread throughout the countries of the Mediterranean. Lamb and Goat pies were the original, then came fruit pies and soon after with bird pies... "Four and twenty blackbirds baked in a pie..." It was the Romans who developed the bird pie into the full blown art that was found at the table of royalty. These pies had the dough put into a frame for support, be it a hollow rock, a deep dish or clay mould.

Diphilus of Sinope, the principal poet of Athenian Comedy, in Athenaeus III, said, "bread made of wheat is more nourishing and digestible than that made of barley." Bread was the early catch all name for all baked goods and included, cakes, pastries, cookies, breads, rolls, matzot, pan breads.

With the advent of the Hellenization attempts in Israel many of the coastal areas joined in the race to produce fancy baking for use in hospitality functions separate from the religious events. Here we see the development of the personal banquets and the house party that was limited to the lucky numbers of four people, seven people and eleven people. A great many Greek and Roman writers of the period wrote of these parties.

The spirit of the party swept the total area and found itself well implanted in the Fertile Crescent, in fact history reports that NEBUCHADNEZZAR was not want for banquets of fine food and drink. On special occasions cakes and pastries were made with honey, boiled fruits, pressed and dried fruits. Sugar as we know it today was unknown in the Middle East during the Biblical Period. (See Sugar section) Confections were made of honeys, dates, almonds, pistachio nuts, sesame seeds, poppy seeds and gum arabic. Some sweets were baked in cake flour and some were rolled in crushed nuts.

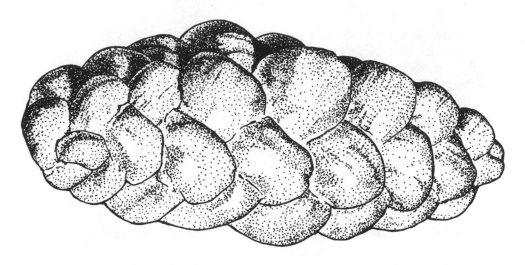

Bread — Challa

E. Banquets

When the kings ate (I Kings 5:2, 3, 4, 7, 8) everyone ate. The banquets were attended by the multitudes in the area, high and low. The quantities and variety of foods was a sight for all eyes. The king's table was the focal point for all political affairs and the major social event of the season of the year. Naturally the Harvest Banquets were far more lavish with a wider variety of fresh foods than the winter or spring holidays. Bakery goods were varied and bountiful.

Josephus wrote of Herod, King of Judea and his wife Mariamne, that their parties were of major importance. Masada, and the Northern Palace hosted many parties. A typical menu was Pine Nut soup, (Tyche soup) Roast gazelle and buck, duck and goose, vegetables of many variety's, dates and figs in sugar and syrup, drink of pomegranate juice and breads of many kinds. Josephus (Joseph ben Mattathias) was a military leader and historian of the period 37 CE to 105 CE. The son of a priestly family, educated in the Pharisees schools. He was considered a traitor when he surrendered the town of Jotapata to Vespasian. His historical works History of the Jewish Wars, Antiquities of the Jews, Against Apion, and Vita, were the only source of Jewish history for this period to survive to modern times, and thus have become the basis for all knowledge of the period. Thackeroy's translation of the Jewish War was of great importance to the research of this work, as was Josephus' autobiography.

Banquets of the Antiochus period would usually consist of seven courses: Hors d'oeuvres, gustatio • 3 entrees of fish, fowl, vegetable mixed with fruit • 2 roasts of lamb and animal of the field (venison) • Desserts, figs and date cakes • Custards, dormice rolled in honey and poppy seeds • Damson plumbs in pomegranate seeds • After the meat course Mulsum, a honey wine was served. Music played on the harp was the background. Agrippa and Gaius Caligua lead a wild and feast filled life in the Galilee. Parties and feasts were the way of life. Agrippa was poisoned while eating at the "games" in Caesarea.

Amos 5:21,22 speaks of the feasts and indulgence of the Israelites. Most of the strict religious groups were not in favor of the many feasts and dances being held in the name of religion. Rabbi Judah (Judah I) and Emperor Marcus Aurelius had many meetings and interviews which took place at sumptuous banquets which these men gave for each other. No record of the menu comes down to us, but we can assume that the foods were full and varied, if "Apicius de re Coquinaria," the first full cookbook is any basis. "Coquinaria" was written by a Roman chef in the Imperial period. M. Gabius Apicius, the chef, lived 80 B.C./40 B.C. His book Apicii Caelii... Coqulnaeia, was reprinted by G. Humelbergius in Zurich, in the year 1542, later Martini Lister of London (1705) translated the complete work, with commentary. It is reported that the Vatican Library has an original copy.

Apicus reportedly killed himself when his standard of living was reduced to the princely level when some investments turned bad. His annual income was reported to be a half ton of gold. Apicius used many sauces, usually thickened with wheat starch and spiced with a wide variety of herbs and spices. One major spicing product was "liquamen," a fermented and salted fish sauce. This same fish sauce was found in Greece, Rome, Canaan, Egypt, China, India and was used by the Israelites.

A number of the Roman cities, Leptis, Pompeii, Magne, to name some, had factories to make liquamen. These cities bottled the sauce for export. These sauces were very important to the food chain since they are very nutritional, containing high levels of vitamins and trace minerals.

Sweets play a very important part in "Jewish Cuisine." Since the earliest of times cakes and sweets were part of the holiday and festival celebration. The bible speaks often of the cakes and sweets as part of the "special" feasts. Since the earliest of history in Egypt, Greece, Rome and Israel the sweet table was the highlight of the banquet.

#3
SOUFGANIOT - POUNCHIKOT
DONUTS (Doughnuts)

$2/3$ cup Sour Milk
$1/2$ cup Sugar
2 Eggs, beaten
2 Tbsp. Butter, soften
$3/4$ tsp. Salt
1 tsp. Baking soda
$3/4$ tsp. Nutmeg powder
$1/4$ tsp. Cinnamon powder
$2^1/2$ cups A.P. Flour
1 cups Jam (Flavor of your choice)

Blend all ingredients except jam, add additional flour as needed to make a stiff dough, set aside and let rise one hour. On a floured board roll out 3/4" thick. Cut with a donut cutter, or a glass depending on if you want the thick stuffed donut or the more modern one with a hole in the center. Some of the countries roll the dough into 3/4" ropes, 5" long, tied into loose knot. Deep fry in hot oil 425'. Cover pot and brown on each side. Remove to paper blotter. With pastry tube poke hole in side of the donut and fill with jam. Can be dusted with powder sugar or frosted.

Note: Some cooks like a very light consistency, so you may eliminate the baking powder and substitute one cake of yeast. In the olden days beer was used to lift dough.

#4
Lehem Egozim Tamarim
Fruit Bread

1 cup Oil (Wesson or corn oil)
3 Eggs
2 cups Sugar
2 tsp. Vanilla extract
2 cups Zucchini, shredded, unpeeled
1 cup Dates, chopped
1 cup Figs, chopped
1 cup Nuts, chopped (Pine Nuts and Walnuts are best)
2 tsp. Baking Soda
$^1/_4$ tsp. Baking Powder
1 tsp. Salt
1 $^1/_2$ tsp. Cinnamon
$^3/_4$ tsp. Nutmeg
$^1/_4$ cup Cold water

Beat eggs, oil, sugar and vanilla until thick. Stir in all remaining ingredients a little at a time, alternating a little of each until all is used up. Pour into a well greased, floured loaf pan. Bake at 350° for one hour. Turn out to cool. slice and serve with tossed salad as a light lunch. This type of meal was very typical of a meal served around Like Kinneret during the Biblical period. Grain, fruit, nuts and spices were easily obtainable, and the breads became of great importance for trade and personal table use. This was a very healthful meal, full of the nutritional building blocks so vital to good body growth. Hallot Lehem (Todat Shelmov) Leviticus 7.14, "cakes of leavened bread given as acknowledgement of peace."

In 330 B.C. Archestratus the poet, wrote "Hedpathia, Hesiod of the Gourmets," an account of the gastronomical customs in the middle east, and contained considerable information about the foods of Lebanon, Israel and Egypt. This book was translated from the Greek into Latin by Ennius the Roman, under the title "Hedipathetica." During the same period, Temachidas of Rhodes, wrote a number of gastronomy works under the common title of "Suppers Descriptions." Athenaeus, who wrote "Doctors at Dinner," listed a number of culinary arts authors in the work, to name a few; Euthydemus, Archytas, Mitreas, Locris, and Dionysius. Unfortunately, all of the latter authors works were lost in the destruction of the great Library of Alexandria in the 7th century A.D.

In the early Greco-Roman period, the craft of chef was elevated to new heights with the establishment of a two year culinary school where the art of cooking and food preparation was taught. Upon completion, a very difficult examination was given. Those who completed the examination received a certification as chef, and commanded large wages. Kodamus, founder of Thebes, completed such a school and worked as a cook at the Palace of Sidon, before going to Thebes. Some of the graduates of the Cooks School were, Aghis of Rhodes, Aphtonites, Chariades of Athens, and Nereus of Chios. Each of these chefs specialized in a particular food presentation, be it fish, vegetable, venison or dessert. Once such recipe known to have been eaten by Alexander the Great is Fried Lamb Liver.

#5
Fried Lamb Liver

1 ¹/₂ lb. Lamb Liver, cut 1" cubes
¹/₂ cup. Virgin Olive Oil
1 tsp. Salt
¹/₂ tsp. Pepper
1 tsp. Oregano, dried, crumbled
2 Tbsp. Parsley, chopped
2 Lemons, juiced

Heat oil in fry pan, add liver and sauté for five minutes. Add all except parsley and mix well. Sauté 7-10 minutes (check for done). Add parsley, mix well. Serve with rice or Burghul.

At the winter Palace, Masada, "King Herod gave great care to the improvement of the place after the high priest Jonathan completed his work — for the plateau was rich in soil and was more workable than any plain, and the King reserved it for the cultivation of food — he cut out of the rock numbers of great tanks to hold water — and stores of food including great quantities of corn, wine, oil, pulse of all varieties and dates in great heaps." (O.T.)

In the Greco-Roman Museum in Alexandria, Egypt, you can clearly see a floor mosaic showing a family eating while begin entertained by musicians, and off to the side people fishing. In downtown Alexandria is located the complete remains of a Roman Theatre equipped with a full dining room for the use of the Princes and Roman Legion commanders.

Food and food related materials are in high evidence throughout the early Egyptian religious writings. In the Desheri at Saqqara, a funerary chamber contains on the North and South walls, lists of foods, breads, beer, meat, poultry, as well as pots and pans needed for the after life. Jars and bottles were specifically identified containing these foods. Jar handles were engraved with the name of the food item.

The colors and art work are still clear and vivid. The Mastaba of Neferma'et has a high base relief at the entrance, with vivid picture groups featuring geese, lambs, goats, ducks, peacocks, turkeys, sheep, figs, grapes, dates, rolls and breads. All itemized as to the specific quantities being donated to the prince and contained in his tomb. The peacock was an important gala banquet item during this period, but in later periods the peacock was used as an artistic representation of Jesus, and not as food. The hunting and fishing scenes are found in great abundance throughout the old kingdom and well into the middle of the Joint Kingdom periods of Greco-Roman influence. A painted limestone False-door in the Tomb of Ankhires, overseer of the works of the king, enumerates the offerings to be partaken of in the afterlife — over 100 foods and drinks in picture form. Some difficult to identify but generally we are looking at all the foods known to man during this period.

The Egyptian agricultural economy of the later Dynasty (600 BC onward) was based on a system of canals and water lift stations (Shadoofs) and water wheels (Sakiehs) run by either oxen or "happy and content slaves" walking the wheel spokes - even today one can see the poor native repeating the process of 3000 years ago. It is of great interest as you travel the countryside to see an ancient water system miles away from the nearest water of today. It is quite obvious even to the untrained eye, that hundreds of miles of water ways and lift stations have been lost to the advancing and shifting sands of the desert and lack of maintenance and general upkeep. In watching the lift stations at work one can observe that without extra care the clay jars of the Sakieh are broken and must be replaced. Fortunately the local clay is the source for making new jars. The problem is of time to remanufacture, not of cost. This same lift system can be seen in the more remote areas of Israel.

As you tour the "out back" regions of Egypt it is hard to believe, based on what you can see today, that up to about

5000 BC the land was heavily forested and supported a huge animal population of diverse breeds. Through the lack of care and knowledge the area was denuded as a source of cheap fuel and quick construction. During the Pleistocene era the country was subtropical and had many lakes and streams, covered with small animals and birds. As the trees and shrubs disappeared the weather became dryer and wild life died out, and then the land died and turned to sand and arid desert. The modern Egyptian has little desire to reclaim the desert as have the Israeli. In Israel you will see hundreds upon hundreds of miles of reclaimed desert yielding all sorts of diverse crops, plants and trees. Perhaps some day soon with the development of a new middle class there will be a desire to work for the total good of the country and its hungry masses throughout Egypt. So far however the Egyptian government has refused the offered assistance of the Israelis to teach them the methods for reclaiming the land.

During the Masada siege it can well be assumed from historic evidence that Eleazar ben Ya'ir, the warrior chief and his co-defenders at the austerity breads as well as roasted nuts, as part of the daily diet. The ramparts and walls contained a variety of vegetable gardens and fruit trees watered from the cisterns.

#6
Roasted Nuts

1 lb. Almonds, shelled
¹/₂ lb. Pistachio, shelled
¹/₄ lb. Pignolia, shelled
¹/₄ lb. Walnuts, shelled
1 Tbsp. Olive Oil
3 Tbsp. Course Salt
1 Egg White beaten

In deep fry pan heat oil and add nuts, stir often. When nuts are nicely warm inside, turn heat up and brown the nuts on all sides. When golden brown turn into a bowl and add egg white, coat nuts well, add salt, mix and turn out on flat surface. Spread out to dry. Add more salt if desired. Eat as adjunct to salad or as health snack.

As we examine the foods of Israel we see that for every food there is a blessing, and for every holiday there is a food. The interrelations of food to God and God to food can best be exemplified in Leviticus 2:1-4, "and when thou bringest a meal offering baked in the oven, it shall be unleavened cakes of fine flour mingled with oil, —" for that matter the full chapter expounds on the foods, and reflects that the left over foods shall be eaten by Aaron and his sons, the priests. Here we see fully how the foods and procedures became part and parcel of the people along with the blessings and prayers of the foods, this is the blending of the fabric which is the people of Israel. In Deuteronomy 8:6-10, the Jews are told that if they keep the laws and commandments of "the Lord Thy God," to walk in the ways, and to fear Him, "they will have all types of foods produced on the good lands, and in great quantity." Again we see food and the religion co-mingle one into another.

F. The Craft Developed

Early Greece took the basics of bread making and perfected mixed breads, spice breads, and assorted specialty breads that can be found described in ATHENAEUS's writing titled "DEIPNOSOPHISTAI." Later Roman soldiers captured Greek bakers and took them to Rome where they practiced their art. True commercial baking developed in Rome with the invention of the hourglass mill — thus milling and baking developed side by side. By 500 B.C.E. the Romans had established army type field kitchens and bakeries. 300 years later they had the wheels of the welfare state well greased (Annona System) and in 125/123 B.C.E. the bread dole and free circuses were the way of life throughout the Empire. Rome set up Mill/Bakeries in each neighborhood of

2,000 inhabitants. In the larger metropolitan areas the bakeries worked round the clock to produce bread and rolls for the people.

"MORETUM"

The poet Virgil gave the recipe for one early bread "Moretum" in one of his writings. This round unleavened bread was baked in the oven and when well browned was coated with olive oil and vinegar, then covered with raw onions and sliced garlic, and eaten while still hot. A derivation of the basic recipe was later enhanced with yeast. This same bread later became the Italian Schiacciata, which found it's way into Israel with the Roman Legions. This same bread developed in Naples under the name Lagano or Laganum. Schiacciata cut into strips and added to soup or stew was the early Tagliatelle which was called Farfel in Jewish cooking.

The early Moretum was often mixed with chopped olives or honey and chopped pine nuts and baked. Later called Torta Rustica this bread developed into the bakery delight called Panettone which can be found throughout the area today. Horace the Roman poet, spoke of his favorite Lagano being added to soups and stews. Horace, according to his writings, loved food and drink.

#7
Moretum

TOPPING
$^1/_4$ Cup Olive oil (fine Virgin)
6 Toes Garlic (cut thin)
$^1/_4$ tsp. Salt
$^1/_8$ tsp. Pepper

BREAD DOUGH
6 $^1/_4$ Cups Bread flour
1 tsp. Salt

2 pkg. Dry Yeast
¹/₂ Cup warm water
1 ¹/₂ Cups tepid water
¹/₄ Cup Olive oil

Blend warm water and yeast, let set ten minutes. Blend in 1½ cups flour. Cover and let set 1 hour. Blend in all other ingredients. Turn out onto lightly floured surface and knead with the palm and heel of the hand. Push firmly with the heel of the hand to blend well, and force out the air bubbles. The dough should be smooth and elastic. Cover with a clean dry cloth and let rise 30 minutes. Cut with a sharp knife into six equal portions. Roll into smooth balls, cover again and let rise 2 hours. Press each ball into 1/8" thick circle. Place into 400° oven for 10 minutes, coat with olive oil and toppings, eat hot.

From Rome the improved bread art form spread back throughout the barbarian lands east and north. Bread and baking were here to stay, as a matter of fact the art has changed very little in the basics in the past 2000 years. The ovens have become more sophisticated but the principles remain as they were at the height of Roman baking, when they produced 61 different varieties of bread.

RECIPES OF THE BIBLE

Cereal grains are part of the grass family. They are raised for their starch seeds. The most common cereals of history are: Wheat, Barley, Oats, Rice, Corn, Rye, Millet, Maize, Sorghum and Flax.

Grain storage houses were found in many of the Tell's, excavated ruins, throughout Egypt, Israel, Lebanon, Jordan and Iraq. They show traces of the two major grains, Wheat and Barley.

Most of the early grains had to be lightly toasted before they could be threshed and ground. Later with the development of the hybrid grains with more gluten, this was no longer necessary.

TYPICAL FOODS

Parched grain (roast ears of corn) was a major food of yesterday and is still enjoyed today. A Biblical lunch was roasted ears, bread and sour wine (Ruth 2:14). Pulse, (Legumes) can be shown as the second most used food. Pulse or dals, would be beans and lentils, followed by other members of the bean and pea families.

Lentil (Adashim) Pottage is still prepared today in Syria and Yemen as it was then. Horse beans, Fava, (Ezekiel 4:9) were used to make cholent, and sometimes, bread. Chicory and endive, the bitter herbs of Passover; and mustard greens, radishes and cucumbers were the main dinner vegetables. Vegetables were often eaten alone, but on good days some meat was added. Olives were not only eaten as a relish, they were often eaten as a main dish with cheese. Figs were dried for winter fruit and eaten fresh from the trees as a summer fruit.

Stuffed vine leaves of many varieties were eaten under various names: Dolma, ma'Amoul, Kahk.

#8
WARAK INAB MAHSHI — ALAY GEFEN
STUFFED LEAVES

1 lb. Chopped Lamb or Goat
3 Onions, minced
1 cup Rice, raw
$1/2$ tsp. Salt
$1/2$ tsp. Pepper
2 Tbsp. Mint, chopped fine
24 Grape leaves
1 cup Water
2 Tbsp. Oil
$3/4$ cup Vegetable stock, liquid (retain for pot)

Mix all but leaves, blend well and set aside. Dip leaves in boiling water till tender. Lay leaves out flat and trim off stems. Place tablespoon of mixture on leaf. Roll up tightly and tuck in ends. Place in greased dish. Place weight on top of rolls to keep them in place. Pour vegetable stock in. Cover tightly and steam slowly for 1½ hours. Add water if required.

#9
YAMS AND APRICOTS

6 Yams, peeled, cut 1/2
12 Apricots, remove pits, cut 1/2
1 cup Water
1 tsp. Cinnamon

Place all together, mix well. Place in covered dish and bake slowly for two hours. When just cool, serve as a relish with stuffed leaves.

Job 23:5 "— they go forth to their work, seeking diligently for food."

#10
OF MEUDE
AMULATUM ALITER
CHICKEN STEW

1 4 lb. Chicken, well cleaned, disjointed and boned
4 Leeks
2 heads Dill, fresh, chopped course
¹/₂ tsp. Salt
¹/₂ tsp. Pepper, fine grind
¹/₂ tsp. Celery seed
¹/₂ cup Rice, par boiled
¹/₂ cup Raisin wine
1 cup Water (boil bones for 20 minutes,
*   remove bones, strain)*

Place chicken, leeks, dill, salt, water in a covered pot and simmer slowly for 1/2 hour. Add all remaining ingredients, cover and simmer 1/2 hour. Mix well and serve with warm bread.

#11
BETACEOS VARRONIS
PARSNIP STEW

8 Parsnips or Oysterplant, cleaned
3 cups Mead
$^1/_2$ tsp. Olive oil
1 Chicken, cleaned, cut up

Trim parsnips, cut into 1/4's, place all but chicken in covered pot and simmer 1/2 hour, add chicken, simmer 1 hour. Serve with warm bread and green salad.

Deut. 8:3 "Man may live (eat) on anything that the Lord decrees."

#12
LIVER SAUSAGE

2 lb. Liver. Skin and veins removed. (Lamb or Goat)
3' Casing (Intestine, well cleaned, turned inside out)
24 Pepper Corns, crushed
1 cup Lamb broth
$^1/_2$ cup Flour
2 Tbsp. Oil
12 Laurel leaves
1 tsp. Salt

Fry liver in oil until done. Chop, place in mortar and grind until smooth, use up all the pan juices. Blend in flour, pepper, salt, and mix well. Add broth and blend well. Stuff casing. Tie off every 4" and cut sausage. Wrap links in laurel leaves. Hang and smoke for 4 - 5 hours. Finish off for service by frying in oil and serve with rice.

#13
PHEASANT DUMPLINGS

3 Pheasants, cleaned, cut in half. Remove all fat and
   trimmings for stock pot
$^1/_2$ tsp. Pepper. crushed fine
$^1/_2$ cup Wine
$^1/_2$ cup Stock, strained
2 piece Bread (1/2 cup) minced

Simmer stock, wine, trimmings. Roast pheasant until cooked. Remove meat, add bones to stock, add some water. When stock has simmered for twenty minutes or so, strain off liquid. Mix meat and liquid, add pepper, bread, and crush together to make a stiff forcemeat. Spoon dumpling mix into boiling water and cook for five minutes. Serve with rice or bulgar.

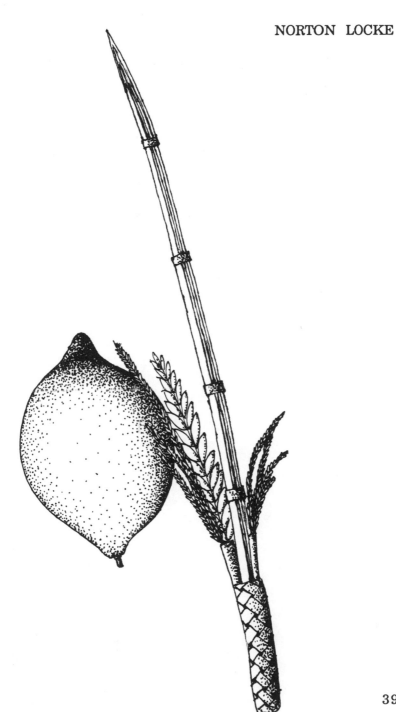

Festivals and Holidays

"and Moses proclaimed the festivals of the Lord unto the children of Israel." O.T.

"Everything in its season." Starting with the new moon, Rosh Hodesh, the major holidays are celebrated. The one day holidays are celebrated for two days to be sure the date and time is correct as specified, they then also added an extra day on the larger holidays. Pesach became eight days, Sukkot became nine days, etc. It was only the fast days that remained as they were, one day; this gave more time to the feast and became a built-in safety factor for the Fast. Each season has a feast.

"THE DAYS AND MONTHS"

The names of the Jewish days and months are not named for Pagan Gods or Heavenly Bodies, as are the modern calendar names. The Jewish calendar numbers the days; and the months were named for the kind of work performed in that time of the season. Later the names became Babylonian. Starting with the New Year, Rosh Hashanah, the calendar is set up fall, winter, spring, summer.

1st Quarter, Tishri, Heshvan, Kislev

2nd Quarter, Tevet, Shevat, Adar. (Leap Year — Adar Sheni)

3rd Quarter, Nisan, Iyar, Sivan

4th Quarter, Tammuz, Av, Elul

and the feasts follow these seasons.

The Hebrew Lu'Ah calendar is a Lunar Calendar. The Lunar year has twelve months of twenty-nine or thirty days, with seven Leap Years of thirteen months (with the thirteenth of thirty days) in each cycle of nineteen years. The

Hebrew year, according to tradition, began with creation so 1990 is 5750, 1991 is 5751, 1992 is 5752 and so on.

The Gezer calendar, 10th century B.C.E., found at the Tell Jazar (Tell Abu-Shusha) speaks of the annual cycle of agricultural activities in Israel. (Joshua 10:33.16:10). The signs of the Zodiac and the four seasons of the year {Tishri, Kisslev, Nisan, Tammuz} shown in the form of the bust of a winged woman are the corners of a fantastic mosaic found in the Synagogue at Bet Alfa in the Jezreel Valley. Built in 518 C.E. by the artist Marianos, the mosaic shows a series of pictures in the Biblical reference and follows folk art developed by the Jewish villagers of the Galilee.

MOED
"The Holy Days"
The Most Important Holidays in the Jewish Year

Rosh Hashanah	New Years	Tishri, September 11 -October 10
Yom Kippur	Day of Atonement	Tishri, September 11 -October 10
Sukkot	Feast of Tabernacles	Tishri, September 11 -October 10
Simchat Torah	Rejoice the Law	Heshvan, October 11 - October 10
Hanukkah	Feast of Lights	Tevet, December 8- January 5
Purim	Feast of Lots	Adar, March 7- April 4
Pesach	Passover	Nisan, April 5 - May 4
Shavuot	Feast of Weeks	Sivan, June 3 - July 2
Tisha B'Av	Fast of Av 9th	Av, August 1 - August 30

Jewish Festivals and Holidays fall on different days in the secular (Gregorian) calendar. As an example in 1990, the Jewish Year 5751, Pesach begins on April 10, Shavout is May 30, Rosh Hashanah is September 20, Yom Kippur is September 29, Sukkot is October 4, Hanukkah is December 12 and Purim is March 11.

JEWISH FESTIVALS AND HOLIDAYS
Calendar — 6 Year Sequence
1991 (5751) - 1996 (5756)

Pesach	Shavuot	Rosh Hashanah	Yom Kippur	Sukkot	Hanukkah	Purim
5751-1991						
Mar. 30	May 19	Sept. 10	Sept. 18	Sept. 23	Dec. 3	Feb. 28
5752-1992						
Apr. 19	June 7	Sept. 28	Oct. 7	Oct. 12	Dec. 20	Mar. 19
5753 - 1993						
Apr. 6	May 26	Sept. 16	Sept. 25	Sept. 30	Dec. 9	Mar. 7
5754 - 1994						
Mar. 27	May 16	Sept. 6	Sept. 15	Sept. 20	Nov. 28	Feb. 25
5755 - 1995						
Apr. 15	June 4	Sept. 25	Oct. 4	Oct. 9	Dec. 18	Mar. 16
5756 - 1996						
Apr. 4	May 24	Sept. 14	Sept. 23	Sept. 28	Dec. 6	Mar. 5

Should you need long range forecasting of the calendar let me suggest that you buy a copy of "The Standard Guide To The Jewish and Civil Calendars" by Fred Reiss, Behrman House, West Orange, NJ, 1986 at your local book seller.

THE SABBATH IS
THE FOURTH COMMANDMENT OF GOD
The Most Important Of All Holidays

Special meals are prepared. The good clothes are worn. Three meals are eaten, whereas during the week, two are usually eaten. Study is stressed and the family group, in rest, is the usual program. (Exodus 31:15) "Six days shall work be done; but the seventh day is a Sabbath of solemn rest, —." The age of TANNAIM of the common era raised the Sabbath to a higher level than was previously the norm. The Sabbath became more of a communal celebration, than in the AMORAIN age, the 3rd century C.E. The Friday evening service was added to the festivities, and we see that the communal

activities have grown up to the modern times. Isaea 58:13
"You shall make the Sabbath a Delight."

The KIDDUSH, has always been the most important
prayer for the sanctification of the Sabbath. After the meal
Z'MIROT, table songs are sung.

The favorite foods of history: fish spiced with pepper and
garlic, goose and chicken broiled with fruits, fruit cakes,
cholent of meat and beans, challot is baked fresh and eaten
warm. Gefilte fish is eaten as an appetizer by European Jews
and baked fish by Oriental Jews.

The HASKALAH has cast a shadow on the Jewish tradition and observance in modern times, however we do see a
"Re-birth" of the tradition in the young, and a strong return to
the more orthodox aspects of the faith. The eating of fish is a
tradition of the earliest of times as a symbol to the devout for
salvation and redemption. From the Jewish symbol of the fish
for salvation came the Christian symbol of the fish as the sign
of redemption.

SABBATH FISH

*2lb. Carp, cut into steaks 1 ¹/₂" thick (you can use
   any fatty fish)*
6 toes Garlic, crushed
1 tsp. Salt
*¹/₂ tsp Paprika, black pepper, curry powder
   (blended together)*
¹/₂ Lemon, juiced

Lay out fish steaks and sprinkle lightly with lemon juice,
then sprinkle herbs and spices over both sides. Set aside in
the refrigerator.

Mix Sauce
2 Red peppers, hot. mince and sauté lightly
3 toes Garlic, crushed
4 med. Tomatoes, chopped
2 Tbsp. Cilantro (Israeli parsley)

$^1/_2$ Lemon, juiced
$^1/_6$ tsp. paprika
$^1/_6$ tsp. black pepper
$^1/_6$ tsp. Curry (Camoon)
$^1/_4$ cup Tomato Paste with 1 Tbsp. water mixed in

Add all the sauce ingredients to the red hot pepper, sauté, mix and continue to sauté for about ten minutes. Press through a ricer or run in a food processor for one minute. Set sauce aside to mellow.

Place fish steaks in a roast pan so edges just touch. Bake in a 400° oven for ten minutes. Pour sauce over fish, return to the oven and bake five minutes. May be served either hot or cold. This dish may be kept refrigerated for several days if required.

This recipe, with a few variations, can be found in most parts of Israel, Lebanon, and Egypt.

"Lord Thou has put all things under His feet; sheep and oxen — the beasts of the field; the fowl of the air, and the fish of the sea; "(Psalm 8:7,8)

TISHOH B'OV
(TISHA B'AV)

The 9th day of the month Av. This is a fast day commemorating the destruction of the Temple at Jerusalem as well as a number of bad things in the life of the Jewish people. This is the usual day to visit the cemetary.

PESACH - PASSOVER

The oldest of the Jewish holidays, begins on the eve of the 14th day of the month NISAN.

Pesach started as the spring festival of the shepherds, with the ceremony of the OMER. The first cut sheaf of barley as a gift to God. Later the combined festival of the harvest and the deliverance from Egypt produced one major holiday that has come down fully intact to modern times. The Messianic hope became part of the spirit of the holiday.

In Leviticus 25:10, the Bible commands the Jews to celebrate Pesach and, "tell their children in every age, the story
of what the Lord did at that time." The foods of the first Seder:
The Afikomon, a glass of wine, a bit of lettuce, tart sauce,
Haroses, roast lamb, baked fish, Matzot, beet soup and dumplings. These are the foods of the season.

Symbols of the Seder:
Roasted Bone (Zero'a), represents the sacrificial lamb.
Roasted Egg (Beitzah), represents the festival offering.
Bitter herbs (Maror) represents the bitterness of bondage.
Green vegetables (Karpas) is the first course meal of
    free men.
Salt water, the tears of suffering
Haroses represents the bricks the Israelites made for
Pharaoh in Egypt. Exodus 12:8 speaks of the Sheep roasted
on a rod and eaten with the unleavened bread, Hallot Matzot,
unleavened cakes mingled with oil as an acknowledgement of
God's goodness (Leviticus 7:12).

Passover was the "Last Supper" of Jesus of Nazareth, and
is without question the most important of all of the holidays
and festivals of the Jewish faith, other than the Sabbath.

Passover is important to Jew and Christian alike, as God
responded in several places in the Torah with this law of
carrying Passover forward to each generation... for ever!

Jesus, according to Matthew and Luke, was born into a
Jewish family, the son of Mariam-Bat-Jochan (Mary), in Bethlehem, and later moved to Nazareth in the Galilee. His
given name Yeshua (Joshua) "the help of god" was Joshua-
bar-Joseph. He was the son of Joseph, a carpenter. His
brothers were reportedly named, James, Joseph, Simon, and
Judas, his sisters were not identified by name, but were
thought to be Martha and Mary. Miriam (Mary), according to
Sholom Asch in his book "Mary," was a devout Jew and served
in the Temple two years.

According to Luke, Joshua was born 7 B.C.E. during the
census of Saturninus, Governor of Syria. His birthday is vari-

46

ously reported to be April 19, May 20 and November 17. The date December 25, was later chosen based on the winter solstice - when the days began to lengthen, and, it was already the day when the festival "Mithraism" was celebrated. (The birthday of the sun). The evangelists tell of Christ's youth in the Jewish environment of his home and his religion. He attended the synagogue and studied the Torah, for his Bar-Mitzvah learned the Scriptures, the Prophets and Psalms. He read Daniel and Enoch. He traveled to Jerusalem for the Passover and enjoyed the foods and rituals of all the Jewish festivals. By the very nature of his training and associations he would have followed the laws of "fit" food, and the dietary laws.

Because Joshua and eleven of his twelve deciples were all Jewish, they looked forward to Pesach — Passover, the visits of family and friends to celebrate the holiday of freedom for their people. The story of Moses was retold and the unleavened bread (Matzo) was eaten for seven days as is required in the law. The meals were prepared and eaten under the Laws of Kashrut. Some meals were dairy. Some meals were meat and other meals were fish, eggs, and fruit. Wine was the drink of the meal, but always as a beverage for ritual, and not as a cocktail as we know it today. Matzot the mainstay of the holiday, Exodus 13: 6,7, was used as the bread and the basis for cakes and cookies.

As was the custom, for the first night, a room in an Inn or Hotel would be rented so that all the friends and relatives could sit together for the Passover feast. On the other nights the feast was in the home. The order of the service and progression of the foods is strictly controlled, and starts with the leader washing his hands. Then the story of the Exodus from Egypt, with Moses, is read. The table is set with three Matzot placed in compartments of a ritual covering. This is to signify the Cohen (Priests), the Levi (Caretakers of the Temple) and the Israelites, (the people). The Matzot recalls the haste to leave Egypt. The roasted shank bone of the lamb (or if a vegetarian meal a roasted turnip) represents the blood the Israelites were told to put on their door posts, to mark their homes, so the angel of death would pass over them. The bitter herbs (Horseradish) is a reminder of the bitter life of slavery in Egypt. Charoset symbolizes the mortar and brick the slave toiled with as he was pushed to work harder. A glass of wine is placed in front of each person. A large glass of wine in the center of the table is the cup of Elijah the prophet, who it is promised, will plant hope in the heart of the downtrodden. It is the prophet Elijah who will precede the Messiah and will announce his arrival with peace and freedom for all men. The meal is told of in Exodus 12: 3-11, and is required to tell their children the story of each year so that they will never forget. Exodus 12:26, 27; 13:14; and Deuteronomy 6:20,21. We are told that for the Passover anyone who is hungry may come in and eat. This is the Law. So the Seder is one more commandment of the law the Jews are required to keep, and the Christians have all but erased from their heritage.

"Exodus 11:14 Passover "and this day shall be unto you for a memorial, and ye shall keep it a feast to the Lord; throughout your generations forever."

Jesus (Joshua) practiced the law (Matthew 26:2) and followed it fully. The Torah, the first five books of the bible are the basis of Jewish life. It is written that Jesus said, "For verily I say unto you. Till heaven and earth pass, not one jot or tittle of the Law shall in no way pass from the law, till all be filled." (Jot or tittle - vowel and accent marks of the Hebrew language). His teachings, with those of Matthew, Mark, John, and Simon were all of their common Jewish faith. They inherited and used the rich moral laws of the people.

We see that they preached as Jews to the Jews, the New Testament says "go not into the way of the gentiles, nor into the city of the Samaritans." Jesus, in suggesting modifications and mitigations of the Judaic Law did not, supposedly, think that he was over throwing it, but rather making it more modern - reformed. He is reported to have said "I come not to destroy the Law of Moses but to fulfill it." Jesus was an Orthodox Jew and studied under the most strict of the Sects.

Jesus's "Last Supper" was the Passover where he ate the foods and said the blessings as required in the Law. This is the Seder the Jews have repeated for the past 3000 years when Moses lead the Israelites out of the land of Egypt. For Jews this is their history, for non-Jews it will perhaps help them to understand their belief a little, as well as those of a man called Jesus. It was many years later that the followers of this reformed Judaism broke away from the faith and founded their new religion... Christianity.

The upper storey of David's building (King David's Tomb) is, according to historic tradition, the place where Jesus celebrated the first night of Passover. The meal was held in the Coenaculum (The dining hall) Mark 14 "Where is the guest chamber where I shall eat the Passover with my deciples?..." The plan of the Cenacle shows the stairway, the big hall, and two small rooms. It was Rabbi Benjamine of Tudela in 1173 C.E. who rediscovered the Tomb. Leonardo da Vinci in 1496 painted his "Last Supper" based on his reflections from David's Tomb.

50 A.D., with the writings of Paul, is the period in history that Christianity broke away from Judaism and the Gospels were written. Now there was a distinct ending of Judaism and Christian interrelationship and coexistence, as Paul relates in Romans 2:28,29. The true break and separation of Judaism and Christianity developed when the Christians rejected the Halakah (Legal Judaism). This arbitrary selection has been the basis for friction ever since. Unfortunately for the Jews, the Christian does not know his roots, and has mistakenly persecuted the Jew as a Heretic.

SHAVOUT
(Shevuoth)

The festival of weeks, the Pentecost.

The 6th day of the Jewish month of SIVAN, according to

the Pharisees, is the wheat harvest, weeks ending the harvest.

The home and the synagogue are decorated in green and all are fragrant with plant and flowers of the season. The holiday originally called HAG HA-KATZIR, the feast of harvest, was also called HAG HA-BIKKURIM, the day of offering the first loaves of bread from the new crop. The first loaves are offered 50 days following the offering of the OMER at the end of PESACH.

At the time of the second Temple, Shavout took on a two fold meaning, the observance of the pact between God and Noah (Mankind) that there would never again be a general flood, and the giving of the TORAH on Mount Sinai.

Shavout is usually the day for confirmation. This is also the day that the book of Ruth is read. This could actually be called the birthday of the Jews.

Dairy foods, milk, cheese, yogurt, cheese cakes are the main foods of the holiday. Fruits of many varieties and kinds are eaten. Blintzes are the most popular of all the foods served on this holiday and can be traced to the earliest times of Jewish history, then into the Greek and Roman periods. Each people since, into modern times, have claimed the invention of this wonderful food.

ROSH HASHANAH

Nehemiah 8:10, "Go your way, — for this day is holy unto our Lord;" The days of Awe, the Jewish New Year, is celebrated on the first and second days of the month of TISHRI, became so designated after the Babylonian Exile, with the splitting of the Days of the In-gathering. The Pentateuch states, "In the 7th Month, in the first day of the month, shall be solemn rest unto you, a memorial proclaimed with the blast of the horns, a holy convocation." This was the beginning of the year according to the movement of the moon. The literature of the TANNAIM, in the period of the destruction of the first Temple, speaks of ROSH HASHANAH as the day on which mankind was judged in the heaven and man's fate was settled.

These are the Days of Awe. Ancient history relates the custom of TASHLICH, of going to the lake or river and throwing away your sins into the deep water and cleaning yourself. This ritual is still practiced today by more Orthodox people.

Rabbi Jacob Ben Moses Halevi (Maharil) said, "Jews go to the stream on Rosh Hashanah to remind God of the worth of Abraham and Isaac." Since the ancient Hebrews were farmers, it is natural that the New Year would correspond to the "first day of creation" or the planting of the new crop and the sprouting of the seed. The holiday symbolizes man's desire for a year of fullness and prosperity for all men.

In ancient days Abraham sacrificed a ram in place of his son Isaac, so the tradition of roasting and eating a sheep's head as the main dish has been carried forward. Honey, apples and spice are the second foods of the holiday, reflecting sweetness for the New Year.

YOM KIPPUR

This Holiday started in the period of the Jewish Kingdom and was refined after the Babylonian Exile. The date is the 10th day of the month of TISHRI.

The day before Yom Kippur is called KAPAROT. The feast of Kaporos, consists of Kreplech, Chicken Soup, and Tzimmes. This meal is eaten by 11.00 a.m., so as to allow the last meal to be eaten no later than 4:00 p.m. followed by the fast. The pre-fast meal is Rooster (chicken) soup, of a freshly killed fowl.

Candle lighting plays a very important part in the ritual. The highlight of the Evening service is when the Cantor sings Kol Nidre. The N'Ilah, or concluding prayers of the Yom Kippur service indicate the closing of the gates of Heaven where the individual has the last opportunity to do penance and plead for a successful new year.

Following N'Ilah, a short break and then a light meal

51

breaking the fast is eaten. "L'SHANAH TOVAH TIKATENU V' SECHOSEMU", O.T. "May you be inscribed and sealed for a good year." This is the wish of the Holiday. It is recalled in the TANNAIM, "All are judged on Rosh Hashanah and theirfate is sealed on Yom Kippur."

SUKKOT
Hag-Adonai, Hag-Ha-Osif, Zeman Simhatenu

Exodus 23:16, "The feast of the ingathering, at the end of the year"

The feast of the Tabernacles — The Autumn Festival begins on the 15th day of the Month TISHRI and lasts nine days. During the festival three (3) other special days occur.

The 7th Day, HOSHANA RABBA— The second time of AWE

The 8th Day, SH'MINI ATZERET— The second holiday of the Diaspora

The 9th Day, SIMCHAT TORAH — Rejoicing in the Torah, the first five books

This is the festival of the In-Gathering, HAG HA-OSIF, and of HAG HA - SUKKOT, the festival of the booths. Some call it God's Festival, since it is the Thanksgiving for the harvest and was the oldest of the festivals.

This was a very happy time and the songs and rejoicing filled the land. The Book of Judges talks of the Daughters of SHILOH (Shiloh, on Mt. Ephraim) holding a dance in honor of the Festival of God. Elkanan, father of Samuel, made pilgrimage to SHILOH with all of his family to partake of the festival. History reports that some of the prophets and sages, were not happy with the tone of the fun making and took strong exception to the bacchanalia of the festival.

Sukkos was the biggest time for the pilgrimage to Jerusalem. The harvest was done and some free time was at hand. Time for a party and to see old friends. today Sukkot is less of a harvest festival and is more of a Torah Festival, a religious awakening. The foods are, long loafs of Challah with braided ladders on top, Kresplech and soup. The symbols are the Lulav and Etrog. here we see all the foods of the harvest used both as food and as decoration.

"—go forth into the mount, and fetch olive branches, branches of wild olive, and myrtle, and palm, — to make booths, — " Nehemiah 8:15.

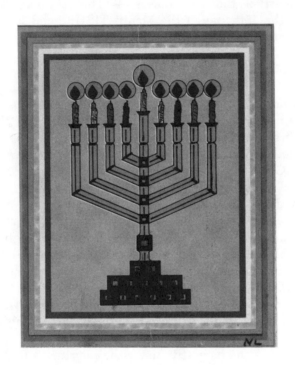

HANUKKAH MENORAH LIGHTS, KIRIAT-GAT

HANUKKAH

The eight days beginning on the 25th day of the month of Kislev. This is a commemorative festival and recalls the revolt and victory of the Hasmoneans. This was not a major holiday, but has taken on major family involvement during modern times. JUDAH MACCABEE and his brothers are the heros of the holiday for it was on the 25th of Kislev they rededicated the altar of the Temple after defeating ANTI-OCHUS EPIPHANES and the Syrian kingdom. Josephus Flavuis was the first to speak of the festival of the "Lights". Hillel gave the order of the lights, of increasing a candle each night. The meaning of dedication, has increased over the years, and the older meanings have diminished.

The story in the Gemarra (Talmud), relates that the Greeks defiled the oil in the Temple. When Judah won the battle he searched the Temple and was only able to find enough pure oil to burn one day — one small flask bearing the seal of the High Priest. A miracle occurred and the one day supply of oil burned for eight days.

The (SIVIVON) DREDLEC, is the spinning top used in the favorite game of the holiday. The top is also called Trendel, Trenderel, Werfel, but the game is the same.

The foods are Pancakes, Pudding made of cheese. Cheese pies and cakes. The foods are all linked to the story of Judith feeding cheese to the ASSYRIAN leader HOLFERNES, who ate and drank much wine, became drunk, then Judith cut off his head. The story is harsh, but the foods are sweet.

The Pancakes, Latkes, according to folklore relates to the flat cakes baked by the wives of the Maccabees during the great battle, when they needed to bake food quickly for the troops. Here we have the original "K" ration.

It is interesting to speculate, but, had the Maccabees not won the battle, there would have been no Christmas for the Christians. The Hebrew faith would have died out and Christianity and Muslim would not have happened. The world might have lost the one god concept and sunk back into idol worship.

THE MENORAH

The seven-branched candelabrum called the Menorah was one of the sacred vessels of the Holy Temple. Its design was commanded in the Book of Exodus. The Menorah has seven branches, and seven separate lamps. The Torah tells us that "The soul of man is the lamp of the Lord."

Here is a facsimile of Maimonides' own sketch of the Menorah in the Holy Temple.

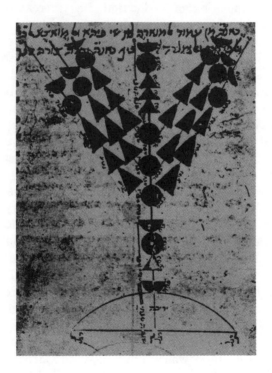

PURIM

The 14th Day of the month of Adar. The day before is the Fast of Esther and the day after is SHUSHAN PURIM.

The book of Esther tells of the reason for Purim. Though it is not of true historical events, it is an allegory, that speaks of the war the Jews must carry on, from time to time, against the enemies that would seek to destroy them. We can look to the book of Esther as a historical novel written during the time of the second temple. The book is as topical today as it was 2000 years ago. Purim is the symbolic name given to Jewish deliverance. The MEGILAH, the scroll, is read and acted out each Purim.

The foods are hamantashen, marzipan fruits, and sweets of many kinds. gingerbreadmen, nahit and wine.

Esther 2:18 "then the king made a great feast unto all his princes and his servants, even Esther's feast;—"

TU-BI-SHEVAT

The 15th day of SHEVAT is the new year of the trees. All are asked to plant trees in Israel and, in the Diasporah, at your home. The trees suggested are fruit trees and trees of the forest.

The foods of the season are nuts, figs, dates, cherries and apricots. Grandma Rose used to sing a folk song, "rozhinkes mit mandlen" raisins and almonds, having to do with this holiday. Bokser, St. John's Bread, is eaten.

SIMHAT TORAH

A new holiday, only 1000 years old. It marks the end of the reading of the Torah, the last chapter of Deuteronomy, and the starting over from the beginning with the first chapter of Genesis. The celebration is like that of a wedding. Symbolically Jews are married to the Torah.

The foods are all those of a happy time.

MINOR HOLIDAYS

ROSH CHODESH

The first of each month, synonymous with the new moon.

LAG BA - OMER

The day that Manna began to fall from heaven, and, the

remembrance of the Bar Kochba rebellion against Rome. The foods are Bob, Nahit and Fava.

CHAMISHOH OSOR B'OV
Midsummer day, the beginning of the grape harvest.

CHAMISHOH OSOR BI - SH'VAT
Mid winter day, the festival of the wood offering to God. St. Johns Bread is eaten.

There are other minor holidays, some are only observed by Eastern European Jews, some by only the oriental Jews and some other holidays that only the Central European Jews observe. They all can be called religious festivals but they are not part of the full Jewish fabric.

Personal festivals, celebrations and MITZVOT'S such as the miracle of birth, circumcision, (Brit Milah), redemption of the first born son (PIDYON HA-BEN). Bar and Bat Mitzvah, marriage, death and burial, are all part of the Jewish life cycle.

Of all the religions of the ancient world only Judaism developed the idea of a single, all-powerful god. It is interesting to note that all the major religions of the world developed in this small area of the world, and at about the same relative time.

From the Near East came; Judaism, Hinduism, Buddism, Confucianism, and Taoism. From Judaism developed Christianity and then Islam (called Muhammadanism). Looking around us we can see that all of these religions (Philosophies) have carried forward to modern times in one form or another, and that all are firmly rooted in the life of the East and it's never ending circle of planting and the harvesting of crops, as well as the basic thoughts and ideas of Abraham, presented in the melting pot of the Fertile Crescent.

With the development of Christianity, after the death of

Jesus (Joshua), we see the food relations carried forward, in the fish of Fridays tradition, and the Eucharist/gratitude of the communion, utilizing the Holy Scripture injunction of Mazza and wine, to show favor.

The same Mother-Religion relationship is interspersed in the Religion-Food tradition of the Islamic faith wherein Muhammad carried forward the many injunctions of Abraham and the early prophets and Rabbis.

We can see the Hellenized/Oriental/Romanized, Middle East struggle to maintain culture and religion, yet embrace the foods and architecture of the social and military invaders that (in geographic order) touched Homs, Tadmor, Palmyra, Emesa, Damascus, Thapsacus, Aleppo, Atakia, Saleucia, Pieria, Antioch, Sidon, Tyre, Tiberias, Nazareth, Caesarea, Apallonia, Jericho, Bethlehem, Beersheba, Petra, Raphia. The resulting revolt of the people against the ruling class spread throughout the region from Greece to Egypt, around Israel to Syria and Asia Minor and back to Rome.

The death and ascension of Adonis comingled with the death and ascension of Christ, Isis rose and fell, Cybele had it's brief period, Hindu influenced invaded Greece, Magi was embraced by some, Askesis by others, and Therapeutae by still others. Above all this din rose the monotheistic religion of the Jews and the rules written in the Torah and spoken of in the Pentateuch.

No people in all the history of man has fought so long or so hard for liberty, as have the Jews. No people have fought against such odds as have the Jews. Often decimated but never broken, the Jews have carried their hope high for all men to admire and emulate. Zelots and Sicarii have appeared in every age, be it Judah Maccabee, Simeon Bar Kokiba, "son of a star, known also as Ben Koziba," or David Ben Gurion, the word of Moses and Isaiah have been carried forward as part of the full fabric of the people who "Walked with God" (Genesis 5:24), and awaited the Mahsiah (Messiah), the people who will inhabit the land "— from the Red Sea even unto the Sea of the Philistines, and from the Wilderness unto the river;—" (Exodus 24:31).   59

Harvest

Harvest

RECIPES OF THE BIBLE

The three foods of "ERETZ-ISRAEL" were DAGAN, corn or grain; TIROSH, new wine; and VIZHAR, oil. Broths, stews and roasted meats the major methods of preparation of foods. ARUHAH was the daily foods, the modest foods. ZEVAH was the worship meal that included meat. KERAH was the festival and holiday meal, prepared for a large crowd of people. LEHEM refers to meals that do not fall into the other categories. Today we enjoy all of them without specific regard to order.

Some other foods of the area and times are Mansaf, cooked rice with cumin and pepper, mixed with cooked lamb or mutton cubes and mixed with Tahina then stuffed into pita bread; Madfun with eggplant layered with chicken, rice, onion, tomato sauce and cheese (mint, salt and pepper are added for spice); Maklubeh, lamb, rice and eggplant mixed together and baked slowly until done; Kusa Mahshi, Eggplant stuffed with mutton and baked; Sfiha, minced mutton seasoned with pepper, then served on pie crust.

Jeremiah 31:12 says, "and they shall come... in the height of Zion, ...To the corn, and to the wine, and to the oil, and to the young of the flock and of the herd;" the foods of Zion.

Mallah, in the Jordan valley of Israel, was a very early village where hunting and gathering of seeds developed into early cultivation and subsequent row farming. Here we see culinary standards developed and implanted in the culture. Genesis 26:12 tells of Isaac being engaged in seasonal agriculture in the western Negev.

Cooked foods of the Bible were often broths (Judges 6:19) of vegetables and meat combined as they cooked to produce a nourishing blend of flavors.

#14
HEALTH BROTH

3 cups Pole Beans, cut in half
2 medium Onions, chopped
2 cups Squash, chopped fine
1/2 cup Lamb or chicken, chopped
2 Tbsp. Oil
1 tsp. Salt
1/2 tsp. Pepper
1/2 tsp. Nutmeg
1/4 tsp. Ginger
1 tsp. Sugar
1 Tbsp. Lemon Juice
3 cups Water

Boil beans in water 20 minutes, replace liquid as required. Sauté meat in oil 'till lightly browned, add onions. Simmer 15 minutes. Add all herbs and spices, blend well. Combine beans and water with meat. Add squash, bring to soft boil and simmer 10 minutes. Add lemon juice, stir, simmer 5 minutes. Portion into bowls over broken bread chunks.

Stews, 11 Kings 4:38, were a combination of meats and beans cooked slowly, such as Hamin or Cholent. Recipes for various stews will be found in the Recipe section of the book. When cooking any of these dishes remember to invite company over to taste the recipes. 1 Kings 13:7 — "Come home with me and refresh yourself."

"Once when Jacob was cooking a stew, Esau came in from the open field, famished. And Esau said to Jacob, Give me some of that red stuff to gulp down, for I am famished. Jacob said, First sell me your birthright. And Esau said, I am at the point of death, so what use is my birthright to me? — Jacob then gave Esau bread and lentil stew; he ate and drank."

#15
RED LENTIL STEW

2 cups Brown Lentils
2 Onions, minced
1 tsp. Salt
$^1/_2$ tsp. Pepper
$^1/_4$ tsp. Cayenne Red Pepper
1 medium Red Bell pepper, chopped medium fine
6 cups Water
1 cup Venison or Kid, cubed 1/2"

Combine all ingredients. Mix well, cover in pot and slowly simmer for three hours. Replace water as required. Serve hot with warm bread.

At the birth of Isaac, Abraham prepared a great feast, "and for every joy that followed a feast was prepared." We can assume that at these feasts, lentil stews and venison, kid and goat were in high evidence.

FISHING

Numbers 11:5 shows that the Jews of history liked fish. smoked fish and skewered (Kebab) fish were favorites. Fish roe (Nehemiah 13:16) were pickled and salted for local food and for export. Pliny in "History Naturalis" speaks of Garum Castimoniale (Kasher Garum), Jewish style fish.

Fish of 43 varieties were gathered in the Sea of Galilee, (also known as the Sea of Tiberias or Lake Kinneret) located in the Jordan Valley by the tribe of Zebulun (Deuteronomy 33:19). Nehemiah conducted trade in fish with Phoenician merchants. Josephus talks of the huge fishing industry of the Israelites that flourished in the Sea of Galilee. Fish was baked, broiled, boiled, salted and sun dried. The roe was prized, salted or mixed with sauces. Often the roe was pressed into sheets and eaten dry or mixed with rice.

Acre, Akko, (called Ptolemais by the Greeks) is in the

Valley of Zevulun. Genesis 49:13, "Zebulun shall dwell at the shore of the sea, and he shall be a shore for ships." AKKO some say got it's name from the Greek "Aka" (Cure). According to the ancients, Hercules was sick and found a cure for his ills from the herbs grown in the area. Fishing in the region was so famous that an ancient saying was, "who needs to bring fish to Akko?" The Crusaders named the city, St. Jean d'Acre. This Canaanite seaport is located on the northern hook of Haifa bay, and has been of major importance to the spice trade as well as the home port of a large fishing fleet. (Judges 1:31). The port of Akko was used by the Greeks, Romans, Crusaders, Moslems and Hebrews. Allotted to Asher during the Israelite period. Akko is considered by some as the beginning of the Israelite tradition on the sea.

The seafood eaten was limited by the biblical injunction, "These may ye eat of all that are in the waters: Whatsoever hath fins and scales..." (Leviticus 11:9). In (Numbers 11:22) "— all the fish of the sea be gathered together —", (Nehemiah I 3:16) "— men of Tyre brought in fish, —" the reference is of hope of redemption and is a mainstay of the Sabbath meal, since fish is a mystical symbol of fertility and immortality. Fish with garlic was of historic significance as it related the religion to the hope of redemption.

#16
KUTAP
BROILED FISH

1/2 lb. Striped fish or Black bass, cleaned
2 Tbsp. Olive oil
3 Apricots, chopped fine
3 Figs, chopped fine
1 slice Bread, chopped medium
1/2 tsp. Saffron

Wash fish and pat dry. Par boil fruit 5 minutes, mix with bread and stuff inside of fish. Sew shut. Skewer fish. Rub

with oil. Sprinkle saffron over. Broil over hot fire, turning all
the time. Do not let burn. Cook 15 minutes. Baste 3 - 4 times
with oil and saffron. Serve with rice or geres. The fish must
be fresh to produce the best results.

*Song of Songs 2:13 "The fig tree putteth forth her green
figs."*

#17
AMNUN METUGAN KATZUTZ
FISH PATTIES

*³/₄ lb. Fish fillets, ground or minced (Amnun is St. Peter's
    Fish, a local favorite)*
1 Onion, minced
2 Eggs, beaten
3 Tbsp. Matzo meal
3 Stalks celery, minced
4 Tbsp. Oil
¹/₄ tsp. Salt
¹/₆ tsp. Pepper

Mix all except oil together. Blend well. Divide into six
equal parts. Press into patty shape. Heat oil and fry on
medium heat until golden brown. Serve with rice and salad.
Pepper sauce can be poured over.

#18
EGOZIM MEVUSHAL BAKALA
NUT STUFFED FISH

12 fillets White fish
¹/₂ cup Pine nuts, (Pignolia)
¹/₄ cup Almonds, minced
4 large Spanish onions, chopped fine
1 ¹/₂ cup Long grain rice
1 cup Olive oil, light virgin oil

$^1/_4$ cup Dried currants
$^1/_2$ tsp. Cinnamon
$^1/_4$ tsp. Allspice
$^3/_4$ tsp. Salt
4 cups Cold water

Heat oil in pan until hot, add onions and sauté until golden brown. Add pine nuts and almonds. Stir for 3 minutes. Add rice, currants, cinnamon and allspice. Stir and blend well for 2 minutes. Add 2 cups cold water, stir. Bring to boil. Cover. Reduce heat and simmer for 15-20 minutes. Set aside and allow to cool for 20 minutes. Lay out fillets of fish. Lightly dust with pepper. Place heaping tablespoon of rice/nut mixture on fillet. Spread out. Roll fillet up like jelly roll. Tie with string. Lay rolls on a rack in a pan. Add 2 cups of water. Bring to a rolling boil. Cover pan. Reduce heat and steam for 12-15 minutes. Can be served hot or cold.

Note: You may use all pine nuts or all almonds if you desire.

Moses was commanded to place a "Hin of olive oil" in the "Tent of Meeting" as an offering to the Lord. (Exodus 30:24) A Hin was a measure of approximately 6 liters or about 7 pints. 7 was a mystical number that reoccurs throughout the "Holy Scriptures."

#19
MULLOS ANETHATOS
MULLET STEW

3 lb. Mullets, cleaned, fillets
2 Tbsp. Oil
$^1/_2$ cup Fish broth
$^1/_4$ cup Wine
6 Leeks, sliced
3 Sprigs Coriander, Fresh
3 Heads Dill, Fresh

8 *Pepper corns*
1 *Tbsp. Vinegar*
2 *Tbsp. Raisin Wine*
1 *Tbsp. Flour*
2 *Tbsp. Oil*

In a greased casserole dish layer in fish, alternate leeks, coriander, dill. Be sure some is under each piece of fish. Sprinkle oil over. Add wine and broth. Cover and simmer for 15 minutes. Grind pepper corn, wine and flour, sauté into roux. Pour over fish. Heat until flour thickens. Serve.

#20
BAKALA AFUY
BAKED FISH

3 *lb. Fish (Hake or Tunny are the best, but you may*
   use the fish you like)
3 *Toes Garlic, crushed*
$^1/_2$ *tsp. Salt*
$^1/_2$ *tsp. Pepper*
1 *tsp. Lemon Juice*
$^1/_2$ *tsp.Paprika*

Wash fish and blot fairly dry, sprinkle seasonings all over. Layer into a well greased pan. Sprinkle lemon juice over, dust with extra paprika. Bake at 350° for 20 - 25 minutes. Serve with rice and vegetable greens and vinegar.

#21
PAPAS SIVE NAPOS
TURNIP SALAD

12 *Turnips, cleaned, cut* 1/4*'s*
1 *quart Water*
1 *tsp. Cumin*
3 *Tbsp. Flour*
1 *Tbsp. Oil*

2 Tbsp. Vinegar, wine
¹/₂ cup Stock

Boil turnips in water until soft, strain off water. Crush turnips and flour, then add oil and mix well. Add remaining ingredients. Heat and simmer 10 minutes. Serve with fish meal as an aid to digestion, so says Pliny.

#22
PATINA DE ABUA SIVE APUA
SMELT CUSTARD

2" Fish fillets, boned (use smelts or sardines)
1 tsp. Red peppers, crushed or use pepper corns
3 tsp. Flour
1 cup Fish broth, made from all the trimmings
2 Tbsp. Oil
4 Eggs, beaten
3 pieces Sea weed, well washed
¹/₄ cup Milk

In a greased casserole dish lay in fish. Sprinkle flour and pepper over each piece. Add broth, oil and eggs, milk and smooth top. Lay sea weed over top. Place in a water bath and steam for 45 minutes. Serve with rice.

Other Foods of History

Every household had a vegetable garden, (1 Kings 21:2) and the main meals came from this garden. Watermelons and the melons of Persia were consumed as a tonic against the heat. A green striped melon, Sekhep, was popular (Numbers 11:5) in Egypt and Israel after the deliverance. Helawi, a condiment of sugar cane and sesame, was used on nuts and grain.

#23
ALITER DULCIA
SWEET NUTS

3 cups Nuts, cut meat in half
1 cup Honey
1 Tbsp. Flour
2 tsp. Oil
1 cup Raisin wine
1/2 cup Milk
1/2 tsp. Pepper, fine grind
2 Eggs
1/2 cup Honey
1/2 cup Nuts, chopped

In a fry pan on medium heat, mix flour and milk to make a soft roux. Add 1/2 nuts, honey, wine, blend and simmer for about 5 minutes, be sure wine and honey are well blended. Whip eggs and pour into nut mixture, blend and stir. Remove from the fire. Add honey and stir. Sprinkle nuts over. Serve.

God said, (Genesis 1:29) "See, I give you every seed-bearing plant that is upon the earth, and every tree that has seed-bearing fruit; they shall be yours for food."

#24
KABBAB KETZITZOT
GRILLED MEAT
(Kebab)

1 lb. Lamb, ground medium
1 lb. Beef or Venison, ground medium
3/4 tsp. Cumin
1/2 tsp. Salt
1/4 tsp. Pepper
2 Onions, minced
1 bunch Parsley, chopped

³/₄ cup Water

Mix all together and knead well to assure that all is fully blended. (some people add 1/4 cup crushed matzo or matzo meal). Roll into ball, cover and refrigerate overnight. Roll out into 1" x 6" fingers. Press firmly together. Fry on medium fire. Roll and brown all sides. Serve with rice and a green salad. The fingers can be placed on a skewer and roasted over a hot fire turning often so they do not burn. You may use any combination of meats.

Kebab, is a historic dish that can be traced to the earliest times. It often consists of small pieces of fat lamb, usually breast, marinated in oil and vinegar. It is grilled on skewers and served with rice or grain. Sometimes pieces of vegetables were alternated on the skewer with the lamb. Aubergines "Hatzilim" (eggplant) was the most popular of the vegetables, followed by yams, okra, capiscums, beans, and peas. The single most enjoyed "starter" or appetizer was stuffed grape leaves (Alay Gefen), and then stuffed spinach or cabbage. Tihini (Sesame seed paste) was the sauce of primary use, followed by zhug and zum and schug. Pita (chapati — flat bread) the common bread and mazza the religious bread.

#25
SCHUG SAUCE
YEMEN HOT SAUCE

3 medium Hot green peppers, minced
5 toes Garlic, minced
1 bunch Parsley, minced
1 tsp. Cilantro (Coriander Leaf) Fresh, minced
¹/₂ tsp. Salt
¹/₄ tsp. Pepper
1 tsp. Water
1 tsp. Fresh lemon juice
Combine all solids and crush into a pulp. Add liquids and

blend well. Mixture should be loose. If overly thick, add more water. Let sit several hours to age and allow the flavors to blend. Serve with meat or use as a topping for Falafel. This spicy mixture has been used since the earliest times and is a favorite of the Yemen peoples. A similar sauce can be found in the Moroccan and Persian food system.

#26
ZUG
COZBARA SAUCE

4 cups Cilantro (Collantro, Cozbara)
4 toes Garlic
10 small Hot green peppers
2 tsp. Salt
$^1/_2$ tsp. Black pepper
1 tsp. Curry
2 Tbsp. Water

Combine all ingredients in a blender and chop 2 minutes. Add juice of 1 lemon, blend. Remove and set aside for flavor to blend. Refrigerate, then use as sauce with meat or fish. Easy does it, this is hot!

#27
KEBAB PEPPERS

2 large Green bell peppers
2 large Red bell peppers
1 medium Onion, chopped
3 Tbsp. Olive oil
$^1/_2$ tsp. Salt
$^1/_4$ tsp. Pepper
1 Tbsp. Vinegar (cider)

Skewer peppers and roast over hot coals, turning often. When skins are fully blackened, not burned, about 10 minutes, remove from fire and peel off skins. Slice in 1/2 and remove seeds and stem. Slice meat into bite size chunks. Combine all ingredients and blend well. Eat with Kebab fish or lamb. Can be stuffed into pocket bread as a light lunch.

Man gathers wood and on part, "he roasts meat, he eats the roast and he is sated;" (Isaiah 44:16)

#28
KEBAB LAMB

2 lb. Lamb breast, Cut 2" cubes
$^1/_2$ cup Oil
$^1/_4$ cup Vinegar
2 Beets. Peeled sliced

Mix oil and vinegar, combine with lamb and tumble well. Allow to sit for 2 hours. Skewer alternating with beet slices. Cook over hot fire turning often. When nicely browned remove and serve over rice or burgul wheat. Can be eaten as "Forspeisen" appetizer or as a main meal.

Burgul (Burghul) is a wheat product. This is regarded as the original form in which wheat was eaten. The grain is soaked in water, then dried in the hot desert sun until fully dried, then crushed into one of three textures: course used in stews and cholent, medium used in Kibbeh, fine used in Tartare or cereal or geres.

The Bible, and the commentaries of later writers talk of the various foods and their methods of preparation as well as the combinations of foods eaten at any given time. The grains were often reduced to Grits — Geres, and were eaten mixed with water or weak wine as a gruel (Thick soup). The grains were ground into Geres, flour (Kemah), and fine flour (Solet), using a hand mill, (quarm).

Kishshuim, bread and cucumbers, were eaten as a lunch or late evening supper, often with Abattiah (Watermelon). Abattiah (Numbers 11:5) are eaten as a meal ending, desert.

Hazaret (Leeks), a member of the Allium family (onions and garlic) are eaten raw with bread or as a relish with meats. Leeks are found in most stews and cholent.

Job 30:4 shows the poor people eating the young leaves of the Orach (Mulluah) plant. The leaves were boiled or eaten raw with vinegar poured over.

The fruit of the Mulberry tree (Shikmah) and the date palm (Tamar) along with (Botnim) pistachio — nuts, were the foods of the poor. Olives (Zayit) and (Rimmon) the pomegranate, rounded out the diet and filled in the food chain.

Milk (Chalav) Deuteronomy 32:14, cream (Shefot) 11 Samuel 17:29, Cottage cheese (Halav) and cheese (Gevinah), (Job 10:10) were the foods of milk from "animals large and small." The milk foods could be found in all diets, rich and poor. Cakes and pies as well as pressed cakes were in vogue. Milk and its by products had to come from a "clean" animal, as outlined in the law.

Boaz's reapers ate roasted ears of corn, bread and sour wine mixed with water. (Ruth 2:14) Lentil pottage, a stew of Jacob, was made of lentils, brown or green, onions, horse beans, chicory and beets, eaten with brine soaked olives and bread. For dessert, dried grapes — raisins, (Numbers 6:3). Esau (Genesis 25:28) cooked his father's favorite food, "Savory Food," venison. Hebrews in the wilderness ate fish, cucumbers, melons, leeks, onions and garlic. (Numbers 11:5).

#29
HAMAN MAHSHI
STUFFED PIGEONS

3 Pigeons, cleaned
3 Tbsp. Oil
1 cup Rice, cooked
$1/2$ tsp. Salt
$1/4$ tsp. Pepper
1 cup Mutton, cooked, minced

1 tsp. Nutmeg

Mix rice, mutton, onion, nutmeg, salt, pepper. Set aside to mello flavor. Wash birds and blot dry. Stuff with mutton mixture. Sew bird shut. Rub bird in oil and dust with salt and pepper. Spike with skewer and roast over medium hot fire. Turn often so bird does not burn. When golden brown (twenty minutest) remove from fire, cut in half and serve with the stuffing on the side.

#30
PARTRIDGE KEBAB

6 Young tender Partridge, cleaned
3 Tbsp. Olive oil
$^1/_2$ tsp. Salt
$^1/_4$ tsp. Pepper
3 Tbsp. Wine vinegar

Wash and dry Partridge. Place on skewer. Mix oil and vinegar and rub over the birds. Pour remaining oil mixture inside the birds. Sprinkle salt and pepper over. Grill over hot fire turning often. When birds are well browned remove and serve with fruit compote. Cooking time is about 20 minutes. You will need to experiment with the cooking time.

Another traditional lamb dish is the tartare of the holy land. This is a dish that is made quickly and then eaten with relish.

#31
KEUFTEH — TZAVAR
Kibeh (Bisenieh) Nayeh

$^3/_4$ lb. Very lean lamb, ground or minced fine
2 medium Onions, chopped fine
1 cup Bulghur (Pre soaked 15 minutes) (Burgul - Burghul)
$^1/_4$ tsp. Cayenne pepper

¹/₂ tsp. Salt
¹/₄ tsp. Pepper
1 bunch Parsley minced
¹/₂ small Green pepper, chopped fine
2 Tomatoes, chopped fine

In a deep china bowl combine all ingredients except tomatoes. Knead for 8-10 minutes. Occasionally dip hands in water, work and blend mixture. Form mixture into patties. Place on serving plate. Sprinkle tomato over the patties. Serve with bread and green salad. (Raw, Nayeh: cooked, Bisenieh).

I Samuel 2:15, says that the wicked sons of Eli preferred roasted meat (Zelah) over that which was boiled or cooked in other fashions. Genesis 27:6 says that Rebekah was a good cook, in fact she could cook kid so that it tasted like the prized venison.

#32
ROAST KID

1 5 lb. Haunch of Goat, well cleaned (If lamb is used,
the item is called shawarma)
3 Tbsp. Olive oil
1 tsp. Salt
¹/₂ tsp. Pepper
1 Tbsp. Hyssop (mint)
2 toes Garlic, sliced

With a sharp knife (Ma'Akelet) cut deep slits into the meat and insert garlic slices. Rub with oil. Dust with herbs and spices. Place spit in position over fire. Rotate slowly until meat takes on an all over even dark brown color, approximately 1 1/2 hours. Baste often with drippings mixed with watered wine. Slice off meat in thin strips as you would do "Hero." Place in pocket bread and serve with lettuce greens and sauce such as Zug or Tihina. 1/4 cut melon is often served as side dish, with a piece of fruit cake.

Fruit was often dried and pressed into a solid cake like mass, Kamr Al — Din, flat cake of apricots, raisins or figs were eaten by all peoples with meat or as a food for the desert trail. One can still see the old men sitting around the fire take a "plug" of fruit cake from their pocket, cut off a small piece and mix it with a bite of goat or lamb hot from the fire. The comingling of flavors is a taste treat.

"These are the animals you may eat: the Ox, the Sheep, and the Goat:" Deuteronomy 14:4.

Prepared as a compote, figs, (TE'ENAH) were eaten year round and were a good source for vitamins and minerals. The bible often talks of Fig Cakes. Isaiah used figs as a medicine for humans (II Kings 20:3) as well as the animals. Dates, figs, grapes, olives were dried and used as food for the traveler on the long caravan routes. Dried fruits and camel's milk was the food that kept men alive for weeks on the trail, in the sands of the desert.

Compote was an easy way to prepare the fruit, so that they would not spoil in the heat. It was noted that through the use of the sweet compote or the citrus compote — confiture, health was improved.

#33
CITRON CONFITURE

Since the earliest of times citron (Etrog) was used as a salad topping, as a sauce for lamb, an aid for fertility, a sauce for strength during pregnancy. Etrog, known as the Median Apple was the basis for this recipe.

2 Etrogs, sliced thin
1 Lemon, sliced thin
2 Oranges, sliced thin
1 Grapefruit, sliced thin

4 cups Water

4 cups Sugar

1 tsp. Cinnamon

Cut fruit in half, remove seeds, cut very thin. Cover with water and let rest overnight. Turn several times. Pour off water. Add sugar and cinnamon. Simmer for 1 hour, stir several times. Pour off into glass jars. Cover tightly.

THE GRASSES

A. **BARLEY** is recorded 5,000 B.C.E. in Egypt as well as Phoenicia (Lebanon). In 3500 B.C.E. we see mention in Mesopotamia (Iraq). In the period of 3000 B.C.E., Israel, Ethiopia and South East Asia all show a substantial use of this grain. Barley was the chief bread grain of the Hebrews and early Greeks. It was heavily used for the flat breads and porridge, also as pearl barley in soups and broth.

The Sumerian codified book, "Farmers Almanac" from the period 2500 BCE, states that the barley seed be planted uniformly "two fingers deep", and "use one shekel of seed for each Garush of land." A garush is a row planted about seven yards long. The grain is reported to be rich in yield, and would compare to the yield experienced in a modern farm using all the newest procedures.

B. **WHEAT** shows itself growing wild in Phoenicia and Israel as well as in China. Two of the original Wild Wheat, Einkorn and Emmer, can still be found growing in Syria, China and Turkey as well as the upper Jordan Valley. Durum Wheat is a cross of these other wheats and is highly prized as a bread grain. Wheat has become in modern times, the largest single cultivated crop in the world. Used primarily as leavened bread, cakes, pastries, spaghetti, and macaroni. Wheat is easily stored and transported.

"Corn shall make the young men flourish, and new wine the maids." (Zacharia 9:17)

The grain, the edible part, had to be separated from the hard bran coat that is encased in a double sheath of chaff. In the wild grain this is very hard to do, and takes considerable effort. When the ear is slightly warmed (roasted) the process is easier since the outer chaff becomes brittle and falls away when rubbed, as in a Quarn. History indicates that "fire pits" were used to heat rocks that were used to roast the grain. Some Tells reflect a "roasting" floor, that was used for this procedure.

The roasted, ground grain was too dry to swallow, so they were mixed with water or wine, kneaded into a paste and eaten as "maza." Later the maza was cooked on the hearth stone and became the flat bread. This early flat bread had to be eaten when hot, because as it cooled, it hardened, and became heavy, virtually indigestible. This bread developed into the Cholla that has come down to modern times.

(Numbers 15:17-21) and the Lord spoke unto Moses, saying, "Speak to the children of Israel, and say unto them: When you come into the land whither I bring you, then it shall be, that, when ye eat of the bread of the land, ye shall set apart a portion for a gift unto the Lord. — Of the first of your dough ye shall give unto the Lord a portion for a gift throughout your generations." The commentary "Man doth not live by bread only" (Deuteronomy 8:11) is not only a figurative statement of the need for spiritual foods, but an indication that the health of the people required the full scope of the variety of the food chain, that of wheat, barley, vines, fig trees, pomegranates, olives and honey for a good life. (Deuteronomy 8:10)

C. **RICE** originated in China more than 5000 years ago and became a major food and trade item throughout Asia and the Middle East along with spices.

D. **RYE** was grown in TURKESTAN and travelled into Israel and Jordan by camel caravan. It is grown mainly on the poor soils that cannot support wheat and barley. Used in bread and as an animal feed it was not considered a very important grain for trade. Rye (Spelt) bread was found in many Egyptian tombs.

Primitive Wheat

E. **OATS** to a lesser degree could be found from Egypt, through Israel, Jordan to southern Turkey. It was used in cakes and porridge.

F. **FLAX** was short lived as a food grain. It became used as animal feed and the straw as bedding material. The oil was used in lamps.

G. **MILLET**, a small seeded annual cereal grain, was a forage grass. The Kaoshan people of Taiwan and the Han people of China, were the millet farmers of history, and fed the crop into the trade routes of Macao and Arabia. Some millet was grown in Mesopotamia and Judah.

H. **SORGHUM** originated in Africa, and was a trade crop to the Roman fleets and the Arab caravans.

I. **MAZE** — CORN, Isaiah 62:8 "Surely I will no more give thy corn to be food for thine enemies, — "; Joel 2:24 "and the floors shall be full of corn, and the vats shall overflow with wine and oil." In an Egyptian papyri, it says, "I have obeyed the message of my lord Rameses in which he said, 'give corn to the native soldiers, and also to the Apuri (Hebrews) who bring stones for the great tower of Pa-Ramessu.'"

Demeter, the sister of Zeus and the daughter of Cronus, was the Greek goddess of "the fruitful earth." She gave the

Prince of Eleusis, ears of corn and the necessary knowledge to cultivate it. The Athenians claim that they were the first to know of corn, and that they passed the information on to the other nations. It should be noted that the corn reference in Egypt and Canaan (Israel), was most probably an expression of plenty, rather than that of the specific grass plant, Corn of the Americas. No tell has reflected the corn plant in the lands of the Fertile Crescent. Corn and the "Roasted Ears", probably refer to wheat which had to be roasted so that the seed could be crushed and eaten.

"The pastures are clothed with flocks; the valleys are covered with corn." (Psalms 65:13)

Maze, Indian corn, "corn of the Americas," was the major cereal grain of the new world. Maze, that we recognize, did not find it's way into Europe and the Middle East, China and India, until well into 1500 C.E. via the return of Columbus. Maize spread throughout the old world in less than fifty years from its introduction to the court of Spain. Corn, as we know it, only developed minor use in the middle east.

The nutritional value of the cereal grains was very important to the health of the peoples in the Middle East. It was the major protein source for body growth. Fruits, berries and nuts filled in the missing links in the food chain. The Mideast did not highly refine the cereal grains as did Rome and Europe, so the full food value of the cereal was utilized for body growth. It is interesting to note the migration of a particular grain from country to country.

Prior to manual cultivation, seeds were distributed mainly by the wind. The grains evolved various wind movement structures: from burs, umbrellas, silken threads, flat wings, roller bodies, etc. So early development was random. Only after man began to selectively collect and plant seeds did we see rows of plants and trees. Each year he would gather the seed, choose the best for planting, as stock seed, trade the remainder in the markets where they found their way into new lands, and the cycle started anew.

J. **FITCHES,** a forage herb (Ezekial 4:9) also known as spelt (Isaiah 28:25) is a wheat of the Triticum Spelt family. It contains two small kernels and was ground for bread. The red kernels added a dark color to breads and, with the development of milling, was eliminated from the recipes.

So we see that the seeds of the grasses were the paramount foods of the peoples of the land. (Genesis 3:18,19) "Your food shall be the grasses of the field; by the sweat of your brow shall you get bread to eat, —."

Cultivation

Cultivation

A major area for this early cultivation was the Plain of ESDRAELON in the Galilee where wheat, barley and olives became major crops for home use as well as trade.

The Jordan River Valley in the Huleh region produced barley, melons and squash. The combined areas became major trade and export stations whose routes flowed into Judea and Samaria. Trade crossed and recrossed the land of Canaan; gold and ivory from Assyria, spices from Arabia for the Hittites, silver from Asia Minor, fish and grain from the Galilee, then into the established trade routes to Egypt and Lebanon.

This land was indeed the land of Milk and Honey. God said, "Let this earth bring forth grass, herbs, yield seed, fruit, trees yielding fruit," — and it was so. And God said, "Behold I have given you every herb bearing seed which is upon the face of the earth, and every tree on which is the fruit yielding seed, to you it shall be for food." (Genesis 1:11,12,29)

Mesopotamia can be singled out as the center of the wheel that produced true selective farming and cattle production. Perhaps this was Eden described in Genesis. The lush bottom lands of the Euphrates River and Tigris River supported fine crop yields that led to trade throughout the spokes of the wheel.

Lachish, conquered by Joshua in 1230 B.C.E., was a rich farm region where they grew corn, grapes and olives along with various vegetables. This area has been reborn in modern times as a major agricultural area.

The spinning and weaving industry dates back to the earliest times and seems to be a house craft that developed in conjunction with the "Grasses" harvest. The development of "Gauze" (linen) apparently takes its name from the town of

Gaza, where it was first manufactured. The fabric was made into blouses in the city of Pelusium, for local use and for trade.

With the development of the iron tools came the need to maintain the cutting edges, and thus the smithing trade. I Samuel 13:19,20,21, "Now there was no smith to be found in all the land of Israel; for the Philistines said, 'Lest the Hebrews make themselves swords or spears;' but everyone of the Israelites went down to the Philistines to sharpen his plowshares, his mattock, his axe or his sickle; and the charge was a pim for the plowshare and the mattock, and a third of a shekel for sharpening the axes and the setting the goads." We can easily assume that the trade of iron work and smithing was soon thereafter a trade of the Israelites.

According to mythology, Ceres made the infant Triptolemus the teacher of men in the use of the plough. "He shall teach men the use of the plough, and the rewards which labor can win from the cultivated soil."

PEAH — corners. Leviticus 19:9,10,11, states that the corners of all fields shall be left for the poor to harvest for their food. This law also holds true for the gleanings of all crops — when the harvest was done, any crop left, be it wheat, grapes or olives, these crops were for the poor so they could eat and not have to ask for food.

In conjunction with cultivation, Deuteronomy 15:1,2,3,4, and Exodus 23:10,11, speak of allowing all fields to sit and rest in the 7th year of the planting cycle so that the earth could regain its strength. This was the beginning of crop rotation and the rule of allowing the land its Sabbath so it could rest and regain the strength for growing. We find all nations have adopted this rule to one extent or another. When a planting cycle does not follow the law, the crops are reduced and eventually the land dies.

Here we see the beginning of sound agrarian systems based on the laws expressed in the Torah, and expounded upon in the Mishnah (the written books of the Oral Law) and the Gemara (written commentary and juristic opinion of the

Oral Law). Section 1 of the Mishnah, Zeraim, (seeds) contain laws relating to agriculture and animal husbandry. With the Diaspora, the rules (Halakah) had to be defined more precisely and codified for all future generations to follow.

The basic crops of the area wheat, barley, chickpeas, millet, lentils, turnips, onions, garlic, leeks and cucumbers with a variety of green vegetables with an occasional meat of the field and fish of the stream, all washed down with a local barley beer.

The Greek writer Archestratus spoke of his travels to "all lands and seas to taste carefully of the delights of the belly." He wrote several cooking books, and assisted in the development of haute cuisine for the rich Athenians. The poor Athenians, according to Alexi of Thurii, ate, as did most of the local natives around the Mediterranean, grasshoppers, wild pears, pulse, turnips, beechnuts, iris flowers and barley paste. The Athenian foods could be found in all the sea port areas of Caanan and Egypt.

#34
ROMAN BEETS

12 Beets
6 Leeks, cleaned and chopped
¹/₂ cup Raisins
¹/₂ tsp. Cumin
¹/₂ tsp. Coriander
1 quart Water

Bring beets to a boil, simmer 20 minutes. Add all remaining ingredients and simmer 20 minutes. Can be served as is or with a yogurt topping.

#35
SELEK
BEET SALAD

6 Beets, peeled and sliced thin
1 tsp. Mustard seeds, crushed
$^1/_2$ cup Olive oil
$^3/_4$ cup Vinegar
$^1/_2$ tsp. Dill, chopped
Mix all together and let set overnight in a cool place.
Tumble and serve as salad with mixed greens.

Beetroot (Beets) Beta Vulgaris, is the same family as the
sugarbeet and swisschard. The beet has been heavily used
since the earliest of history, both as a fruit and as a vegetable.
The Greeks, Mesopotamians, Egyptians, Hittites, all used
the beet in their diets.

#36
MELAFAFONIM SALAT, QUESHU SALAT
CUCUMBER SALAD

12 Cucumbers, washed, cut $^1/_6$ lengthwise
4 Onions, cleaned, sliced thin
$^1/_4$ cup Mustard seed
$^1/_4$ cup Olive oil
2 cups Vinegar
1 tsp. Celery seed (Kill)
$^1/_3$ cup Salt
1 Tbsp. Sugar
Mix onion, salt, cucumber and let sit overnight. Drain
and wash cucumber and onion. Add all remaining ingredients blend well and pour over the cucumber mix. Blend well.
Place in jar or crock. Use the second day.

"The Israelites ate delectable vegetables" (Numbers 11:15)

#37
HIMINADOS
BROWN EGGS

6 *Eggs*
1 *cup Water, cold*
1 *Tbsp. Olive oil*
$^1/_4$ *tsp. Pepper*
$^1/_6$ *tsp. Salt*

Place eggs in a baking dish. Blend all ingredients and pour over eggs. cover with brown paper (or use loose plate). Bake in slow oven 6-8 hours (250°). Eggs will be nicely brown on the outside and tender inside, peel eggs and serve. Usually eaten as a starter with cheese. The egg, according to the Greek writers represents the total world with all it's parts: the shell, earth: the albumin (white), the water of the world: the yolk, fire: air sack, life. Total perfection.

#38
SHAKSHOUKA
EGGS AND TOMATOES

5 *Eggs, beat 4 whips with fork*
2 *medium Onions, minced*
6 *Tomatoes, chopped fine*
1/2 *tsp. Salt*
1/4 *tsp. Pepper*
1/4 *cup Olive oil*

In a large fry pan heat oil and sauté onions until lightly golden, add tomatoes, cover and simmer slowly 15-20 minutes. Add spices, stir. Pour eggs over mixture. Cover and simmer five minutes. Be sure eggs are set. Serve over rice with warm bread on the side.

A. "THE HEBREWS"

The Fertile Crescent, the land of the Hebrew tradition of

Genesis is where civilization began and where it grew and expanded. The Hebrews, were a group of people belonging to the Aramean branch of the Semetic family. The Hebrews, variously called, Apiru, Hapiru, Habiru, Khapiru, Apuriu, and Habiri, are the people of the book, who have been identified before the 13th century B.C.E. living in Canaan. The Canaanites called the people who migrated from beyond the Euphrates, Ebers - Hebrews. These were the descendants of Shem, forefather of Abraham. The Hebrews were positively identified in a clay tablet found in Tell-el-Amarna with the inscription "Habiri."

These are the Israelites, the linchpin of civilization. The Israelites perfected foods in two avenues, ceremonial and common fare. The two became one and became the basis of the relationship between man and God, nature and God.

Among these Hebrews were the forefathers of the Israelite conquests. They were the clans from which sprang the Tribes of Israel. Asher, Naphtali, Zebulum, Issachar, Manasseh, Ephraim, Dan, Judah, Gad, Benjamin, Reuben, Simon. Here we learn of the Law. Of the foods, spices, herbs, of the will of man, and the way of the people who were sweet with "The taste of honey and cinnamon" O.T.

B. THE JEWS

People of the tribe Judah (Yehudah) were called Yehudim, which translated reads Judaioi, Judaei, Juden. Over the years of history the names and terms of identity for the Israelites became mixed and the terms interchangeable. The twelve tribes became of one name — Jews.

The first king of the people Israel was a farmer. Saul, son of Kish, of the tribe of Benjamin, who was a farmer in Gibeah. In his middle years became the hero of Jabesh Gilead by defeating the Ammonites and was declared king by the people - the first King of Israel. Saul was killed at the battle of Mount Gilboa and David became king after a rather brief fight with Ishboshet for the throne.

Under David, (the keeper of flocks), of the tribe of Judah, the Israelites were reunited, the capital of Jerusalem was established, and the Philistines were driven out of the land. David and his son Solomon solidified the kingdom and established the Temple in Jerusalem.

C. THE ISRAELITES
"GOY KADOSH"

The Israelites were people dedicated to, and continually working toward, holiness following the historic precepts of the Patriarchs. The traditions of these people have been carried forward to the present day. The foods of the people, being a part of that history have also been carried forward, and added to so that at any point in time their history is the sum total of the complete experience, and not of a single moment. This is the reason that the fabric of the people is so rich and full... all the experiences, those of joy and travail are the warp and weave. The foods eaten today are all interwoven with Abraham, Isaac, Jacob (known as Israel), Joseph, Moses, Egypt, Canaan, Greece, Rome and later Spain, Portugal, Germany, China, Russia, Norway and America.

Goy Kadosh can be dated back to its beginning when God said to Abraham, "Get thee out of thy country (Ur) ... and from thy father's house, unto the land that I will show thee..." (Canaan). Later when Abraham was tending his fields in Egypt (Gohen), he again was told by god, "I will give unto thee and to thy seed after thee ... all the land of Canaan ...and I will be your God." Abraham returned to Canaan.

There is considerable conjecture as to which Ur Abraham indeed came from. Ur of Mesopotamia or Ur of Syria, which was located near Haran. The Bible (Deuteronomy 26:5) states that Abraham was a wandering Aramaean, which would make him a Syrian, then the Bible says that Abraham grew up in Ur of the Chaldees, which would make him an original Iranian. Both the Urs of history had a rich agricultural background, and could easily fit into the story of Abraham and his migration down to the "Promised Land." I am sure that the development of Tell Ebla (Tell Mardikh) will reveal much interesting material from its huge recently discovered but yet to be translated library. This library (circa 2300 BCE - 2200 BC. Describes the city of Ebla and its population of some 300,000 persons. This city was the center of a huge agricultural economy. On one clay Eblaite Cuneiform a warehouse of mention contained 548,500 measures of Barley. That is enough food to feed 18,000 meals, 3/4 cup size. The city records 30,000 "men of trade", farmers, bureaucrats, artisans, and scribes.

It was said that in Canaan, Abraham's tent had four doors, so that a traveler coming from any direction could easily find entrance for food, drink and shelter. This was the first known Hostel or Hotel, so indeed Abraham established the Hospitality Industry. Abraham pitched his tent at Beth-El (Genesis 12:8) or some say a stone throw away at Ai (Ha-Ai).

Abraham started the Jewish agriculture history in Canaan, centuries later his descendants could still be found on the land, some as semi-nomads with their flocks and others as steady farmers. In the period 100-150 C.E. the Romans drove the Jews off the land and into the cities, however there has been a continuing history of Jewish farming from those early days up through today.

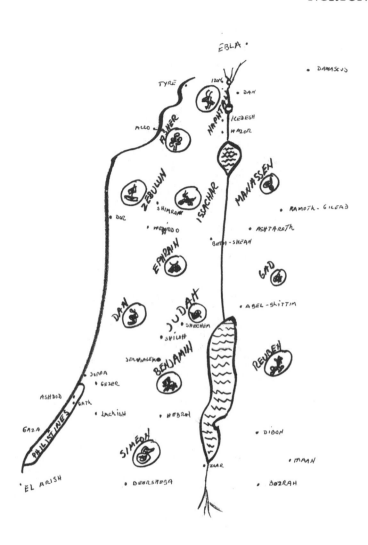

The tribes of Israel with land allocations.

91

Camel Caravan

Spices - Seasonings

Salt, fruit sugar, pepper, M.S.G., have been used as flavor agents since the earliest recorded time. These items have been used to make food more palatable, and to preserve the foods. Written history has shown that man has continually searched for compatible combinations of foods and flavorings to make food taste better, as well as look better. The shelf life of food was increased with the addition of salt and peppers. This eliminated the necessity of completing everything at one sitting. Food could be kept for days and in some cases weeks or even months. In ancient days they had very few refrigerators or freezers. The extension of food holding was exemplified by ANTIOCHUS who was famous for his heavy use of spices at his lavish banquets, some that lasted for weeks at a time.

Not only was spice a main point of the food culture, it became a most important part of the religious life. "Take choice spices; 500 weight of solidified Myrrh, — 250 of fragrant cinnamon, 250 of aromatic cane, 500 — by the sanctuary weight - of cassia, and a hin of olive oil. Make this a sacred anointing oil — with it anoint the Tent of Meeting, —." The Tent of Meeting was the Tabernacle built by Moses in the wilderness. Ohel Moed, Mishkan — (Exodus 25.26) built and decorated by Bazalel and Oholiab, rested in Shiloh before moving to the temple in Jerusalem.

Spices yesterday and today are bought in an Attarine, a small shop of shops, located in a spice selling street, or at the spice gate of the city, usually located on the main route into the town.

With the introduction of new spices the art of cooking improved and the number of recorded parties increased. Conjecture implies that as cooking improved it became more of a fashion to give parties for friends and guests. Theognis, the Greek elegiac poet, in the fifth century BCE wrote, "one finds many companions for food and drink but," he states, "few for hard work." The spiced foods added the festive touch lacking in early history.

The Phoenicians, the Arabs, King Solomon, King Hiram of Tyre, were all very heavily involved in the spice trade. The famous Queen of Sheba brought into Israel a tremendous train of camels loaded with herbs and spices from her home, the area now known as Yemen. Spices of many colors and flavors abounded in the "secret" spice lands. Sesame, ginger, chili peppers, cumin, coriander, hyssop, sage, fenugreek, just to name a few, are the spices of the Middle East. Through commerce they all found their way into Greece, Rome, Spain, then into the north countries with the Vikings. Later the nine crusades carried the spices, herbs, and food ways of the Holy Land into all of Europe.

Later still, Nicolo Polo and his son Marco began their seventeen year journey to fully unlock the secrets of trade in Cathay, Indochina, Burma, India and Mongolia. Marco Polo's book was the end of the "Fertile Crescent" control of the spice trade and it set the stage for the competitive dash around the world by Spain, Portugal, the Dutch, and, finally, England. This flood of exploration was to find the shorter route to Marco Polo's world of spices, herbs and gold.

SPICES

The following is a listing of the spices of antiquity with their major location and mention of some medicinal properties:

Allspice; Pilpel Angli, from the Pimento Tree, Asia and Caribbean Islands.

Anise; a seed, cousin of parsley, Egypt and India, used to cure coughs.

Caraway; Kimmel, Asia Minor, another Viking favorite brought into the north countries early in history. Used as a stomach cure and throat lozenge.

Cardamon; Hail, a seed of the ginger family, India, a favorite of the Vikings.

Cassia (akakia) (malabathrum); cousin of cinnamon, used in baking.

Citron; the golden apple of Hersperides, used as diet aid, used in jam in an herb used as a spice.

Celery seed; Smallage, Asia, Homer's favorite, used to aid rheumatism

Cinnamon; Cassia, Bark of the Chinese "Tree of Life", China and Ceylon, an aphrodisiac of history (Tarchin)

Cloves; Ziporen, flower bud from Moluccas, Indonesia. (garifallo)

Coriander; Cousbera, "Manna from heaven", see Numbers 11:6,7,8,9. Was listed in the Medical Papyrus of Thebes 1552 BCE. Used to cure flatulance. (kollantro) Used in meat and pastries (Gintz) (Gad)

"Now the Manna was like coriander seed and the appearance of Bdellium — and ground it in mills (quarm) — and made cakes that tasted of it if baked with oil." (Bdellium/Bedholah a gum resin similar to Myrrh)

The Song of Songs 3:13,14 talks of the chief spice "Thy plants are an orchard of Pomegranates, with pleasant fruits, Camphire with Spikenard, Saffron, Calamus and Cinnamon, with all trees of Frankincense, Myrrh and Aloes."

1800 years before Christ, Joseph was sold by his brother to "a company of Ishmaelites come from Gilead, with their camels bearing spice, herbs, and balm and myrrh, going to Egypt."

Condiments found in King Tut's Tomb show quantities of black pepper, juniper berries, beetles, raisins, dates, ground date stones, fruit of Persia tree, fruit and seed of Nabq tree, coriander, barley, melon seed, onion, Acacia bark, tar, henna, hemp, and several barks and seeds. Other condiments were too decomposed to be properly identified.

The Pharisees paid tithes of mint, anise and cumin.

Cumin; Camon, Egypt and Israel (Kezah) (kimino) used to spice meats and cheese (Chaman).

Curry Powder Mix; There are six distinctively different powders, India.

Fenugreek seed; Hilbe, aids digestion, Southern Mediterranean. (Chaiman)

Four Spice; Cinnamon, nutmeg, cloves, ginger, mixed equally together.

Garlic: Shum, from the Garden of Eden according to legend. Found throughout the Mediterranean, Mullucc, India. The Jews of Egyptian bondage brought garlic with them in the Exodus. Garlic has been held near sacred by the Hebrews, Greeks and Egyptians. The Greeks used it for Temple purification. Egyptians used it to invoke the gods. The Hebrews used garlic as part of the wedding ceremony. It has been from earliest times used as an antiseptic.

Ginger; Zangvill, Rhodes and Egypt.

Horseradish; a root of the Mideast, condiment, used to clear the nose and head.

Lebanese spice; 1 tsp. Cayenne, 2 tsp. Paprika, 2 tsp. Cinnamon blended well.

Mace; Koshet, the outer skin of Nutmeg. Used in baking.

Mahlab; ground cherry pit kernels, an aromatic spice for meats and fruit.

Mustard seed; Clardal, Sinapis, Greece, China Cylon, use as a poultice.

Moroccan Spice; 1 tsp. Coriander, 2 tsp. Cumin blended well.

Nutmeg; Egoz Muscat, nut of Mulluccas and India.

Paprika; Pilpelet, ground sweet red pepper, India.

Poppy Seed; Pereg, Western Asia, Israel.

Pepper, black; Pilpel, the master spice, green berries, Asia.

Pepper, white; Pilpel, ripe berries, Asia.

Joshua brought pepper from Nazhana (Nizhana) in the Upper Galilee to prove to Hadrian that Israel lacks nothing. Pepper corns were used to cure halitosis. Used as a medium of exchange, pepper came to be called "Black Money." In the Biblical period pepper was expensive so a substitute was often used by the poor people, the seed of the bitter Vetch (Eccles 6:1).

Red Pepper; Shata, Cayenne, (Biber), Middle East.

Salt; The spice for making a covenant (II Chronicles 13:5) was obtained from the mines of Sedom or from evaporating the waters of the Dead Sea. Melah, salt, was a major spice of the Bible. "Sedom or Sodom Salt" is a rock salt gathered in the southern extremity of the Dead Sea and is often mentioned in the Talmud. Taricheae on the Sea of Gennesaret was the major location for making salted fish. Elisha cured the poisonous springs near Jericho by throwing salt into them. Salt was used in the preparation of the "Show Bread" and was also used in conjunction with every sacrifice by the priests. New born children were rubbed with salt.

Saffron, Za'faran; used as a hair pomade by the Assyrians, a perfume by Antiochus and as a dye by the Phonecians. The Egyptians concocted an anointing oil from saffron, cinnamon, cassia and myrrh. Used in cooking to produce a bright yellow color and a soft exotic flavor...

A city of major spice importance was En-Gedi. Due to abundant water and a warm and friendly climate it was renowned for growing many rare and costly spices. History shows that the city built terraces, aqueducts and reservoirs for growing of its crops, then had to build strongholds and watchtowers to protect their valuable crops. The town flourished during the Israelites, Hellenistic, and Greco - Byzantine periods. En-Gedi was pointed out by Josephus as a major producer of "Opobalsomon" Balsam.

Saffron saffrin (Corcoom - Koorcoom); (Kirkoum) center of the crocus flower. Song of Solomon 4:13,14,15.

Sesame Seed; Susum, Assyria and Israel. Herb used as spice.

Tumeric; Karkum, root of the ginger family, India, called oriental saffron.

Taklia; Coriander garlic, in equal parts fried together in thick roux

Vanilla Pod; Asia, a flavor for baking and custards

Zaatar; a mixed spice for Pita.

In addition to spices, foods were enhanced with the use of herb plants. They were used fresh or dried. Since herbs have such a distinct flavor, they were used in small quantities and carefully. Many of the herbs have been used as medicines since the earliest times. Each herb was used for a different cure by the Egyptians, Greeks and Hebrews. The color or texture of the herb was a key to the medical use to which it was put. Some nuts are part of the herb culture.

HERBS

Apsinthos; Wormwood, Hemlock, Gall. A bitter herb, used to strengthen digestion.

Balsam; Israel, leaf of the shrub. Used in stew and soup.

Basil; Raihan. Called Tulasi in India. Pliny called it a medicine for the heart.

Balm; of the mint family (Menta) tastes like lemon

Bay Leaf; Alei Dafna, of the laurel tree. According to legend Daphne turned into the laurel to escape Apollo.

Caper; bud of the caper bush, used as relish. (Nasi) grew in and around the Temple at Jerusalem, can be found today growing in crevices of the Western Wall.

Capsicum; Chillis, small pepper, smoky pepper flavor.

Chervil; See Git, Native of Russia. Brought to Rome, then to Israel by the Legion.

Chives; Bazelit, part of the onion family. Used as aid to purify the blood.

Citron; Kitron, juice used as spring tonic and in baking for flavor. (Etrog)

Dill; Shamir, part of the parsley family, called "Evil Eye" throughout the Mediterranean; used to cure head colds. (Djinns) (Samit)

#39
DILL SQUAB WITH KASHA

4 lbs. Squabs, cut in half (you may substitute with
    chicken or game birds)
1/4 cup Olive Oil
1/4 cup Pine Nuts, shelled
5 medium Carrots, cleaned, cut in half
2 medium Onions, sliced
1/4 tsp. Pepper
1/2 tsp. Thyme
3 Tbsp. Dill, chopped (fresh is best)
2 cups Dry White Wine
1 cup Chicken Stock (you may use vegetable stock)

2 medium Eggs, lightly beaten
1 cup Kasha (Buckwheat Groats)
1/2 tsp. Salt
1/4 tsp. Pepper

Heat oil and brown the bird on all sides. Remove bird from oil and set aside. To the oil add carrots, onion, herbs and spices. Sauté lightly until onions are golden. Add wine, stock, and stir. Bring to a rolling boil. Remove from fire and add the bird. Mix well. Set pan aside. In a heave sauce pan add Kasha and pour egg over. Blend well over medium heat as you add salt and pepper. Continue heating as you stir for three (3) minutes. Combine Kasha and bird. Add nuts, blend evenly. Cover tightly and place in a pre-heated oven 325°. Bake for fifteen (15) minutes, check for doneness; serve with warm Pita bread and green Israeli olives and a tossed salad with vinegar dressing. I have seen this recipe prepared with Squab, Chicken, Turkey, Pigeon and wild bird. One recipe I saw prepared in Jerusalem was made with the addition of 1/4 cup pepper grass, another recipe from Bethlehem used Israeli Parsley (added, chopped fine) in the Kasha blend. You might want to try each of the variety items to see which you like the best.

Fitches; a forage herb (Ezekial 4:9), (Isaiah 28:25) Spelt, is a wheat of the family Triticum Spelta, containing two red kernels (Emmer)

Fennel; Shashoram, used in baking, one of the nine sacred herbs. North Mediterranean. Used as a stomach medicine.

Hyssop; (Ezobh) a drug, curative (Numbers 19:18). Used for its oil, from the Evergreen shrub. A cure for coughs and colds. Used in purification.

Hell; seed of the celery plant, used in soup and stew, a breath sweetener.

Leek; Crousha, a long onion, as a blood tonic.

Lemon; used since earliest times as an herb, a fruit, a pickle, cooking flavor. As a strengthening elixir for pregnant women.

Lovage; of the parsley family, tastes like celery.

Juniper; used to cure meats. Curative for kidney ailments.

Khubeisa; Haalamit, Bread of the starving. Herb used as a vegetable.

Marjoram; of the mint family. Lebanon, Israel, Egypt. Used as a cure for inter chills.

Mastic; Greek resin, favorite of Turks. Flavor in baking and wine making.

Mint; Menta, Ovid wrote that mint was used to sweeten the smell in the house of Bacchus. (Nane)

Myrhh; Though a gum resin, is used as an herb to add flavor. Used as a curative for ulcers.

Nutmeg; Sweet spice of India.

Onion; Bazal. A bulb, used to cure the cold and make roasting meats sweet to the taste. Gave strength to the blood.

Oregano; Savory of the mint family, Lebanon, Turkey, Greece.

Parsley; Petrazilia. Greek mythology says Hercules wore garland of parsley to build his strength. Used as a cure for kidney and bladder complaints.

Peppergrass; of the mustard family, has horseradish flavor, used to replace parsley.

Pimento; Camba. Sweet red peppers.

Pine Nuts: Pinones. From the Pignolia Tree, a mountain pine tree.

Purslane: Succulent herb of Portulaca family.

Rose; triantafillo, strong flavor used in fowl, desserts, and candies.

Rosemary; Rozmarian. Evergreen mint from Israel and Lebanon. Used as stimulant for the hair and for nervous stomach. (dendrolivano) used for fish, meat.

Sage; Salvit. From Dalmatia. Used as a gargle to cure laryngitis and tonsilitis.

Sesame; Halvah candy and Tahini sauce is made from the crushed seed.

Sorrel; Hamzitz. Used in soups and salads.

Sumac; Zaater. Used in bread making.

Tarragon; Korianite. Unknown in ancient days, but used heavily today.

HERBS, SPICES, SEED FLAVORINGS

Scheherazad opened the pirates cave of gold by using Sesame — "Open Sesame." The sesame was crushed into an oil, and the oil was used to grease the hinges on the cave door so that it would open easily, or so the story goes. Herbs are used as foods, as seasonings, as recipes for curing ailments, also as dyes and scents. So you see that at any given meal you can be intaking very important vitamins and minerals, making the food taste better, and look better as well as improving it's holding qualities.

Most herbs should be eaten fresh for maximum benefit, but dried they do help, and better dried than left out completely. In cooking with herbs, they should be added toward the end of the cooking cycle so that their full benefits are retained and not boiled away.

Dill, thyme, marjoram, parsley, used properly will help to reduce the need for "TUMS" or "Alka Seltzer" after a heavy meal of fish or stew, for that matter when ever you overdue on saturated fats the herbs will help what ails you. The herbs have a capacity to rework fats so that they do not lay heavy in the stomach. Parsley is a wonderful source for vitamins and the trace minerals that are so necessary to good health, and according to Pliny, it aids a full belly.

It has been found that eating undercooked vegetables and herbs aid in the elimination of catarrh and cholesterol. The herbs ingested in their raw state or al-dente act as a mild diaphoretic, as well as a carminative. Their alkaline salts counteract the fats of many foods. They are not a cure all but they sure do help, as can be testified to by the medical reports of ancient Greece, Rome, Egypt, and China.

Fennel used in the preparation of fish is a centuries old aid to digestion. A stomach tonic for infant's colic, that has been used since early Israeli times is this elixir: Steep 1 tsp. Anice, 1 tsp. Caraway Seeds, 1 tsp. Catnip. Strain through fine sieve and serve the liquid slightly warm to the child, or for that matter to grandad when they have the stomach "Humors." It tastes good even if it doesn't work every time.

Measles were cured says Pliny, by making a tea of 2 tsp. Catnip, 2 tsp. Marjoram, 1/2 tsp. Saffron. Strain and serve six times daily.

Sachets of sweet herbs are wonderful in a dark closet or dresser drawer. Bags of mixed herbs and spices and bags of ground rinds of lemon, tangerine and orange peel, mixed with clover, cloves, all-spice and hung in a damp room would remove the odor as you worked in eliminating the water. The bride always made a bag of Rosebuds, lavender, Cinnamon sticks and cracked nutmeg to pack in the clothes chest.

Have a dandruff problem, no problem, early doctors took a tsp. each of Rosemarie, Sage, and stinging nettles, mixed in a quart of warm water, set aside for six to eight hours, strained and then rubbed into the scalp. Rinsed out with rain water and by magic, no more dandruff ...they also said that it would grow hair in the spots that were beginning to thin out.

Chamomile is used to flavor wine and as a tea to help the gall bladder rid itself of stones. Pliny said "Use for all gastrointestinal problems, disorders." It tastes good and you will not have morning-after mouth.

Fennel water is a stimulant for poor eaters, young or old. Parsley ground up in a meat loaf provides a major supply of vitamins A, C, B complex, and the minerals calcium, copper, iron, manganese. The Chinese Herbalists say that Parsley is a must for a woman with a child. When someone has a very bad cold Barley soup with coriander is even better than chicken soup.

In our ultra modern society where we have only to open cans and heat frozen dinners, we are finding more health problems being traced back to poor nutrition. Facts are facts, we can eat better, eat for less money, feel better and look better if we get away from all those highly processed, chemically altered, canned, boxed, and frozen, prepared foods and cook from scratch. Listen to the ancients who lived to ages of 150 years or more by eating the good foods of the land.

SUKAR

Sugar; though neither a spice nor herb, it is used as both in the flavoring of foods. Heavily used in baking and candy making, it has become a major "spice."

Sugar in various forms can be found in many of the oldest recipes, however due to its cost it was not used in every day cooking by the masses. Honey or date honey was the substitute for "refined" sugar.

Tawahin es- Sukar, a ruin of a sugar mill, has been found outside of Jericho, and another one has been found near the town of Zo'ar (Sogher) near the Dead Sea. Some authorities say that the name "Sugar," comes from the town name, Sogher.

Sugar preserving is the age old method of keeping vine ripe fruit from spoiling. The easiest method of extending holding time for fresh fruit is to mix it in varying concentrations of sugar and water. The concentration determines if the fruit is to be a preserve, jam, conserve, marmalade or "canned" for travel.

Usually "canned" fruit is in a sugar/water ratio of ½ and ½. Preserved fruit is in a sugar/water ratio of ⅔ and ⅓. **Preserves** try to save the shape and texture of the fruit. **Jams** puree everything as fine as possible, simmer it down and then add the sugar. **Marmalades** use everything of the fruit (usually citrus) except the seeds and keep nice firm pieces in the mix. **Conserves** are mixtures of several fruits and often add nuts to the mix. Almonds, walnuts, hazelnuts were common. A typical recipe of the ancients:

#40
ORANGE, CITRON MARMALADE

4 Oranges
1 Citron
2 Lemons

Wash all fruit. Slice all very thin. Remove seeds as you go. Place in a crock pot or stainless steel bowl. Add 1 1/2 quarts water, cover and let sit overnight to soften the fruit. Bring to boil, simmer for 1 hour, set aside to cool. Cover and let set overnight. Add 3 cups sugar. Bring to boil, stir well. Simmer for 1 hour. Taste for cups sugar. Bring to boil, stir well. Simmer for 1 hour. Taste for proper flavor. Some people desire more sugar and thin slices of ginger root. If you add sugar or ginger, again bring to a boil and stir well. Pour off into a glass jar or crock. Use up as needed in the next two weeks.

You may change this basic recipe to a conserve by adding 2 cups currants or 2 cups pitted sour cherries and 2 cups sugar to the last boil. Then stir in 1/2 cup nuts. Blend well and portion out as before. This addition becomes more of an Oriental or Indian dish.

#41
MUHALABIEH, FLAN, ZABAGLIONE, SABAYON, EGG PIE
SWEET RICE CUSTARD

6 *Eggs*
3 *Tbsp. Honey*
1 *cup Milk*
2 *Tbsp. Butter, melted*
1 *cup Rice, cooked, hot*
3 *tsp. Sugar*
1 *tsp. Cinnamon*

Pour butter over rice and mix well, set aside. Beat egg yolks with sugar, milk and cinnamon and cream well. Place in a double boiler or in a water bath. Stir over medium fire until just before boiling. Stir until mixture thickens then add rice and mix well. Be sure rice is fully coated. Pour into bowl and allow to cool and fully set. Beat egg whites stiff. Portion out custard and put dollop of egg white on top. Pour crushed pomegranate seeds or raisins over top.

Custards were a very important part of the cuisine of early China, India, Egypt, Mesopotamia, the food has come down to modern day fairly well in tact. Custards were made with fruits, legumes, grasses, berries, seeds and select herbs. Alexander served custards at all state functions, as did the Kings of the Israelites.

Sugar; the white crystalline sweet substance is known as sucrose, and is a member of the large family called carbohydrate. In ancient days the source of "commercial" sugar was from the sorghum cane, the Wild Date Palm, and the honey comb.

Sugar is formed in nature through photosynthesis. History indicates that sugar cane was brought into Asia and the Middle East from Africa, during the period 1000 BCE through 400 BCE and was recorded in the activities of India and Anatolia, as well as Mesopotamia. The early name "Sakara", and "Khannda", has come down to modern times as sugar and candy. Persia in the period 35 BCE to around 490 AD has many references to the solid form of sugar.

The Old Testament refers to the sweetness (sukariyot — Sugar) in bread, and the taste of honey.

The Chinese introduced the methods of extracting sugar from cane to the Arabs during the Chou period, approximately 770 BCE. The Arabs spread the culture throughout the Fertile Crescent. Early Egyptian writing talks of sugar manufacture.

Sugar was scarce during the Biblical period and therefore was treated as a luxury reserved for the Kings and Potentates. Sugar could be found moving with the spice trade.

Sugar cane is a giant perennial grass of the Saccharum family. The sugar beet has been grown for centuries in Mesopotamia and Israel, but only in modern times has it been used for other than cooking, use as a vegetable.

The date palm is indigenous to the area from Egypt to Persia, and is found in 30 distinct varieties. The Israeli palm, "Phoenix Doctylifera" can be traced to the earliest recorded history. The fruit of the tree, the date, is a one seed berry, oblong in shape, contains 50% sugar, and about 2% protein 2% fat, 2% mineral matter and the balance of weight in water and fiber. The palm is not only a major supplier of sugar and syrup (sirup), but the trunk supplies lumber, the mid ribs of the leaf supply material for weaving as well as furniture and basket making. The leaves are used as fuel, the fruit stalks for making rope. Date sugar is made from the sap of the tree and the pressed fruit. The date palm plays a major role in the celebration of the Feast of Tabernacles ...Sukkot.

The Mandrake must be mentioned, though not an herb or spice it had a place in the flavor world of both. Called the "Love Apple," it is a plant of the potato family, ground and used as a drug for surgery and a poison if used improperly. Worn as a Talisman to guard against the evil eye it was used by the Greeks (Javan, Iawones) and Egyptians as well as the Hebrews. Its appearance is that of a yellow plum like fruit with soft pulp. (Genesis 30:14,15) The Mandrake was credited with producing fertility.

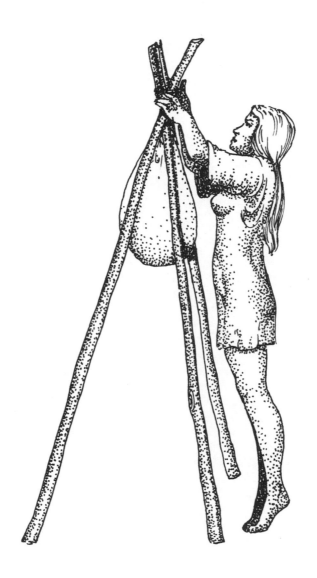

Woman With Goatskin

Eating Habits and the Development of Cuisine

In the period from 5000 BCE to 4500 BCE it was not uncommon for the locals to cook a meal (GIPA) in the cleaned and scraped stomach of the animal just killed. This method of cooking produced the first example of the casserole. The skin would be oiled then stuffed with cut vegetables, meat chunks and water, closed up and affixed on an "A" frame positioned alongside the fire. Often the bones of the animal would be added to the scant wood supply to produce a longer lasting fire that was necessary in the slow cooking, simmer, of this cooking method. The Scythians were particularly noted for this method of cooking. The method migrated into the north countries and found its way into Scotland as "Haggis", into Hungary and Slovenia as "Mogen" and could be found with the Vikings as well as the Visagoths and Goths. Stuffed stomach became a basic food of all the areas.

The locust played an important part in the local diet, when dried (toasted) it is eaten much like pop-corn is eaten today (take a bag to the theater). The locust was a great benefit to the diet as it contains 75% protein, 20% fat and the balance is nutrients, vitamins and minerals. The item is still eaten in parts of Africa and in the remote parts of the Middle East where farming production is in a state of decline.

As we become more involved in the foods of the country we must ask the question who cooked the food? "Lehem" referred to a general meal, and this was always cooked by woman. Kerah or Zevah, large festival or religious meals were more often than not prepared by groups of cooks, primarily men, so as to lend more importance to the preparation and the service of the foods. This tradition has been carried down to current times. Women cook the home meals but when we go out for "fancy" foods, the kitchen is usually run by men.

Eating habits of the Middle East during ancient times had a high incident of vegetarianism. Some due to religion and purification, but mainly due to the limited availability of meat to anyone outside the upper classes. This is why we find a preponderance of vegetable dishes carried forward into modern times.

In Judaism the forefathers of the Hebrews were strict vegetarians, that was changed with Noah's flood. Since then, meat has been permitted, but only under the laws of Kashrut, the blood had to be removed, since this was regarded as the "life source." This was the first of what would become the Jewish dietary laws. Later, some animals, fowl and fish were prohibited. Ascetic Jews discouraged meat eating on the grounds of it being cruel and gluttonous. Some early Christian Monastic orders and Muslim Sufi Mystics also stressed meatless diets.

The Laws of Noah

The Noahide laws apply to all peoples. These laws were encumbent upon Noah and all his descendants — the whole human race — and were commanded by God to be observed.

In the seven laws, the people were to refrain from;
a. Idolatry
b. Adultery and Incest
c. Bloodshed
d. Blasphemy
e. Robbery
f. Social Injustice
g. Eating flesh from a living animal

#42
AFUY HATZILIM KISHUIM
Baked Mixed Vegetables

2 small Eggplant, peeled, sliced

110

4 *large Zucchini, scraped, washed, sliced*
6 *medium Potatoes, peeled, sliced*
1 *medium Red Pepper, cleaned, sliced*
9 *Tomatoes, sliced*
2 *medium Onions, sliced*
8 *Okra, tops removed, sliced*
1 *¹/₂ cup Olive oil*
1 *tsp. Salt*
¹/₂ tsp. Pepper
1 *bunch Parsley, chopped*
1 *cup Hot water*

Arrange all vegetables in a well greased baking dish. Sprinkle salt over, add pepper. Add olive oil, sprinkle parsley over and then add the hot water. Cover and bake at 325° for 1₁/₂ hours. Remove cover fifteen minutes before done to produce a crust. Serve with warm pita bread and a bottle of Adom Atic — slightly sweet red wine. Here is a typical main meal vegetarian dish that can be traced into the earliest days prior to the recorded history of the land and is as modern as today.

1. KASHRUT

The dietary laws of the Hebrews, called KASHRUT, is the law of "fit" food. Leviticus 11:1-43 tells what can be eaten. The law is specific as to animals, fish and fowl that may be eaten. Leviticus 11:44,45 explains why the Israelites must be observant, and in Leviticus 20:25,26 expounds why the children of Israel must be holy. The injunction is very hard to follow and for this reason it is thought that keeping Kosher is a test of personal strength, for the regulation of the individual's life, the establishment of self control and the proving of the mastery of self to one's self.

Other non-Judaic religious groups of the area also follow the basic laws of Kashrut as part of their beliefs and life style, as did the early Christians.

Dietary Laws

"Tahor" — clean, and "tame" — unclean, can be traced to Noah and the instructions from God. "Of clean beasts take seven and seven —, and of the not clean only take two and two —." The seven clean animals are ox, sheep, goat, hart, gazelle, roebuck and pygary, plus wild antelope and mountain sheep of the high lands. 42 animals are specifically listed as unclean. 24 birds are listed as unclean and some are specifically listed as clean, including: pigeons, turtle dove, palm dove, hen quail, partridge, peacock, pheasant, house sparrow, duck and goose. All reptiles are unclean. All fish with scales are clean including carp, trout, salmon, herring, sturgeon and swordfish.

Liberal Judaism leaves it to each individual whether or not to observe Kashrut according to his own judgment. Orthodox and most of Conservative Judaism does not allow this flexibility in accepting the law.

Leviticus 11:3, "Whatsoever parteth the hoof, and is wholly cloven-footed and cheweth the cud, among the beasts, that may ye eat.." Pork therefore was specifically rejected by the Bible, and was expounded on in the written commentary of the elders.

Leviticus 11:7 and Deuteronomy 16:8 both make specific prohibition against eating the flesh of pig and boar. The pig is pointed out by name as not being allowed as food. Idolatrous worship used the pig in high sacrifice. In Isaiah 66;4 the words are loud and clear against the eating of "swine's flesh." It is easy to see from the many references in the Sacred writings why the observant Jew and coreligionists refrain in their eating habits.

The dietary laws had a definite sequence of development from Noah. Beginning with A. prohibition from eating living animals. Then progressing to B. Tahor, purity C. Fit/Unfit animals.

The specific biblical reference that are so important to the Dietary Laws are Leviticus 11:9. "These may ye eat of all that are in the waters: Whatsoever hath fins and scales...", Leviticus 11:3, "Whatsoever parteth the hoof, and is wholly cloven-footed, and cheweth the cud, among the beasts, that may ye eat." Ecclesiastes 9:7, "Eat thy bread with joy." Deuteronomy 12:21, "when you kill of the heard" refers to the method of slaughter. Leviticus 17, 12, speaks of the blood removal requirement, and lastly is Deuteronomy 14:21, "for though are a holy people unto the Lord thy God. Thou shall not seethe a kid in it's mothers milk."

No matter which meal is prepared or eaten, at the ending of the meal the prayer after eating is said, (Birkat Ha-Mazon) Deuteronomy 8:10, "Thou shall eat and be satisfied and bless the Lord thy God —." This prayer, the "Birkat" is called the Grace of Moses, who recited the words (this benediction) when the manna fell from heaven.

Pork eating by the latter day followers of Jesus (the revised religion) came into being as a rejection of Judaism in general and the reform practices of Jesus specifically, as well as the new independent religion of the Diciples of Christ, and their reinterpretation of what they perceived as the teachings of the "Rabbi from Nazareth." It was in the city of Jaffa (Yaffo) that the Christian stories of Tabatha and Simon the tanner were written. (Acts 9:36-42, 10:10-19) "Peter stayed in the house of Simon, and while asleep on the roof, had a dream." This dream was interpreted to allow Christians to eat of the flesh of "unclean animals," even though that was a direct contradiction of the word of Jesus and the teaching of his Jewish born disciples. The split was now complete and non reversable.

The Koran emphatically states that all "good" things are allowed, and refers to those foods of the "people of the book" in categorical fashion. The Koran forbids in specific terms: corps, blood, meat of swine and of animals slaughtered as offering to others than God.

Luke, the only gentile among the Apostles of Christ, acted as a devout Jew, making it very clear (in the N.T.) even after the Pentecost that they remain faithful to the practices of

Judaism, (Luke 24:53, Acts 2:42,46; 3:1) and follow all the laws and teachings of the Holy Scriptures.

Later at the "Council of Jerusalem (Acts 15:2-5) the leaders of the new church decided that it would be easier to make converts if they followed Paul's radical position and forget the Law, so that it would be easier to gather in Gentile converts. History shows Paul to be the winner in this ancient battle for political power. Through Paul's ramrod tactics the "Universal Church" was firmly established and the groundwork was laid for the Diaspora of the Jewish people, the Galut. It is interesting to note that Paul, the most orthodox Jew of the thirteen disciples, was the most outspoken for the abandonment of the Laws, so that they could convert the Gentiles, when he found he was unable to convert the Jews.

Fowl of various kinds were eaten with relish; roosters, chicken, quail, squab, turkey, goose, pheasant, partridge and duck, just to name a few of the birds eaten from the Noahide period through the Roman periods. Roasted goose was perhaps the most important and the most popular of all the birds. The goose was the major bird of the period of Egyptian captivity. Fowl were almost always roasted, though some were baked and some boiled.

Exodus 16:13, Quail, a food given to the children of Israel by the Lord God. "At dusk ye shall eat flesh, and in the morning ye shall be filled with bread; — and it came to pass at even, that the quails came up, and covered the camp; —"

#43
QUAIL IN RICE

5 Quail, cleaned and cut in halves
1/2 cup Olive oil
2 medium Onions, minced
2 Tbsp. Parsley, minced
1 tsp. Salt

114

$^1/_2$ tsp. Pepper
2 cups Rice, pre-cooked
$^1/_2$ cup Vegetable Stock
1 cup Water

Heat oil and brown birds on all sides. Add onions and cook until transparent. Add parsley, salt, pepper and mix well. Add stock, cover and simmer 20 minutes. Add rice and water. Cover and simmer for twenty minutes. Check for tenderness. leg should easily separate from joint. Historic writing shows the quail to be a favorite food. Easy to catch in nets or by hand when asleep on the ground. The quail was a tasty meal for rich and poor alike, and combined well with most vegetables beans or starch.

#44
BAKED PARTRIDGE

4 Partridge, cleaned and cut in halves
$^1/_2$ cup Olive oil
1 tsp. Salt
$^1/_2$ tsp. Pepper
2 toes Garlic. minced
1 cup Dry red wine
2 Lemons, juiced

Wash and blot bird dry. Dust with salt and pepper. Brown well in hot oil. Add all remaining ingredients. Cover and bake for 1 hour in 325° oven. (Can be cooked on top of the stove with a tight cover and low heat for about 3/4 hour.) Check for doneness. Serve with rice. This basic recipe can be found in the full scope of the Greek and Roman cooking. They most probably borrowed the recipe from the Jews of the Biblical period.

The cleaned feet of the birds, be they wild or domesticated chickens, turkeys, doves, partridge were cooked in the soups for flavor, or used to make a simple gelatin dessert which found its way into all countries as a simple delight for the poor. Later the dish found its way into the Americas as a "Happy" dessert for young and old alike.

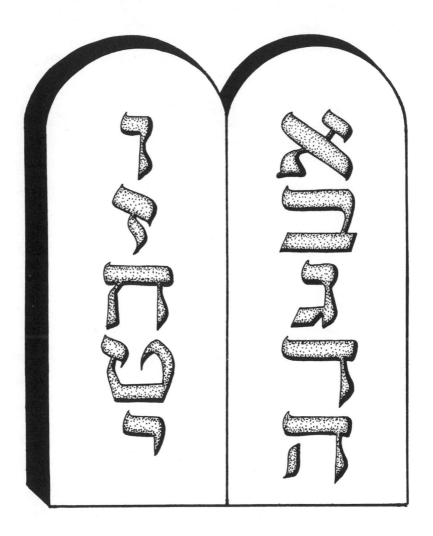

Ten Commandments

2. THE FOODS

An interesting feature of Middle Eastern foods is that the area from Egypt through Israel and Lebanon to Turkey and Greece have many similar dishes with often times similar names. Differences that do occur in these dishes are the use of varying amounts of the common spices and the addition of different herbs. Even though there is a commonality in foods each cultural area developed a "local" cuisine that is truly their own. As example, unleavened bread and cakes of the Israelites (Exodus 12:38,39) can be found in all the countries though under various names: Hamez, Serbian bread, Persian flat bread, Pan bread, Matzo, Ta, Pan. It should be noted that all of these areas use the same cooking methods: frying, baking, boiling, grilling steaming and the same basic foods, meat: goat, lamb, sheep, oxen, calf, bullock; vegetables: cucumber, sweet potato, white potato, celery, pumpkin, squash, onion; fruits: especially the citrus family: and the list goes on.

Based on this commonality it is easy to understand how food combinations in a geographical area would follow similar patterns in their meat and vegetable dishes. More variety and difference can be found in sweets and baked goods as shown in custards, sweet cakes, flaky pastry and breads, and that due to the available spices and flavorings found in the particular town or state.

Religious dietary laws outlines allowable combinations and this played an important role in dictating what items could be eaten.

We see that cereal grains and beans played a major role in highly populated regions and arid desert regions due to a lack of meats and a shortage of certain vegetables. Area adjacent to rivers and seas broadened their diets with fish and sea foods. Salted and dried foods were the "refrigerator" of the day. Fruits and vegetables lent themselves to drying and sugaring while meat and fish held well with salt.

Toasted seeds are a most important adjunct to the food chain of the middle east. Where meat is not found in great abundance in the diet of the poor classes it is natural to find meat protein substituted by pulse and seeds. Melon, pumpkin, and sunflower seeds are found in the diet throughout the area.

#45
GARINIM
(Seeds)

Roasted seeds
1 cup Seeds (Raw)
1 $^1/_2$ cup Water
$^1/_4$ cup Salt (do not over portion)
Wash seeds and remove all pulp. Drain and blot dry. Place all in a sauce pan or heavy skillet. Bring to a soft boil, stir often. When all salt is dissolved, reduce heat and simmer 20 minutes. Drain and blot dry. Spread out on a sheet pan and place in a 300° oven. Roast 20-25 minutes. Seeds should not turn dark brown. Shake pan often so seeds do not stick. Remove and cool seeds.

Identification of many food items enjoyed in the pre-Roman/Greco period are vividly shown in the base reliefs and temple carvings from the Upper Kingdom as well as the Lower Kingdom of Egypt during the period 5000 BCE-4000 BC. One such example, the tomb of Unis-Ankh, son of the Pharaoh Unis, overseer of Upper Egypt, shows an artistic and hieroglyphic parade of foods worthy of a king's son. Here can be seen wine, birds of the field, domesticated animals, fruits, nuts, grains, plus some of the serving vessels and jugs from the period. The religious interplay of foods and the after life cause the very best foods and drink of the land to be included with jewelry, personal treasures and even select servants and concubines to be interred with the noble person. The thought was that once the journey to the next world was completed, a party would be held to celebrate the transformation. Many of

118

these items can be viewed today in the Egyptology exhibits of museums.

Many private memorial tablets (stelas) from the middle kingdom (found at Abydos) show banquets of food and partying; beer, breads, the left leg of cows and goats, rolls, sweets, fruits, melon, and various other foods of the area. It should be noted that the left leg indicated the favorite for the favorite, or the very best part for the great leader. Wild ducks and geese show in almost every stela, both for the princes and the upper class. A favorite method of cooking duck was in stew.

#46
WILD DUCK STEW

1 3 lb. Duck, cleaned, washed, cut into quarters
$^1/_4$ cup Olive oil
$^1/_2$ cup Parsley chopped
1 Bay leaf
2 tsp. Salt
$^1/_2$ tsp Pepper
1 Lemon, juiced
1 cup Okra, cut
$^1/_2$ cup Water

Brown duck in oil until nicely colored on all sides. Add parsley, bay leaf, water. Cover and simmer for 3 hours on a slow fire. Add more water if required. Add salt, pepper, lemon juice, mix well, cover and simmer 1 hour. Add okra, cover and simmer 1/2 hour. Serve over rice, with warm bread.

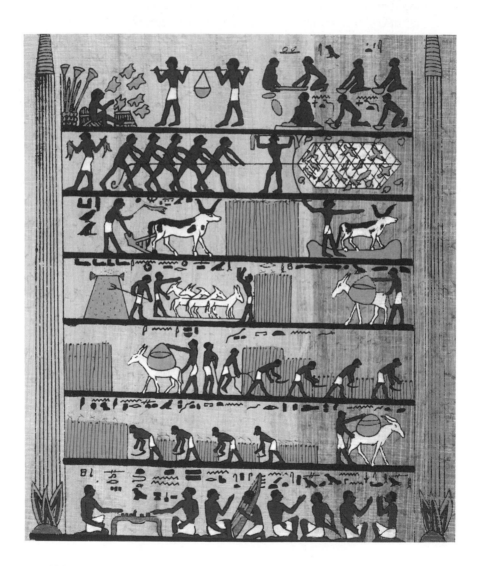

3. TRADE

Trade was the key to the full development of cuisine: vegetables for Thrace, Euphrates and the Nile Valleys as well as the Jordan Valley; fruits and nuts from Egypt, Jordan, Israel; poultry in the form of partridge of Maloy, cochen chicken from India, brahnos and langshan's from China, white leghorns from Assyria and various birds from the field, olives, dates, figs, and grapes from Israel and other countries throughout the region. A drawing of a Rooster was found on a seal dated 600 BCE, found at tell en-Nasbeh, near Jerusalem as were glass plates and juglets.

In ancient times glass for decoration, jewelry and table use was manufactured around the outlet of the River Belus close to Akko. Pliny indicates that the special sands found on the seashore of Haifa and Akko was the very best for glass manufacture. Plates and dishes, as well as jars were produced for food service and storage. Many of these glass pieces found their way into the full trade cycle. As the art of glass work improved the style and shapes improved, and the uses for the work increased. Once such plate set was found fully intact in the Bar — Kochba dig.

At the excavation of the tell-Hazor, with its twenty strata, many cities were found built one on top of another. Here we see a historic span of 3000 years, (Joshua 11:1-5) The tell has it's beginning with the early bronze age, then Joshua; followed by the periods of Sisera, Deborah, Solomon, Ahab, Jezebel, as well as others of the Israelite history. Here have been found, among other things, a complete sequence of the jars, pots, vessels, stirrup jugs, juglets, bowls, tall-neck Bilbils, all in the various mediums of clay, pottery, glass, ivory, bone, stone, bronze, brass, iron, silver, and gold. Here we see how serving and storage of foods improved from generation to generation.

Other major foods of the Middle East were beans, peas, milk and cheese.

A. BEANS

Beans (Polim) are a seed or pod of the tribe "Phaseoleae." The beans of the Old World, as mentioned in the Bible, are all of the species Vicia Faba, and come down from the Broad Bean or Windsor Bean. They are seed-propagated, called annuals. Basically the beans of the family contain 21-25 percent protein, 60 percent carbohydrate, 2-3% fat, and the balance in fiber bulk.

The **Soy Bean** was, and is, the world's most important bean. Born in China, it has a history as a major source of oil, food and bulk, throughout the East and Middle East.

The **Horse Gram**, the Bonavist bean and the Mung bean, native of India, were all heavily used throughout the area during the Biblical period, as they are today.

Carob — The Locust or St. John's Bread, is the pod of the leguminous tree. The pod, called locust, is believed to be the "Locust" that John the Baptist fed on. The pod is 50 percent sugar, primarily used as cattle feed, it is used as food by man during hard times. The pod contains 5-15 dark brown seeds in a sweet pulp. Ground, it is used in bread. The carob gum is used as a gum Tragacanth. The fruit is called "Boxer." All of the beans mentioned in the following list can be found in an Italian or Greek grocery. Major cities may also have an Arab grocery where you can find many of the ingredients.

Beans along with the cereal grains were the mainstay of the food chain.

Asparagus: Bean; Israel, Jordan

Buckwheat: Kasha. Turkestan, Persia, Israel.

Broad Bean: Phul. Major bean of Mideast, baked, ground, fried, boiled.

Calabar Bean: African ritual bean, contains Physostigmine.

Carob: Seed and Pod. Found throughout the Mediterranean.

Corn Pea: also called China Bean, Black eyed Bean, Cornfield Pea from India, China, Israel, of species Vigna

Sinenis. There are 200 varieties of this bean.

Green Bean: Europe.

Hyacinth Bean: India, Iran, Iraq

Horse Gram: Horse Bean, Fava, Indian, Persia, Jordan, known as the cholent bean.

Haricot Beans: Jordan, Turkey, Greece

Kidney Bean: Large red bean high in nutrition. (Sheuit)

Lentils: Used for cereal and porridge. A good source of protein and carbohydrates. Used in soup. Esau sold his birthright, to his brother Jacob, for a bowl of lentils — red pottage.

Lima Bean:

Lubiya: Cow peas, Israel, Jordan

Mung Bean: China, India. As bean sprouts

Peanuts: Bothim. Native of Egypt.

Snap Bean: Greece, Turkey.

Soy Bean: Houmous. The major bean of China, Mongolia, Southeast Asia and the Middle East. High source of protein.

Windsor Bean: Broad bean, Central Europe. Large seed, Mediterranean. Small seed, Middle East.

White Runner Bean: All Mediterranean areas.

#47
WHITE BEAN STEW

4 cups White Beans
8 cups Water
2 tsp. Salt
2 Tbsp. Oil
2 Onions, cleaned, chopped
$^1/_2$ tsp. Pepper
$^1/_4$ tsp. Crushed red pepper
1 Green (or Red) Pepper, cleaned, chopped
1 bunch Parsley, chopped

Bring beans to boil. Simmer 2 hours. Add all remaining

ingredients and simmer 3 hours. Add water as required.
Serve with flat bread.

"What food I eat you will supply for money, —" Deuteronomy 2:28.

Edible — podded bean, variously called, snapbean,
stringless bean, blue lake bean, is the young immature stage.
The mature bean is most often used in animal feed due to the
character change in the bean. The asparagus or the bonivest
bean probably was the "vine" bean, the podded bean, used in
the early Hebrew bean and onion stew.

#48
BATZAL SHEUIT MEUDE
Podded Beans
Bean And Onion Stew

1 6 lb. *Green beans, cleaned, ends off.*
6 *Onions, chopped.*
¹/₄ cup Lentils, washed well
¹/₂ tsp. Salt
¹/₄ tsp. Pepper
¹/₄ tsp. Cayenne pepper
¹/₂ cup Butter
1 *gallon Water*
6 turnips, tops cut off, washed, cut in quarters. Combine
water and green beans. Bring to boil, cover and simmer 30
minutes. Add turnips, onions, lentils and all spices. Stir well.
cover and simmer 1 hour. Stir well, add butter and stir. Cover
and simmer 1 hour. Serve over broken bread in a deep bowl.
Green salad or cucumbers are usually served on the side. The
turnip is interchangeable today with the potato which was
introduced into the area in the 1500's C.E.. Turnip tops are
eaten with vinegar as a salad.

Most of the bean recipes in the area, are for baked or

boiled dishes, however some are ground and mixed with fat and ground meat. Some beans are sweet dessert dishes mixed with honey and spice. You will experience some of each kind in the recipe section of our book.

#49
AFUNA AFUY
Peas Casserole

¹/₂ cup Cow peas, pre soaked
¹/₄ cup Corn peas, pre soaked
5 6"x6" Matzo, rough broken
3 eggs, beaten
¹/₂ cup Nuts, chopped
¹/₂ tsp. Salt
¹/₂ cup Sugar
1 tsp. Cinnamon
¹/₄ tsp. Nutmeg
¹/₆ tsp. Ginger
¹/₄ cup Oil
¹/₄ cup Raisins
3 cups Water

Combine all ingredients and mix well. Pour into greased dutch oven or other covered pot. Bake at 350° for 55 minutes or place on back of Kirayim and steam for 2 hours. The dish will be thick, you may add more liquid if desired.

#50
SALAT AFUNA MEUDE
Puree Pea Pudding

³/₄ lb. Yellow split peas
¹/₂ lb. Green split peas
3 medium Onions, chopped
¹/₂ cup Olive Oil, virgin
2 Lemons, juiced

2 toes Garlic, minced
1 tsp. Salt

Wash peas well, rinse twice. Cover with fresh water. Bring to a boil. Add half of onions, add half of garlic. Simmer for 1¼ hours. Stir often so peas do not stick and burn. Use a potato masher and reduce to a puree. Force through a sieve. Add oil and salt. Mix well. Chop remaining onion and garlic very fine. Portion peas and sprinkle with the onion/garlic mixture. Then sprinkle with lemon juice. Serve warm pita bread on the side. This is a light supper meal designed for 4-6 persons. Olives and tomatoes are often served as a relish. The puree is served hot or cold as taste dictates.

B. MILK

A highly used food, goat milk was the most highly chosen for drinking and making leben. It was easy to digest and worked well in baking and the making of cheese. Sheep milk was the second choice, followed by the animal of local availability, yak, camel, cow, bullock, gazelle and the like. Since water was scarce, milk (Joel 4:18) became the everyday drink. Water when potable was drawn from common community wells or a cistern and carried in leather bags and buckets or clay jars. Often they had to carry the water for miles, so this was an unreliable source of water for family use. The household goat or cow was the easiest and most reliable source of liquid for drink.

Camel's milk was prized because it soured quickly and could be made into leben and yogurt easily. Yogurt was regarded as a tonic for life. Even today we find people 100 to 120 years old in Turkestan, Iraq, and throughout the regional mountains, who give credit for their long years to the goodness of yogurt. Judges 5:25 "He asked her for water and she gave him milk, she brought forth butter in a lordly dish."

Leben is added to fresh milk to make it ferment, thus producing GHAIB (Curd) another food (Job 10:10) product. Ghaib when shaken produces butter. Leben — Matzoon —

127

Filbunke are all basically the same item from different areas. A concentrated milk with the better holding qualities of a condensed (canned) milk. Leben used in cooking does not "break" and separate as does regular milk at lower temperatures.

Smetana is soured milk with added cream used as a topping for vegetables, fruit and in some area over fish. Jajik is yogurt mixed with cucumber and pepper served a slight lunch, served with bread.

Shamenet, sour Cream. Eshel, Sour Milk. Hema, Sweet Butter.

Proverbs 27:26,27 speaks of "goats milk enough for thy food" and in Genesis 32:16 Jacob speaks of "the thirty milk camels" he will give to his brother Esau.

Butter churns (Mahbezah) have been found in many tells throughout Israel, most prominently in the Beersheba area.

(Judges 4:18) Joel was given milk to drink by Sisera, as he was thirsty. "She opened a skin of milk and gave him some drink."

#51
MEUDE ADASHIM GEVINA TZEHUBA
Lentil Stew with Cheese

1 cup Red Lentils (presoaked in warm water 1 hour)
2 slice Bread, day old, minced
1 Egg, beaten
1 cup Yellow cheese, grated
2 medium Onions, minced
3 Tbsp. Oil
1 bunch Parsley, chopped fine
$1/4$ tsp. Thyme, dried
1 tsp. Salt
2 toes Garlic, minced
$1/6$ tsp. Pepper
$1/6$ tsp. Nutmeg

1 Balsam leaf
1/6 tsp. Cinnamon
1/2 cup Stock (Vegetable)

Drain lentils and sauté onions in oil until golden. Add garlic, stir ten times. Mix all ingredients together, blend well. Pour into greased casserole, cover and bake 375° for thirty-five minutes. Serve with green salad and warm bread.

Pliny in (Historia Naturalis) wrote that the spice, the leaf from the Balsam shrub, was in great demand by the Romans, and "protected even unto death by the Jews."

Allicum, an active antibacterial contained in the pulp of the garlic "Toe" helps lower blood pressure and it helps to clear bronchitis. Pliny spoke of the garlic as a curative for the upper body. Odysseus ate garlic to protect himself from the enchantments of Circa.

#52
FRIED CURD CHEESE CUSTARD

1 cup Cottage cheese, drained, large curd
3 Tbsp. Sugar
4 Eggs, separated
1 Tbsp. Lemon peel. grated
1 tsp. Currants
1 cup Flour
3/4 cup Milk

Blend flour and milk together, make a loose dough. Set aside. Beat egg yolks, sugar, lemon peel until it begins to thicken. Blend in cottage cheese. Add flour mixture and blend well. Pour 1/4 of mixture into well greased large fry pan. After bottom has set, sprinkle in currants. Cook on medium fire. When bubbles stop rising, turn over and cook other side. When nicely brown, cut into quarters and top with stiff beaten egg whites and jam. This pancake is still cooked today on a flat rock as it was done thousands of years ago.

C. BUTTER (HEMA)

Produced throughout the Middle East, recorded as early as 2000 BCE. The Scythians and Greeks used butter extensively in their cooking. It is made of milk primarily from goats, sheep and cows. Some countries also use milk of bullock and oxen or other native animals. Gee or semneh, a clarified butter, is used in cooking.

D. CHEESE

Cheese has been eaten and recorded in the Middle East since the 15th Century B.C.E. It was first manufactured, so the story goes, when a traveler put his milk into a sheep stomach bag. Affixing the bag to his saddle horn he left on his camel for a trip to the neighboring town. After eight hours on the march the rennet from the skin caused the milk to become a curd cottage cheese. So began the story of cheese. The kind of milk used determines the type of cheese made. Rennet is still used today in the making of cheese although some cheese making uses lactic acid bacteria as a substitute. David is remembered in the Old Testament taking cheeses to an army captain, as a friendship offering and 11 Samuel 17:27,28 "cheese from the herd" was given to David.

E. VEGETABLES

Peas, asparagus, celery, cabbage, leeks, onions, radishes, cress, garlic, cucumbers, squash, mustard greens, are the base staple vegetables of the Southern Mediterranean shores down to the Persian Gulf and are heavily used throughout the cuisine.

F. FRUITS

Quince, pears, apples, peaches, cherries, apricots, melons, grapes, olives, figs, dates, lemons, tangerines, pomegranates, citron, all surround the Mediterranean shores and are fully involved in the cuisine of the areas. Used primarily to accommodate a vegetable dish and often times as caravan food.

Pomegranates (rimonim) were the emblem of fertility. Solomon decorated his walls, ceilings, pillars and even his furniture with carved pomegranates. (1 Kings 7:20). Saul tarried in the uttermost part of Gibeah under the Pomegranate tree. (I Samuel 14:2).

Leviticus 19:23-25 reminds us that the first three years of life of a fruit tree shall be as if it bore no fruit, and you shall not eat any. The fourth year fruit is only for religious celebration but in the fifth year onward you may eat all the fruit from that tree that you desire.

Fruits as well as the spices were regarded in high esteem and were to be protected from harm, as they, along with the wheat crops,were a gift directly from God. One can easily see that without these basic items the people would not be able to survive. Fruit gave character to many of the early recipes, in fact were we to eliminate fruit from many recipes the dishes would become quite tasteless. The wealthy land owners during times of stress, war, or famine were required by the state to supply fruit to the poor.

During the Bar-Kochba (Kosiba) period one such person has his property confiscated. The directive was specific in nature, "First the wheat and then the fruit were to be taken in custody and extra caution must be taken so that the animals of the herds should not trample them or in no way were they to hurt the crops, and as for the spice orchards, let no one get anywhere near it," so wrote the scribe Shimeon Bar Yehudah. This writing was found in the caves at the Kosiba digs.

Fruit was from the earliest of days regarded as most important to pregnant women and for the improvement in health of the very young children. The very rich used fruit as both decoration at the banquet and also as a fitting climax after the meal. Pliny commented often as to the importance of fruit in the health of man.

The Lord you God gave you, "Vineyards and olive groves

which you did not plant — and you ate your fill," Deuteronomy 6:11.

#53
MISHMESH OREZ MEUDE
Apricots And Rice

$^1/_2$ cup Raisins
$^2/_3$ cup Dried apricots, chopped
2 $^1/_2$ cups Rice, cooked, warm
$^1/_2$ cup Butter
$^1/_2$ tsp. Salt
$^1/_4$ tsp. Pepper
$^1/_3$ tsp. Cinnamon
$^1/_4$ tsp. Nutmeg
$^1/_2$ cup Water

In a sauce pot melt butter, add raisins, apricots, and sauté for 5 minutes. Combine all ingredients and mix well. Cover pot and simmer (steam) on slow fire for 15 minutes. Pour into serving bowl.

This recipe is often served with left over (pre-cooked) lamb breast, chopped medium. The lamb can be served on the side, cold, or, as in Persian cooking, the lamb is added in the mixture during the slow steam period. In other preparation style the rice is served over baked fish.

#54
TZENON SHAHOR
SCHWARTZ RETAYCH
Black Radish

5 medium Black Radishes, peeled and grated
1 Onion, minced fine
1 Tbsp. Schmaltz (Rendered chicken fat)
$^1/_4$ tsp. Salt
$^1/_2$ tsp. Pepper

Mix all together. Let rest 1 hour. Serve on lettuce or stuff into pita bread.

#55
TOUAGEN, ABGUSHT, YAKHNIE
HUBAGRITS
Oats Stew

$1/4$ cup Oats, washed, course grind

5 cups Vegetable stock

1 Onion, minced

2 Carrots, peeled, chopped fine

4 arms Celery chopped fine

1 Turnip, chopped

$1/4$ tsp. Salt

$1/4$ tsp. Pepper

$1/6$ tsp. Celery seeds

2 Tbsp. Schmaltz (Chicken fat) Olive Oil may be used in place of Schmaltz

Note: some recipes use cracked wheat (Graplech) or barley.

Bring stock to boil. Add oats and simmer 30 minutes. In separate pan heat schmaltz and sauté all vegetables. Pour into the stock. Add all herbs and spices. Simmer for two hours. May be thickened with flour roux to fit individual taste. Serve with warm bread and salad. This was a one pot dish throughout history. Place all ingredients in a Kallahat or similar heavy clay pot. Mix well. Place on the back of the fire box and let simmer as the fire slowly burns out. Next day reheat for service.

#56
YERAKOT AFUY
KUKUYE SABZI
Vegetable Casserole

1 Onion, minced

133

2 cups Spinach, chopped fine
2 bunches Parsley, chopped fine
5 Leeks, minced
1 cup Lettuce, (Bib) sliced fine
1 tsp. Salt
$^1/_2$ tsp. Pepper
$^1/_4$ tsp. Paprika
$^1/_2$ cup Walnuts, chopped
$^1/_2$ cup Butter
2 Tbsp. Flour
8 Eggs, beaten

Combine all vegetables, spice, flour. Mix well and be sure that flour is evenly mixed in and vegetables are well covered. Add eggs and mix well. Melt butter in 7-8" cake pan. Pour vegetable mixture into pan. Bake in 325° oven for 55 minutes. Serve with yogurt on top. Garnish with chopped dill.

Beduins Eating

G. MEATS

History shows us that cattle were primarily for trade and the best animals were for sacrifice. Later as the herds increased meat was eaten, but even then mainly on feast days and only in wealthy homes on a daily basis. The poor usually ate meat on Sabbath only.

Abraham's father, Terah, in addition to having a clay factory for idol manufacture was in the livestock business in the city of Ur (Genesis 11:28,31) near the banks of the Euphrates River. In later years Abraham himself raised animals (Genesis 12:16). The main trade routes from Ur were to Armenia and the Persian Gulf as well as to Caesarea in Assyria. After leaving Ur, Abraham settled near Hebron in Mamre. His major food were curds and milk. Meat from bullocks, lambs and kids, (Genesis 27:8,9) and wild game. Meats were roasted, boiled or made into stew. Abraham ate honey, figs and dates. Wheat and barley were made into bread.

When Jacob left Haran he took his livestock: (Genesis 26:13-14) oxen, asses, flocks and camels. This was for trade and for his family's food. We find that the major meat eaten was lamb and goat followed by kid, with some oxen and beef cattle for special days.

Lamb is usually eaten cooked medium well (mevushal heytev) throughout the Middle East and Asia, this in sharp contrast to medium pink (beynoni) in modern America. Age of meat in North America and most parts of Europe is usually 14-16 days. Age of meat in the Middle East is measured in hours, not days. It is called "green" fresh killed. Lamb is more often cooked Kebab (roasted) in the Holy Land, and usually cooked in large, primal cuts. In the Americas you will find more of the sub primal cuts such as chops, roast, stew and cube, shank and the like. The method of cooking is pan fried or baked. Here we seldom use innards, there they are the delight.

Lamb, Karim, is a major food of holidays. Beersheba,

derives its name from the lamb, Beer-Sheba, the well of seven lambs. Bir Al-Sab'. The name comes from Abraham and Isaac who dug water wells at the site and made a treaty with Abimelech the Philistine King — Abraham set aside seven Ewes as a bond of oath — so the name. (Genesis 21:31).

Meat eating was limited due to the expense, and when eaten, all parts of the animal were utilized. The poor class, could afford only the less desirable cuts, those pieces that were not easily sold in the markets, so we see the recipes for the use of the hoofs and hocks as well as the tail and neck. This practice has carried forward through all of history and we find the stews and casseroles.

#57
GOAT CASSEROLE

4 Goat Shanks (if shanks are small add 2 extra)
3 Onions, peeled and cut into halves
4 toes Garlic, peeled and chopped
2 Tbsp. Lemon Juice
1 Tbsp. Vinegar
1/2 tsp. Pepper
2 Tbsp. Flour
2 Tomatoes, chopped
3 cups Water (or watered wine)

Wash shanks and sprinkle with flour. Brown in hot pan. Place shanks in a covered dish. Add all ingredients and bake at 350° for 2 hours. Serve with warm bread and rice.

History indicates that this dish was usually cooked on the back of the stove with the fire banked. The cooking time must allow 6-8 hours depending on the heat of the fire. Vegetables from the garden were added depending on the crop and the time of the year. The favorite vegetables were Afuna (peas), Gezer (carrots), Hatzilim (eggplant), Pilpelim (sweet peppers), Kishuim (Zucchini) and often the green leaf vegetables,

Tered, Petrozilia, and Hasa.

#58
KETZITZOT METUGAN
Fried Patties

1 lb. Lamb (or Goat), chopped fine
1/2 lb. Bread, chopped fine
2 Eggs, beaten
1/2 cup Cold water
3 medium Onions, chopped fine, sauté lightly
2 toes Garlic, minced
1 tsp. Salt
1/2 tsp. Pepper
1 Tbsp. Parsley, minced
1/2 tsp. Spearmint leaves, crumbled
2 Tbsp. Olive Oil
1 Tbsp. White Vinegar
1/2 cup Burghul, crushed
1/2 cup Olive Oil

In a china bowl mix lamb, bread crumbs, egg and water. Blend well. Add onions and garlic. Blend well. Add all herbs and spices. Blend well. Add vinegar and mix. Cover and refrigerate for 1 hour. Roll out 20-22 balls of equal size. Press into patty shape. Press patty into burghul and dust well. Fry in hot olive oil. It may be served in a pita pocket with a tossed salad, or with rice and vegetables.

"She hath prepared her meat, She hath mingled her wine; She hath also furnished her table —" (Proverbs 9:2).

H. HONEY
Honey has been a popular food that pre-dates the time of Solomon. Israel has always been regarded as having a "full" food honey of high quality. Bees were farmed since the earliest of times. (1 Kings 14:3,) "biscuits and a cruse (dibs) of

137

honey was sent as a valued gift from Jeroboam to Ahijan," the Prophet. Nofet Ha-Zufim Debash, "from the honeycomb", was the favorite of foods (Psalms 19:2), and according to Isaiah (7:15) honey comb was the food of the children.

Grape Honey; Devash Anavim, is the concentrated grape pulp which is boiled before fermentation. This was indeed one of the first "sweet foods."

Date Honey; Devash Temarim, is made by soaking the fruit in water for six days, then boiling it into a thick syrup.

Proverbs 25:16, "Hast thou found honey? Eat so much as is sufficient for thee,—", and Proverb 23:13, "and the honeycomb is sweet to thy taste", indicate the constant Biblical reference to this natural food. Psalms 118:12 tells of the gathering of the wild honeycombs, and I Samuel 14:25 speaks of the finding of honey. Historians speak of honey being well sealed in a jar lasting "a hundred years."

Fig Honey, "Honey of the Crag", was the fourth honey talked of in the Bible, (Deuteronomy 32:13) and in the commentary. Those figs not used in the honey process were dried (Samuel 25:18) in the same fashion as were dates. It is felt by the leading scholars that the "Tree of Knowledge of Good and Evil" was the fig tree.

I. WINE

Since the time of Moses , wine has been a major food and drink, as well as an export product. (Numbers 13:21,22,26,27) Israeli wine has been of good quality and much in demand. There are many references to wine (Yayin) throughout the Bible. We are told to use it in moderation. Wine was often mixed with spice (Song of Song 9:2,5). Wine mixed with myrrh was used as a drug.

Judah was the major wine producing area of Israel. Wine was extensively used since water was scarce and often of poor quality. Wine skins were carried on all long trips, and when visiting the Temple as offerings it was also used as payment of taxes. Grapes were squeezed, eaten fresh, fermented for wine or boiled for grape honey. Wine was always to be mixed with water. The method of wine culture has come down through time fairly well intact. The Bible speaks of four major types of wine: sparkling (foaming) wine, Psalms 75:9; Spiced wine, Song of Songs 8:2; Wine of Helbon, Ezekial 27:18; Lebanon wine, Hosea 14:8; and the use of wine houses or banquet halls. Baalhamon was the home of Solomon's vineyards. Hosea speaks of the bountiful wines of Israel in 9:10, 10:1. Noah, the tiller of the soil, was the first to plant a vineyard.

Less than a half hour from Jerusalem stands the Arab village of El Jib, beneath the vineyards and orchards of this simple village lies the remains of the great Biblical city of Gibeon (Giv'on) Joshua, 10:2. Here was located a huge wine storage cellar, estimated to contain in excess of 100,000 liters of wine. Located close by were grape treading basins, fermentation vats and sedimentation vats, as well as jugs and stoppers. The size and scope of this discovery attested to the flourishing economy of this "great City" of the period 1200-1000 BCE. Less than 4 meters away is located another archaeological wonder, "the pool of Giv'on", Samuel II, "Where the 12 men of Saul and 12 men of David met together." Here is carved out of bedrock, a catch basin, stone stairs, balustrade, a tunnel leading to the water room (cistern) fed by an underground spring. This spring is used today as it was 5000 years ago. A marble statue of Tutmosis III found at Deir El Medinah shows the King offering two jars of wine as tribute to Amon-Re. A gift of great value.

Avedat (Ovdat) in the central Negev, situated on the intersection of the roads from Petra and Elath to Haluzah, served as a food and water supply point to the major camel caravans traveling the length of "The River" Jordan. History has shown that Avedat was of major importance in the Indo-Arabian commerce. Many items were off loaded to other caravans and wine and fruits were added to the loads. The town was the site of a large ceramic industry, and a system of dams attest to the agricultural and wine industry in the region. Remains of fruit drying apparatus and, many wine presses can be found in the governments preserved historical site. Just a few miles away from Avadat is the Biblical city of Beersheba. Clay jugs and biblets were transmitted as both a container for wines and spiced fruit and as a main export product in its own right since well made clay products were in great demand.

In Judah, the district surrounding Hebron, the ancients speak of the vintage wines used in the Feast of Booths — Sukkot. Wine was stored in sheep skins with vents on top, so that it could properly age, and the skins would not blow up. Sometimes wine was stored in jars with a light cork. (Jeremiah 13:12,38:11) Ziba and Abigal (1 Samuel 25:18) brought skins of wine to David. It was Solomon who gave servants of Hiram, King of Tyre, twenty thousand baths of wine in exchange for timber to be used in the building of the Temple in Jerusalem. The two major measures for wine was the Bath and the Hin (Isaiah 5:10).

Many wine presses, cut out of the rocks, have been found throughout the mountain regions of Israel. This attests to the wide spread industry of the vine culture and wine production. Once such site is near the village of Mat'a, near the valley of Elah. The town of Gath (II Samuel 1:20) is named for the wine press.

When Abraham first visited Jerusalem, then called Salem, the King Melchizedek, gave him wine and bread. (Genesis 14:18)

(Isaiah 5:1,2.) "My well-beloved had a vineyard in a very fruitful hill; and he digged it, and cleared it of stones, and planted it with the choicest vine...and also hewed out a vat therein,..."

The question as to how grapes, and the resulting wine, came to be located in the "Holy Land" can be explained by the commentary of the ancients that "at the time of creation, Adam, before leaving the garden of Eden, took with him the vines. Later, following the flood, Noah found the vine. He tasted the grape upon it, and finding it good to eat, grew them."

Grapes (Anavim) from the valley of Eshcol, were "the gift of God" to the Israelites, (Numbers 12:23) along with pomegranates and figs. This was the land of milk and honey. Numbers (13:23) "They reached the wadi Eshcol, and there they cut a single cluster of grapes — it had to be born on a carrying frame by two of them." In an attempt to lengthen the useful life of the grapes they were dried in the sun and produced another food that has come down to modern times, the raisin (zemmukim). Wine is cited as one of the good things created for good people. Deuteronomy 32:14 and Genesis 49:11 speaks of wine as "the blood of the grape." Ecclesiastes 10:19 states "A feast is made for laughter, and wine maketh merry."

Since the earliest of times man has wanted a drink other than water, he has searched and found wines of various types, and in the search has found that various grains, fruits and vegetables ferment and produce a heady mixture that when taken in excess can produce drunken states. Beer, mead, raisin wine, apricot wine, barley wine all fit into this experimentation. The Bible cautions us to use this type of drink with care and in moderation.

#59
RAISIN WINE

4 cups Black Raisins
10 cups Water
1 cup Sugar
1 Tbsp. Cinnamon

Grind or chop raisins. Whip in water. Blend well and beat 4 minutes. Add sugar and cinnamon. Bring to soft boil and simmer three minutes. Pour into crock or jar, cover with cloth. Each day stir. Continue for eight days. Strain through double cheese cloth. Squeeze out well to capture all the juice. Place in clean jar, cover and let set for 10 days. Serve.

Numbers 28:7 "an offering of fermented drink (beer) to the Lord" was the libation presented as part of the burnt offering.

#60
MEAD

3 Tbsp. Hops
³/₄ cup Honey
5 cups Water
¹/₂ tsp. Fresh lemon juice

Place hops in a muslin garni bag. Combine all ingredients in a sauce pot and bring to a soft boil. Simmer for 20 minutes. Skim scum every 5 minutes. Cool and strain through double cheese cloth. Place in deep crock or jar, cover top with cheese cloth. Allow ample space in jar for expansion. Allow to ferment for 18 days. When fermentation stops pour into bottles and cork. Store in cool dark room. Serve when cool. History indicated that Amphora jars were often used. The tops were sealed with cork and wax.

J. OTHER FOODS

a. Wild game: The gazelle, the hart, the roebuck as well as four other animals of the herd (?) were eaten and considered savory food.

b. Eggs: (Beytzim) eggs of all "clean" birds and fowl were choice foods and were found throughout the diet of the Middle East. Eggs were usually poached in hot oil or hard boiled as trail food. They were used in baking of breads and cakes and could be found in the cholents and custards. Often the whole egg, shell and all were put in the raw dough of the bread and baked. The egg was a prize of luck and good fortune. The egg, from the earliest of Hebrew tradition has played an important role in symbolizing of the circle of life. We see in the birth and death feasts that the egg is a major food. At almost every major festival the egg is used to symbolize fertility, prosperity and the never ending life of the people Israel.

    c. Cooking oils: Olive oil (Shemen Zayit) was crushed from green olives and was the major cooking oil. Sheep oil, from the rendered fat tail of the sheep was highly prized but in short supply. Semneh, butter clarified and specially prepared was in major use in many countries of the area. Each area had its own name for the product. The sheep tail ALYA (Leviticus 3:9) was important both for cooking and religious practices.

    d. Prepared foods: Assyrian and Armenian influence introduced the Kibbeh and Burghul wheat mixtures to the Israel and Egyptian areas. Meza are the Hors D'oeuvres of the Middle East: Tabbouli, Hummus, Tehini, Wara awab, Samak, Kefta, are just a few of the many items that will be explored in the recipe section of the book.

K. THE CRAFT

The industry of food and food stuffs not only created cuisine, it also set trade customs for the cities and established guilds which carried on into modern times where people were known by their craft. The gates of the city were named for the food item sold: i.e. the craft: the fishgate, the sheepgate, the bread gate and so on. Jerusalem is the best known for its food gates, but all major cities followed the same pattern.

L. FRUITS AND NUTS

Fruit and nut trees supplied a very important link in the food chain, vitamins and minerals that were not in evidence in the heavily vegetable oriented diet of the area. "And from the ground the Lord God caused to grow every tree that was pleasing to the sight, and good for food,"(Genesis 2:9)

Apricot, (Mishmesh) eaten fresh, dried, and in compote. A major fruit of the area.

Apples, (Tapuah Etz) several varieties were grown. Song

of Songs 2:3, "a shady tree growing sweet fruit." and 7:9, "The odor of the beloved is reminiscent of the delicate aroma of the apple —" Throughout biblical writings the apple has rated high for it's smell, looks, and taste. Tufah is the name of the apple to the Arabs. Eaten raw, as apple sauce, cider, garnish, it is a multipurpose fruit.

Almonds, a trail food, used in candy and baking, as a diet aid. (Numbers 17:23) "The rod of Aaron was budded and bore ripe almonds" (Shkedeem). Almonds, in Genesis 43:11 were called, "choice fruits of the land," and were sent to the ruler of Egypt by Jacob. Genesis 28:19 calls the almond by the name Luz, the Arabs call it Loz. Two major types of almonds were recorded in the Holy Land, the Dulcis variety with the pink flower and the sweet nut, and the Amora variety with the white flower and the bitter fruit. The latter type must be roasted to destroy the poisonous alkaloid that develops in the late stages of growth. Major almond cultivation can be found in the Northern Negev. Nut trees were a major cash crop of Athens. The Attic hills were covered with nut trees to the extent that their production of wheat and barley all but disappeared. Ground almonds were commonly used to thicken (tighten) sauces and to add flavor to jelly and jam. Almond Paste and Marzipan were considered a gift from God by many people of the area. Marzipan is two parts almond and one part sugar ground together and lightly cooked over a slow heat until well combined. Almond Paste or icing is one part ground almond and two parts sugar, two egg yolks beaten together over low heat until it become a pliable paste. Orange flour (blossom) water or sour orange juice are used as a flavoring agent with the almond paste

The use of seeds or nuts in a flat bread (cake) was enhanced from the early Egyptian baking through Roman times and comes down to modern times fully intact.

#61
MON CAKES

¹/₂ cup Corn Oil
¹/₂ cup Sugar
1 tsp. Cinnamon
¹/₄ tsp. Nutmeg
3 cups Flour
3 Eggs
¹/₈ tsp. Salt
¹/₂ cup Poppy Seed (mon) or substitute
finely chopped walnuts
2 tsp. Baking powder

Wash mon (poppy seed) and soak three hours. Drain. Mix all together and blend well. Make small balls, roll out thin. Place on greased sheet pan. Bake at 375° until brown — about ten minutes.

" — the Lord giveth you on the sixth day the bread of two days;" Exodus 16:29.

#62
CRANBERRY, ALMOND, ORANGE RELISH

¹/₂ cup Blanched almonds, chopped semi-fine
1 cup Cranberries, fresh and plump, well washed
2 cups Sugar
1 Tbsp. Lemon juice
¹/₂ cup Water
¹/₂ cup Orange juice
¹/₂ cup Orange rind grated
1 Tbsp. Lemon rind grated
1 Tbsp. Honey

Combine all but nuts in pan. Cook until cranberries pop. Stir often. Skim scum from top, bring to soft boil, add nuts. Stir. Remove from fire. Cool and serve.

If you follow the ways of the Lord your God, you will live in "a land of wheat and barley, of vines, figs and pomegranates, a land of olive trees and honey;" You will enjoy the good things of life." (Deuteronomy 8:6,8)

#63
MARZIPAN SHEETS

3 cups Blanched almonds
2 cups Sugar
1 Tbsp. Vanilla
4 Whites of egg, lightly whipped

Grind almonds on fine plate. Mix sugar and ground almonds, grind together on fine plate. In a stainless steel bowl slowly cut egg whites into almond sugar mixture. Let set 5 minutes. Roll out very thin. Cut with cookie cutter. Place in an oven on low heat to dry. You may ice with a royal icing and then dry if you wish. Some people dust with powdered sugar just before the sheet is dry.

Marzipan was an ancient confection and was found in early Mesopotamia, Greece, and Canaan. The Romans used "Marzopan" (Mauthaban) as a pharmaceutical that only a drug dealer could dispense. In the later Roman period Marzipan was used as a filling dough as well as a spread over fruits.

#64
NUT STUFFED DATES

1 ¹/₃ cup Almonds, ground fine
¹/₂ cup Sugar, granulated
³/₄ cup Powder sugar
2 Whites of eggs
1 Tbsp. Brandy
1 Tbsp. Almond extract

¹/₂ tsp. Vanilla extract
24 Dates, slit, seed removed
12 Walnuts cut in half

Mix the almonds and sugars together. Blend well. Turn out on a board. Punch hole in center of ball. Add egg whites and mix well until nicely blended. Punch hole in center and add brandy, almond extract, vanilla extract and mix well. Wrap almond mixture around 1/2 walnut and stuff in date. Squeeze shut. Roll in powdered sugar. Serve.

Song of Songs 4:5 "I have drunk my wine with my milk."

Almond Cookies (Luz Drops)

³/₄ cup Almonds, ground fine
³/₄ cup Sugar, fine powder sugar is best
5 Tbsp. Orange Blossom Water (or use sour orange juice)

Mix all together to make a thick paste. Work until paste is smooth. Pinch into 1" balls (*) wash hands and dry very well. Roll balls in the palm of the hand until smooth and round. Roll balls in powdered sugar. Press 1/2 almond into the top. Place completed balls on a side board to dry and form. (*) A variation of this cookie is to insert a pinch of minced apricot into the center of the ball and then roll it.

Citron, used for sauce and compote. The Etrog of Sukkot.
Chestnut, baked and roasted as a dessert and a garnish for lamb. The chestnut (Castanea) shows strong evidence for heavy use during the Greco-Roman period. Used as a food for man and animal, it had significant importance in the food chain of the Mediterranean area, to China and the edge of the Caucasus. The largest nuts are called Marrons, this name can be traced into the full language of the area. The nut is eaten raw, milled into flour, baked, fed to livestock. The tree bark is used to tan leather, the round wood used for poles, posts and piling. Rashi spoke of the chestnut in his commen-

147

tary.

Date Palm, (Temarim) Used for fruit, wine, date honey, and cattle feed. (Psalm 92:12,14) the branches were used to welcome travelers.

Pliny talks of the reputation of the dates from Jericho — high quality and the very best taste, in chapter 13 of his work "Natural History." David's daughter was named Tamar, after the palm that grows in Jericho and produces the best fruit. In the shade of the palm the Prophet Deborah judged the people (Judges 4:5). This palm was also called Kippah, "The Head", hence the name of the head covering used by the religious Jews. In Isaiah 9;13, the long leaves of the palm are called "Kappot of Palm" and is the Lulav of the Feast of Tabernacles (Lev. 23;40).

Fig Tree, (Etz Teenem) Fruit eaten raw, dried, candied, in cakes and cooking. David talked often of the wonders of the fig. (Teenim) The fruit was used often as a medicine. Syrup of fig is still used today as a drug. Isaiah 28:4 and Jeremiah 24;2, speaks of "the first ripe fig." This is the early fig which appears on the old wood, last year's growth. This was very sweet fruit and was regarded as a true delicacy. The major part of the regular fruit crop was dried for "Winter Fruit" or pressed (1 Samuel 25;18) into "cakes of fig."

Hazelnuts, (Acmidula — Amygdala) were spoken of by many of the early writers. Baked, broiled, ground into flour, the hazelnut had its place in history.

Mulberry (Petel) Tree, produces fruit that tastes like raspberries.

Olive Tree, produces fruit (zayetim) for eating as a condiment, but more importantly its major product (shemen) the oil of the fruit. Olive oil is the primary cooking oil of the Middle East. One tree properly maintained will produce 20 gallons of oil, that's enough of the golden oil to support a family for a year. The olive tree has been in cultivation in Israel for 4000 years. It is said in Greek culture and literature that the olive tree was Athena's gift to the Greeks.

The olive tree is a long living tree, an evergreen of the family oleaceae, and ranges in height from eight feet to well over 40 feet. They have a white flower that blooms in the spring of the year. As the fruit ripens the berry changes from green to straw color, then to red and just before the harvest to black. The black olives are usually crushed into oil. The first squeezing of the oil is called "Virgin Oil" and is the best for cooking due to its clear sweet taste. Second and third squeezings are used in the commercial field and for curing of fish. Third and fourth squeezings are usually used in burning lamps for light and heat. Olives picked just at the moment they begin to turn black are put into brine for salad olives. The brine (salt) makes the olives fit to eat, and extends the life of the olive over a long period of time. The olive tree migrated from Israel all around the Mediterranean and, ultimately, to the New World.

The Talmud says, "It is easier to raise a legion of olive trees in the Galilee than to bring up one child in the land of Israel." Both olives and Israeli children have been raised in this land for thousands and thousands of years.

One can look back as far as the Minoans to view olive culture in the land that the Lord gave Abraham. Olive oil is one of the reasons that the people of this land have from the beginning of their history had almost no vascular problems due to saturated oils. Olive oil and fresh vegetables have a cleansing action on the body, so said Pliny.

#65
MOROCCAN OLIVE SAUCED LAMB

STOCK
1 lb. Lamb bones, cracked
4 medium Carrots, scraped, rough chopped
4 medium Onions, peeled, chopped
$^1/_4$ cup Parsley
3 arms Celery with tops, chopped

1 Tbsp. Fresh basil
1 tsp. Pepper
1 Tbsp. Fresh thyme
4 cups Water

ENTREE
3 medium Carrots, scraped, diced
4 medium Onions, spanish, peeled, chopped
$^1/_2$ cup Black olives, pitted, chopped
$^1/_2$ cup Green olives, pitted, chopped
6 Anchovy fillets, washed and mashed
    (or you can use 1 Tbsp. Worcestershire sauce)
5 toes Garlic, mashed
1 medium Lemon, juiced, remove seeds
3 Tbsp. Cilantro, chopped
1 5 lb. Leg of lamb
3 toes Garlic, cut into $^1/_4$ s, spears

In a deep sauce pot place all of the stock ingredients, bring to a boil, skim, reduce heat and simmer for one hour. As stock is cooking, take lamb and using a thin sharp blade spear the leg and insert a spear of garlic. Rub the leg with oil, dust with pepper and sear the meat in a roasting pan sitting on top of the stove. Turn the meat often to get nice color. Place pan in a 375°F oven for 20 minutes. Reduce heat and roast for 1 1/ 2 hours at 325°F. Baste every 15 minutes with pan juices. Remove lamb and place on a serving platter and place on back of stove to keep warm. Strain the stock and discard the lumps. Combine the stock and the pan juices. Bring to a boil then reduce heat and skim off the fat. Now over a medium heat reduce the juice to a little more than two cups of liquid sauce. Add all of the remaining ingredients as you stir and blend well. Pour gravy into sauce boat. Take to the table and carve the lamb and serve gravy over top, serve a green salad on the side.

Pomegranate, produces fruit for wine and table use. The Pomegranate is a sacred fruit. Used often as an object of art, the fruit is mentioned in the writings of the area. The skin is used to tan leather, as a dye, the seeds for medicine, the pulp is thirst quenching and was taken on the caravan routes where water was not available.

#66
EGOZIM TABBOULEH (TABULEH)
Tomato Salad With Nuts

¹/₄ cup Pita bread, chopped fine
¹/₄ cup Burghul (crushed wheat)
¹/₄ cup Hazelnuts (filbert) minced
1 ¹/₈ cup Parsley, chopped fine
4 Tomatoes, medium, chopped fine
4 Onions, spanish, chopped fine
2 tsp. Salt
¹/₄ tsp. Pepper
¹/₃ cup Lemon juice, fresh squeezed
¹/₃ cup Olive Oil, light virgin oil
2 Tbsp. Mint leaves, chopped fine
6 Romaine lettuce leaves

Place burghul in a bowl in 1/2 cup cold water. Let soak 5-7 minutes. Add pita bread mix and allow to soak 2 minutes. Place in cheese cloth and squeeze out excess moisture. Combine all but olive oil and lettuce. Toss and mix well. Check flavor. Add more lemon juice if required. Add olive oil. Toss. Portion soft ball on Romaine leaves. Serve as salad.

#67
NUT KIBBI

³/₄ cup Burghul (crushed wheat)
³/₄ cup Pine nuts, chopped fine
1 lb. Lamb, ground twice on fine plate
¹/₈ tsp. Nutmeg, ground
¹/₁₆ tsp. Cayenne Pepper

¹/₈ tsp. Paprika, fine
¹/₄ tsp. All spice, ground
1 tsp. Salt
¹/₈ tsp. Pepper
3 small Onions, chopped fine
³/₄ cup Olive oil
1 cup Water

Place burghul in bowl, pour water over. Soak 7 minutes. Add pine nuts. Stir. Place in cheese cloth and squeeze out excess water. Combine lamb and burghul/nut mixture. Knead until smooth. Spread out, sprinkle spices over. Knead together and blend well. Divide into equal size balls. Press balls flat (1/2" thick). Press thumb into center of each meat cake. Fill thumb print with olive oil. Sprinkle onions over top. Serve with pita bread. You may like a heavier taste, if so, sprinkle extra salt over the top.

Pistachio, (Fistuk Haliby) {Botnim} was (Genesis 43:11) "One of the choice fruits of the land" used by Jacob in gift giving. The fruit is often called "Pistakin." The nut is one of the fruit/nuts subject to tithes. The Pistachio was one of the fruits grafted to new root stock to produce a sweeter taste. The nut is found being used in the full culinary scope of the Mid East. It's greenish kernel and delicate almond-like flavor make it a natural in the cooking of lamb and goat. The nut is often mixed with the trail food and developed many uses in baking of breads and cookies.

Pignolia, pine nut, used in cooking meats, as a sauce when ground and mixed with crushed fruits or wine. Pinus Pinea (Isa 44:14) was a food of the poor. Attis the tree spirit was, according to Mythology, turned into the pine tree. The pine tree has been worshipped by many peoples, but in Canaan, Rome and Greece the tree was a source of life and wealth... the tree produced food and a source of trade for other foods. The cone of the stone pine contain a nut seed that yield good protein for body growth. These same nuts (seeds) were used to produce a rather strong wine for local consumption.

#68
HAIS - NUT CANDY

$^1/_2$ *lb. Pistachio nuts, minced fine*
$^3/_4$ *lb. Almonds, minced fine*
$^3/_4$ *lb. Dates, pitted, minced*
1 *lb. Dried bread crumbs*
3 *Tbsp. Sesame oil*
3 *Tbsp. Powder sugar*
1 *tsp. Cinnamon powder*

Combine all ingredients but sugar. Blend well. Pinch off and roll into small balls 1½". Dust with cinnamon sugar. Set aside and allow to air dry for 4-6 hours.

Peach (Afarsek) [Persial Apple] was subject to tithing, "after they began to show red veins." This is a fruit of great culinary importance. Huge peach orchards (Plantations) were cultivated during the Greco/Roman period. Discussed in the Mishnah, the peach is well known. Eaten raw, stewed, boiled, in jam and jelly, the fruit was found on every table in every form that man could think of. Fermented with sugar the fruit would produce a strong drink.

Pear (Agas) (Pyrus Communis) "Crustumina" the pear growing wild in the Upper Galilee, was discussed by Pliney in his "Natural History," and in the Mishnah, it can easily be justified that this soft fruit was enjoyed through the full biblical period and comes down to modern man fairly well intact.

Quince, most probably the fruit of Eve's temptation. Quince is the name of the fruit and the tree. Called three different names; Havush, Parish, and Aspargal. The fruit was given to the sick as a tonic. The fruit cannot be eaten raw, but only after being boiled. Jam, paste, preserves are the traditional use.

#69
QUINCE PASTE

2 lbs. Quince, washed, cut into quarters
2 cups Sugar
3 Tbsp. Lemon juice, fresh squeezed
1 cup Water

Place cut Quince and 1/2 cup water in tightly covered pot. Lightly boil for 25 minutes. Press through fine sieve or screen. Combine sugar and balance of water, boil until sugar is fully dissolved. Add lemon juice. Stir. Reduce heat. Stir in quince pulp, stir well until mixture thickens. Pour into flat pan, spread thin— 1/4" maximum thickness. Allow to air dry for up to 48 hours. Cut and serve.

Sycamore Fig, (Teahnah) a delicate tree with small figs that grow in bunches. Amos 7:14, "I was a herdsman and a dresser of Sycamore trees." This fig lends itself to eating in jams and jellies and was combined with a mixture of citrus and soft fruits to make a full bodied marmalade served with meat and fowl.

Walnut (Egoz) from the tree genus Jaglans, was well known throughout the Middle East, East, and through the land from Canaan to China to the Himalayas and through the Euphrates Valley back to the Jordan Valley. The nut is very rich in oil and has a high content protein. The tree, sometimes referred to as the Persian Walnut, was a very good source of lumber for building as well as food stuff. Some of the trees reached a height of 150 feet tall with a trunk of 5 feet in diameter. Song of Songs speak of "A Garden of Nuts" in Chapter 6 verse 11. Historic evidence shows that the walnut was in great demand as a food source and that the wood was prized as a fuel in the altar fire of the Temple. Josephus wrote of Walnuts growing in the valley of Gennesareth. All parts of the tree were used. The bark for dying cloth, the shells of the nut for children games, the clear timber for building, the select pieces for objects of art and wood carving. Ground nuts were used to thicken sauces of savory or sweet flavors. One such dish is Rahat Lokum (Turkish Delight/Loukoumi).

LOUKOUMI

3 drops Green food color
2 cups Sugar
1/2 cup Hot Water
3 Tbsp. Gelatin (Knox or similar)
1/2 cup Cold water
1 Tbsp. Orange Rind, grated
1/4 cup Walnuts, minced fine

Combine cold water and gelatin, blend until soft. combine sugar and water and bring to a soft boil, stir until all sugar is dissolved. Reduce heat and add gelatin blend. Stir well. Simmer 15-20 minutes. Add orange rind and juice, blend well, simmer 5 minutes. Stir well. Add food color blend in well. Pour mixture through a fine sieve into flat pan, allow mixture to flow out so that it is no more than 1" thick. Sprinkle walnuts over top and allow to chill and firm. Cut into 1" squares and dust with powder sugar. Set out as candy. Some recipes call for a whole nut to be pressed into the top before the mixture begins to harden.

Nuts and Seeds (Agozim V'Garinim) of various types were eaten roasted and lightly salted. It makes no difference what type of nut, almonds, walnuts, pistachios, filberts, pine nuts. They should be shelled and placed in a warm oven of 350°-375° for 10 minutes (long enough for the nut to begin throwing it's natural oil). Remove the nuts from the oven and sprinkle lightly with salt. Allow to cool and enjoy as a snack. Pumpkin, squash or melon seeds can be cooked this same way, but cook them for 20 minutes.

Of all nut-candy (deserts perhaps the best known are Baklava, a dough layered dessert, and Halvah, a complete candy fudge).

#72
ALMOND LAYER CAKE

5 *Egg whites*
$^1/_8$ *Salt*
$^3/_4$ *cup Sugar*
$^3/_4$ *cup Almonds, finely ground*
1 *tsp. Almond extract*
$^1/_4$ *cup Sugar*
$^1/_4$ *cup Toasted Almonds, chopped*

In a glass bowl combine egg and salt. Beat until just stiff. Slowly add 3/4 cup sugar and beat into meringue. Fold in almond extract and 1/4 cup sugar. Add almonds, beat until smooth. Make 4 equal size circles of meringue on paper lined cookie sheet. Bake at 250° for 30 minutes. Remove from paper and place on flat surface to dry. While meringue is drying, make your favorite chocolate filling. Cover tops and sides of meringue with chocolate filling and stack one on top of the other to create a layer cake. You may ice the top layer with an almond flavor icing or put extra filling on top. Sprinkle chopped almonds over top. Refrigerate 4-6 hours. Serve.

#73
TARATOR
HAZELNUT SAUCE

1 *cup Hazelnuts, pulverized in blender*
1 *cup Shelled walnuts, pulverized in blender*
1 *cup White bread hearts, pulverized in blender*
4 *toes garlic, minced*
$^1/_4$ *tsp. Cayenne pepper*
$^1/_4$ *tsp. Salt*
$^1/_4$ *tsp. Dry red peppers, crushed fine*
$^1/_4$ *tsp. Hungarian paprika*
$^1/_4$ *cup Olive oil, light virgin type*

¹/₃ cup Red wine vinegar
1 tsp. Lemon juice, fresh squeeze
5 Tbsp. Cold water
4 Tbsp. Mayonnaise*

In a glass or stainless steel bowl toss nuts, bread, garlic, red pepper, paprika, salt and cayenne. Blend well. Add olive oil and vinegar and toss well. With the back of a fork mash all together. Stir in mayonnaise. Mix well. Add water and lemon juice a little at a time and stir well. Taste to check seasoning. Correct seasoning, chill slightly. Use a sauce over boiled, grilled or stuffed fish.

The Ancients made this sauce using a Mortar and Pestle. The walnuts were home grown and the hazelnuts imported from the North and Northeast Mediterranean lands.

*Mayonnaise is modern, but in the Greco/Roman period a sauce of egg yolk, olive oil and a touch of vinegar was the standard.

M. THE HARVEST

History shows us the importance of a season's end, the harvest, the holiday and rituals of thanks:

Hag Ha-asif, the Harvest Feast, called Sukkot. In Leviticus 23:40 we read of the gathering together of the four species (The Main Parts of the body), "Fruit of goodly trees", citron, called Etrog (the heart). "Branches of palm trees", the Lulav (the spine). "Boughs of leafy trees", the myrtle (the eye). "Willows of the brook", the Aravot (the mouth). Put all the parts together they praise God for the good harvest. The parts combined are the Lulav, and Etrog, and form the symbols of the Sukkot celebration.

The holiday represents the journey of Israel through the desert after the exodus from Egypt and it also represents the final harvest of the season — the in-gathering. (Exodus 23:16).

The Sukkah is symbolic of the temporary houses in the fields of the harvesters and also the temporary houses in the desert (Leviticus 23:42,43). The decor of fruits and vegetables used is that of the harvest. This is the time of great thanksgiving.

It is written that the "70 nations" will enjoy peace throughout the world when we all join in the feast of Sukkot. (70 refers to the 70 languages of mankind, Joshua 8:32)

Sukkot was the major Jewish holiday in the Bible, and is related to the major effort of man, the endless work searching for food. Gifts of the crops were taken to Jerusalem for presentation at the Temple. Favorite foods of the holiday are barley soup, cabbage rolls, baked squash, baked onions, and apple pie. Goose or duck was usually eaten when meat was offered.

For more information about Sukkot as well as the other holidays of the Hebrew faith, turn to the full Holiday and Festival section of this book.

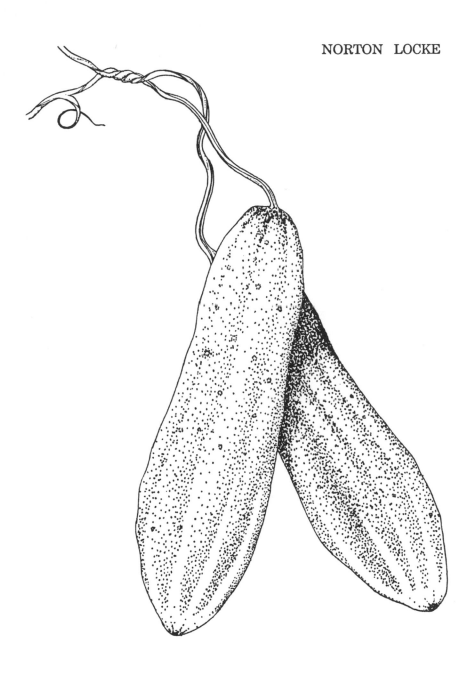

Cubumber and Vine

159

The Land of Milk and Honey

Deuteronomy 8:7 testifies to the fact that when the people are on the land, the land will wax well. "The land is a land of hills and valleys and drinketh water of the rain of heaven...I will give you the rain of your land in its due season, the first rain and the latter rain, and thou my gather in thy corn, and thy wine, and thine oil. and I will send grass in thy fields for thy cattle, that thou mayest eat and be full. "We can see again that the Jews are on the land and modern Israel is blooming and the crops and fields are full.

This is the Land of Milk and Honey. The names of the towns and villages attest to the bounty of the land: Carmel, field of fruit; Beth-Bacherem, house of vineyards; Beit-Shikma, Sycamore House; Gath, Wine press, Beth-Phag, house of figs; Beth-Haggan, house of gardens, Kiryat' Anavim, village of grapes; Marj El-id, valley of the feast; Gethsemane (Gath-Shamna) oil press; Abu-Tor, father of the ox. Mat'a, plantation; Nahal-eschol, village of grapes; Gedera sheepfold; Ein-Karem, spring of the vineyard; Bayit-Vegan, house and garden. Just to name a few.

When visiting Israel today many artifacts of the early history can be viewed in the museums that dot the countryside. The two most important for a full overview are the Rockefeller Museum in Jerusalem, and the Haifa Museum of Ancient Art. Of great importance to the student of ancient art will be Ha-aretz Museum in Tel Aviv with its numerous artifacts of the Biblical period. History lives as you view the cooking vessels, ovens, grinding wheels, vestments, saddle-quern, jars and utensils.

The Jerusalem Biblical Zoo is the most unusual zoological garden in the world, in that it has built a gathering of almost all the 130 animals mentioned in the Old Testament. Located on Mt. Scopus the zoo is currently building a reproduction of Noah's Ark exactly to scale as outlined in the bible. Some of these animals are extinct in the outside world and only exist in the zoo. On the campus of Bar Ilan University, they also have planted only plants listed in the Bible.

POST ROMAN RECIPES

From the Land of Milk and Honey

A. THE BEGINNING
Mezze, Starters, Small Foods

STARTERS
      PICKLES
            SAUCES
                  FLAVORS

Note: • *Dots indicate the oldest recipes*

#74
• ROTEV SKEDEEM
Almond Sauce

1 cup Almonds, peeled, minced fine
4 Tbsp. White vinegar
1/2 tsp. Dry English mustard
1 toe Garlic, crushed
2 Tbsp. Oil
1/6 tsp. Pepper
1 tsp. Water

In a mortar crush together all ingredients and make a smooth creamy puree. Use as topping for vegetable or meats.

#75
• BOB
HOUMOUS

2 cups Chick-Peas, pre-soaked in water 8 hours
5 cups Water
1 tsp. Salt
1/4 tsp. Pepper

Boil peas in unsalted water for 20 minutes. Reduce fire and simmer 35 minutes. Check for tenderness. Drain off water, add salt and pepper. Toss to fully coat. Serve as side dish.

#76
• SALAT GEZER
Carrot Relish

18 Carrots, washed, ground
1 cup Celery, chopped fine
1 Red Pepper, chopped
1 pt. Vinegar
1/2 cup Sugar

2 tsp. Salt
1/2 tsp. Paprika
1 cup Water

Simmer carrot in water 15 minutes. Add all other ingredients. Bring to boil. Simmer 25 minutes. Cool. Bottle. Refrigerate.

#77
PASHTEDAH GEZER
Carrot souffle

1 cup Carrots, boiled, mashed
2 Tbsp. Onion, minced
1 cup Half and half (cream)
2 Tbsp. Flour
1/4 tsp. Pepper
1/4 tsp. Paprika
2 Eggs, separate

Heat 1/2 and 1/2. Whip in flour. Add onion and spices. Stir well. Add egg yolks beaten, add carrot. Stir. Whip egg whites stiff and fold into cream mixture. Pour into well greased casserole dish. Set into pan of hot water. Bake at 350° for 30-35 minutes.

#78
• CHAREIN

1 large Horse-radish root
2 medium Beets, cooked
1/4 tsp. Salt
1/2 tsp. Sugar
1/2 cup Dry red wine

Grate root and beet, add spice and blend well. Add wine. Place in covered jar. Refrigerate, let sit three days. Serve with all meats.

#79
• CHAROSET

6 Green, sour apples, grated
2 Red, sharp apples, grated
1/2 cup Walnuts chopped
2 cups Shelled almonds, chopped fine
1/4 cup Red wine
1/4 cup Honey
1 tsp. Cinnamon
1/3 tsp. Ginger Powder
1/8 tsp. Nutmeg
1 Orange rind grated
3 Tbsp. Orange juice

Combine all ingredients, mix well. Refrigerate. Serve with all meats. Used as biblical injunction during Passover to remind celebrants of the mortar used to make bricks.

#80
REBAT DUVDUVANIM
Cherry Preserves

1 lb. Red Sour Pie Cherries, pitted, retain pits
2 cups Honey
1 cup Water
1 Tbsp. Lemon

Place cracked cherry pits in water, bring to boil for 3 minutes. Strain off water into sauce pot. Discard pits. Add honey, lemon juice, bring to boil, add cherries. Stir well. Simmer 35 minutes. Skim scum from top several times. Bottle.

#81
• ROTEV LEMON
Egg-Lemon Sauce

2 Eggs
2 Lemons, juiced
2 cups Hot stock (Chicken or Vegetable)

Beat eggs for 2 minutes, blend in lemon juice. Slowly stir in hot stock and beat all the time. Stir into the dish to be prepared. This is the basis for Egg-Lemon soup, and as a topping for fresh vegetables.

#82
• MELAFAFON HAMOTZ
Cucumber Pickle

Cucumbers preserved with dill are probably the oldest of pickles. The two major cucumbers of Israel are smaller and rounder than those found in the Americas. The Israeli pickle is sweet, some smooth, some rough and covered with spikes. If we use the Girkin we will approach the proper flavor.

3 lbs. Small girkin cucumbers
1 ¹/₂ cups Dill flours and seeds, chopped
5 toes Garlic, peeled and chopped
6 whole Black peppers (Pilpel)
8 tsp. Salt
2 medium Red peppers chopped
4 cups Water
1 cup White wine vinegar

Wash and pack cucumbers in a glass jar or crock. Alternate layers of cucumbers and dill and garlic. Sprinkle peppers over the top. Mix all other ingredients together. Blend well. Pour over the cucumbers. Seal jars well. Let sit eight days in a warm room (80°), or 12 days in a cool room (60°). These pickles should be eaten within 30 days or they will turn

167

very soft and mushy.

#83
• REBAT TEHENIM
Fig Conserve

1 *1/2 lbs.* Fresh Figs (Dried will do)
4 cups Honey
1 cup Water
2 tsp. Lemon juice
1/4 cup Anis seed
1/4 tsp. Cream of Tartar
6 Apricots, dried sliced thin
1/4 tsp. Lemon rind, grated
1/2 cup Nuts, chopped

In covered sauce pot boil, honey, water, lemon juice, apricots. Stir. Add figs. Cover and simmer 20 minutes. Remove cover, add nuts. Simmer 10 minutes. Pour into hot, clean jar or crock. Cool. Serve.

The fruit of Eve's temptation was in Jewish tradition the fig or citron, but in Christian tradition it was the apple (malum) due to the Latin translation of the Hebrew.

#84
• TEENIM MEVUSHAL
Fig Preserves

3 lbs. Figs, fresh
3 cups Sugar
3 Tbsp. Lemon Juice
3 wedges Lemon peel, scrubbed
3 Cinnamon sticks
3 small Cardamon pods

Place figs in pot, pour sugar over and let stand 3 hours. Place on fire and bring to soft boil, add lemon juice, stir, add peel, cinnamon, cardamon. Stir. Simmer 10-15 minutes until fruit is well glazed. Remove from fire. Into 3 clean jars put one cinnamon stick each, one lemon peel, one cardamon pod. Spoon into jars. Pour hot wax plug. Cover and seal. Cool slowly. Refrigerate.

#85
• TEHENIM METUKIM
Figs, Spiced

24 Figs, washed, stems off
1 pt. Water
³/₄ cup Vinegar
2 cups Brown sugar
1 stick Cinnamon
³/₄ tsp. Mace
¹/₂ tsp. Allspice

Place figs in boiling water for 3 minutes. Add sugar and spices, stir. Add vinegar, stir. Simmer 20 minutes. Figs will be clear. Cool. Cover and let sit overnight.

#86
• FILE POWDER

2 cups young leaves of the red sassafras tree, dried in an oven at a low temperature (150°) until crisp. Crumble very fine. Grind into powder. Mix with 1/4 cup thyme powder and 1/8 cup crushed bay leaf. Use as a spice in gumbo and stew. A good seasoning for fish chowder.

#87
• ROTEV SHOOM
Garlic Sauce

1 full head Garlic
6 Cloves
8 slices French Bread, crust removed, soaked in water,

169

squeezed dry
¹/₂ cup Olive Oil
¹/₃ cup White Vinegar
¹/₆ tsp. Salt
2 cups Potatoes, mashed
1 Tbsp. Chic-Pea Paste

Mash garlic in mortar or use blender. Add potatoes and blend well. Add bread and blend well. Alternate oil and vinegar in small units until fully absorbed. Add salt. Taste for flavor. If too thin add chic-pea paste and blend well. Serve. (Chic-pea paste is 1 cup soaked peas, 1/2 teaspoon salt, mashed smooth and used as thickening agent.)

#88
RABAT ANAVIM
GRAPE CONSERVE

1 lb. Grape, purple, remove seeds
2 cups Honey
¹/₄ cup Sugar
2 Tbsp. Lemon Juice
1 cup Water
¹/₄ tsp. Cream of Tartar
1 tsp. Cornstarch

In a glass bowl place grapes, sugar, cornstarch. Mix well so grapes are coated. Add honey, blend. In a deep pot boil water, lemon juice, add cream of tartar. Pour grapes into pot. Stir. Simmer 20 minutes. Check to see if syrup is thick, is not cover pot and simmer 10 minutes more. Cool. Uncover and pour into a crock.

"— now it happens to be the season the ripe grapes" at the end of July. Numbers 13:20.

#89
• GRAPEFRUIT SOUFFLE

¹/₂ cup Grapefruit sections, chopped
3 Tbsp. Orange Juice
¹/₂ cup Brown sugar
1 Tbsp. Lemon Juice
¹/₂ tsp. Orange Rind
1 cup Milk
4 Tbsp. Flour
4 Tbsp. Butter
¹/₂ Tbsp. Vanilla
2 Egg white, whipped.

Melt butter, add flour and make soft roux, add milk and blend well until smooth. Add grapefruit, orange juice, sugar, lemon juice. Mix well. Fold in egg whites. Pour into greased baking dish. Bake at 300° for 1 hour.

#90
• TEHENIM YERUKIM
Green Figs

2 lbs. Green Figs, trim stems
3 cups Sugar or Honey
2 ¹/₂ cups Water
1 Tbsp. Lemon juice
¹/₈ tsp. Vanilla extract

Boil sugar, water, lemon juice. Cook three minutes. Add figs. Stir and remove from fire. Let sit over night. Bring to boil. simmer 10 minutes. Add vanilla, stir. With slotted spoon remove figs and place in jelly jar. Reduce syrup by half. Pour over figs and seal jars. Store.

Amos 8:2 "and the Lord said: Amos, what seest thou? and (Amos) said: a basket of summer fruit. —"

171

#91
• HILBE
Robiya; Hilbeh

2 Tbsp. Fenugreek Seeds
2 cups Water
2 tsp. Zhug
Soak seeds for 3 hours, pour off water. Grind course. Add
1/2 cup water. Whip together 5 minutes. Blend in zhug.
Check for flavor. Used as a dip for bread and lamb. Hilbe is
often sprinkled on greens for dressing.

#92
D'VOSH
Honey Dressing

2 Tbsp. Lemon Juice
2 Egg yolk
¹/₂ tsp. Salt
2 cups Oil
3 Tbsp. Honey
Whip all together until thick. Use at once.

#93
• HAIMISH
Cucumber Pickled

12 Cucumbers, sliced
1 cup Vinegar
¹/₂ cup Sugar
1 tsp. Caraway seeds
Mix all together and place in a jar. Mix every day for six
days. Serve as a condiment.

#94
• JAFFA REBAT TAPOZIM
Orange Marmalade

12 Oranges, cut in half, sliced thin, seeds removed
1 qt. Water
2 cups Honey
1 cup Sugar
1 Tbsp. Lemon rind, grated
1 Tbsp. Lemon juice
1 Tbsp. Candied ginger, sliced thin

Combine oranges and water. Slowly simmer for 2 hours. Replace water as required. Combine all ingredients, bring to boil. Stir until thick. Remove from fire, cool slightly. Pour into jars and refrigerate.

#95
• KIMA SAUCE

1 lb. Lamb
2 medium Onion, chopped fine
3 Tbsp. Olive oil
2 toes Garlic, pressed
$1/2$ cup Dry red wine
8 medium Tomatoes, chopped
$1/2$ tsp. Sugar
$1/2$ tsp. Cinnamon
1 Bay leaf
1 tsp. Salt
$1/2$ tsp. Pepper
1 bunch Chives, chopped
$1/2$ tsp. Basil
4 Tbsp. Water

Sauté onion and oil until golden. Add lamb and brown lightly. Mix well. Add garlic, wine and sugar. Simmer 7 minutes. Add tomatoes, cinnamon, bay leaf, salt, pepper and stir well. Simmer 10 minutes. Add water. Cover and simmer 20 minutes. Add chives and basil. Simmer 10 minutes. Stir well. Mash tomatoes and stir. Serve as sauce with bread or any meat dish.

"Wine is a mocker, strong drink is riotous;" Proverbs 20;1

#96
SALUT KROOV HAMUTZ

2 medium Tomatoes, peeled, chopped fine
3 cups Sauerkraut, drained, chop course
1 head Celery, cleaned, chopped
2 Onions sliced fine
2 Green peppers, sliced fine
1 cup Chili sauce
1 cup Catsup
$^1/_2$ cup Brown Sugar
$^1/_2$ cup Lemon Juice
2 tsp. Paprika
$^1/_2$ tsp. Black Pepper

Mix all together. Blend well. Place in crock or jar and refrigerate 24 hours. Serve.

#97
• LAMB DUMPLINGS
(Kreplach) Dumpling

2 cups Flour
$^3/_4$ tsp. Salt
1 Tbsp. Olive oil or margarine
$^2/_3$ cup Warm Water
$^1/_4$ cup Lamb shoulders, ground fine
$^1/_6$ tsp. Cayenne
$^1/_6$ tsp. Cinnamon
$^1/_8$ tsp. Nutmeg
2 Tbsp. Margarine

¹/₄ cup Pine Nuts, chopped fine
¹/₂ cup Onion, minced
On a work board mix flour and salt. Make a well in the center. In the well add oil and water, mix the dough. Knead and make smooth ball. Cover and set aside. Sauté lamb and onion in margarine. Add spices. Stir well. Add pine nuts. Stir well. Sauté 2 minutes more. Remove from fire. Punch down dough, knead until elastic. Cut into four pieces. Roll out thin. Cut into 3" squares. Put 1 teaspoon meat mixture in center. fold dough triangle. Press edges shut. Set aside to dry slightly. Put pot of lightly salted water on boil. Drop in dumplings. boil 25 minutes. Remove and serve with tihina sauce as hors d'oeuvres or entree.

#98
• LEBEN
Clobbered Skim Milk

3 cups Milk reduced in half over medium fire
¹/₂ cup Yogurt
Mix well, cover and let sit 5-6 hours until set. Refrigerate until used. Mix well. Can be served as is or mix with fruit cocktail, with syrup, honey, or pour over fresh sliced vegetables.
"Has thou not poured me out as milk, and curdled me like cheese?" Job 11:10

#99
LEMON-OIL SAUCE

1 cup Oil
¹/₂ cup Lemon Juice
¹/₄ tsp. Salt
¹/₆ tsp. Pepper
2 sprigs Parsley, chopped
¹/₆ tsp. Basil

¹/₈ tsp. Fennel
Whip all together. Serve at once.

#100
• LIMONIM HAMUTZIM
Lemons Pickled

6 Lemons cut into quarters
2 cups Course Salt
1 cup Hot Red Peppers
1 tsp. White Pepper
1 cup Lemon Juice

In a crock place layer of lemons tightly packed, layer of salt, sprinkle with hot peppers and white peppers. Repeat layers. Pour lemon juice over. Place a piece of wood or top with weight. Let sit in a cool room for 3-4 weeks. Serve as a pickle.

#101
• RABAT MELON
Melon Preserve

1 lb. Watermelon rind, cubed 1"
2 cups Honey
¹/₂ cup Water
2 stick 4" Cinnamon
¹/₄ tsp. Nutmeg
¹/₂ cup Almonds, blanched slivered
1 Tbsp. Lemon Juice

In square pot combine honey, water, cinnamon stick, nutmeg. Bring to boil, add watermelon rind. Stir well. Simmer 1 hour, add almonds and lemon juice. Stir well and simmer 10 minutes. Skim scum. Serve.

Always help feed the poor "open your hand to the poor and needy — " Deuteronomy 14:27.

#102
REBAT TAPOZIM V'DUVDUVARIM
Orange and Cherry Conserve

4 medium Oranges, washed, sliced thin, seeds removed
  and blanched, cracked
4 lbs. Cherries, pitted
4 Tbsp. Lemon Juice
1 tsp. Lemon Rind, grated
3 cups Honey
1 cup Sugar
1 tsp. Cinnamon
$1/4$ tsp. Cloves
$1/6$ tsp. Nutmeg
2 cups Water

Place oranges and 1 cup of water in large sauce pan and simmer for 10 minutes. Stir often. blanch pits in 1 cup of water, retain water, discard seeds. Set orange pan aside. In separate pan boil lemon juice, rind, honey, sugar. When sugar is dissolved, pour in cherries. Add pit water and oranges with water, stir well. Soft boil until thick. Pour into jars and store.

"I planted me vineyards; I made me gardens and parks, and I planted trees
  in them of all kinds of fruit;" Ecclesiastes 2:4,5.

#103
• MESA

1 cup Black olives (Greek) seeds out
1 cup Goat cheese, crumbled
$1/2$ cup Sweet pickles, chopped large
1 head Romain lettuce, washed, leaves torn in half
2 Tbsp. Olive oil

Mix all together. Eaten as salad or hors d'oeuvres.

#104
• SALAT BAZAL
Onions, Pickled

2 lbs. Tiny Pearl Onions, peeled
1 cup White Wine Vinegar
1 cup Water
1 tsp. Salt
$^1/_2$ tsp. White Pepper
1 tsp. Sugar
1 tsp. Dill

Place all together in an enamel pan. Boil for 4 minutes. With slotted spoon remove onions and place in glass jars. Pour liquid over. Cover and seal. Let age 7-10 days. Use as a pickle.

#105
ROTEV TAPUZIM
Orange Sauce

8 large Oranges, sectioned
3 cups Coconut meat, flaked
$^1/_2$ cup Brown sugar
1 tsp. Lemon Juice

Mix all together. Refrigerate overnight. Serve with meat dish.

#106
• KAVVSH BEYTZIM
Pickled Eggs

24 Eggs, hard boiled 30 minutes, peel, placed in wide
    mouth jar
1 qt. Boiling vinegar
8 whole Peppers
6 whole Cloves

5 *whole Allspice*
4 *toes Garlic*
1 *tsp. Sliced ginger*
Place eggs in jar. Add spice and herbs, fill jar to top with vinegar. Cap and seal. Shake vigorously. Set in cool dark place. Let sit 20-30 days. Use as a pickle.

#107
• ANAVIM HAMUTZIM
Pickled Grapes

2 *lbs. Grapes, carefully cut with stem piece attached*
$^1/_4$ *cup Dry Mustard*
$^1/_2$ *cup Brown Sugar*
2 *pt. Water*
1 *tbsp. Cinnamon*
1 *tsp. Cloves*
$^1/_4$ *tsp. Nutmeg*
In a pot combine sugar, water, cinnamon, cloves and nutmeg. Bring to boil. Simmer 10 minutes. Cool, place grapes in a jar. Sprinkle mustard over each layer of grapes. Pour sugar syrup over and cover grapes. Cover jar tightly. Set in a cool dark area for 90 days. Use as a pickle.

#108
REBAT GLAAT
Pumpkin Jam

4 *cups Pumpkin, peeled, sliced thin*
2 *cups Sugar*
2 *cups Honey*
$^1/_2$ *tsp. Mastic (Mastiche) pectin powder*
$^1/_4$ *cup Almonds, blanched, slivered*
2 *cups Water*
Boil water, sugar, honey. Cook 7 minutes and stir. Add pumpkin. Simmer 45 minutes. Add mastic. Simmer 10

minutes. Add almonds. Simmer 5 minutes. Pour into jelly jars and store, or serve with meat dish.

#109
• QUINCE CONSERVE

1 ¹/₂ lb. Quince, peeled and chopped fine, or grated
2 cups Honey
³/₄ cup Water
1 Tbsp. Cinnamon
1 Tbsp. Lemon Juice

In sauce pan combine quince, honey, water, cinnamon, simmer for 1 hour. skim any scum. Stir in lemon juice. Use as sauce for meat or as spread on bread.

#110
REBAT PETEL
Raspberry Jam

1 lb. Raspberries, washed
2 cups Sugar
1 Tbsp. Vinegar
1 Tbsp. Lemon Juice

Combine raspberries and sugar. Soft boil 5 minutes. Add vinegar and lemon juice. Stir. Soft boil 2 minutes. Remove from fire. Cover and let sit 12 hours. Stir occasionally. Jar and seal. You may use blueberries, strawberries or any other soft berry.

#111
• LOUKOZ KAVYAR SALAT
"Red Fish Eye Salad"
Taramasalat

6 slices White Bread, soaked in water, squeezed dry
1 cup Cold Water

¹/₂ cup Whitefish Roe, salted
¹/₄ cup Lemon Juice
¹/₄ cup Onion, grated
³/₄ cup Olive Oil
Place all in blender at medium speed. Blend for 2₁/₂ minutes to yield a thick puree. Place in lettuce lined bowl. Serve with crackers or demi-rye. History indicates that the roe of the Gray Mullet or Sea Bass (loukoz) were the source of the best roe. Chaboute, a fresh water fish of the Euphrates was the major Mesopotamian product.

#112
• RED PEPPER SPICE

¹/₂ cup Cayenne pepper
¹/₄ cup Cumin
2 tsp. Salt
Mix all together. Blend well. Place in a jar and cover with tightly fitting lid.

#113
SORGUM MOUSSE

¹/₂ cup Sorgum
3 Egg yolks
¹/₂ cup Milk, scalded
¹/₂ cup Heavy Cream
3 Tbsp. 10 x sugar
Beat egg yolks until light and soft, beat in sorgum. Stir in milk. Cook in double boiler and stir until mixture thickens like custard. Remove from fire and cool. Whip cream and sugar until tight then fold into the cool custard. Pour into shallow pan and refrigerate.

#114
• TABBOULE
Bulgur Salad

6 small Pita bread, warm, retain
1 cup Bulgur, cracked wheat, soaked 30 minutes
2 cups Scallions, chopped fine
2 cups Parsley, chopped
$^1/_4$ cup Mint, chopped
2 Tbsp. Dill
2 cups Tomatoes, peeled, chopped
$^1/_2$ tsp. Salt
$^1/_2$ tsp. Pepper
$^1/_2$ cup Lemon Juice
$^1/_3$ cup Olive Oil

Drain bulgur, combine all ingredients, toss well. Refrigerate 2 hours. Cut pocket in Pita, stuff with tabboule and serve, or serve in bowl and put Pita on side.

In about 1100 C.E. Maimonides (Rabbi Moses ben Maimon) known as the Rambam, in his writing Hilchot Da'ot spoke out loudly about good health. He said not to eat overly processed flour as it cheated the person eating it. He also said that it was good for you to eat fresh fruits and vegetables. He was also outspoken about drinking in moderation, and when you drank be sure that it was with food, during meals. Maimonides suggest that we not eat salty foods.

#115
ROTOR AGVANIYOT
Tomato & Oil Sauce

1 medium Onion, chopped fine
2 Tbsp. Olive Oil
2 toes Garlic, pressed
8-10 medium Tomatoes, peeled, chopped
$^1/_4$ cup Dry Red Wine

1 tsp. Sugar
1 tsp. Salt
¹/₂ tsp. Pepper
1 4" stick Cinnamon stick
¹/₂ bunch Parsley, chopped (Retain)
¹/₂ tsp. Basil (Retain)

Sauté onions in oil until light golden. Add all ingredients except parsley and basil, stir well. Simmer 30 minutes. Add parsley and basil, stir. Remove cinnamon. Serve.

#116
REBAT AGVANIYOT
Tomato Preserves

8 large Tomatoes, peeled, chopped
3 cups Sugar
¹/₄ cup Lemon juice
³/₄ cup Ginger, crystallized, chopped
1 Tbsp. Lemon Rind, grated

In silver stone or enamel pot mix tomatoes and sugar. Let sit 1 hour. Add lemon rind and juice. Mix well. Place on low heat. Stir often. Simmer until mixture is thick. Cool slightly and place in glass jar.

#117
• TURNIP, PICKLED

2 lbs. White turnip, washed and peeled, cut into quarters
4 toes Garlic, minced
1 Beet, raw, peeled, sliced
6 Tbsp. Salt
3 cups Warm Water
1 ¹/₂ cups White Vinegar

Layer turnips into large jar, mix garlic and beet between. Blend salt, water and vinegar. Mix well. When salt is fully dissolved, pour over turnip layers. Cap and seal jar. Set in cool dark place and let age 7-10 days. Use as a pickle.

#118
• TURNIP RELISH

5 medium Turnips, peeled, sliced thin
³/₄ tsp. Fresh Lime Juice
¹/₂ tsp. Fresh Lemon Juice
1 tsp. Red Pepper Spice
1 tsp. Salt
In a glass bowl mix juices with salt until salt is liquified. Add red pepper with turnips and mix well. Cover, refrigerate for 2 hours. Stir. Serve.
Isaiah 55:2 "— you shall eat choice food and enjoy the richest viands."

#119
• ZHUG

1 Tbsp. Water
6 toes Garlic
1 tsp. Cumin
1 Tbsp. Dry Red Peppers
1 Tbsp. Coriander
¹/₄ tsp. Cardamon
Grind all together, make pulp. Set aside, use in making zhum. Often used as is for rubbing on lamb or venison before broiling. zhug can be used as a topping for any broiled meat.

#120
• ZHUM

2 cups Leben — Clobbered Skim Milk
2 tsp. Semneh, rendered butter with Garlic and
*   red pepper*
2 Tbsp. Flour

¹/₄ tsp. Garlic
¹/₆ tsp. Salt
¹/₆ tsp. Cayenne Red Pepper

Mix all together, sauté until thick. Top with Zhug. Serve. This dressing is used on all vegetables and as a dip for bread. The use is limited by your imagination.

Soup Pot Over Fire

186

B. SOUPS

#121
MARAK TAPOHEY ETZ
Apple Soup

6 large Apples, peeled, sliced thin
2 medium Pears, peeled, sliced thin
3 Tbsp. Lemon Juice
$^1/_4$ cup Orange Juice
1 Tbsp. Brown Sugar
$^1/_6$ Tbsp. Nutmeg
1 tsp Cinnamon
2 quarts Water

Bring water to boil, add all ingredients. Simmer 25 minutes. Skim the surface. Taste for flavor. Add more cinnamon or lemon to taste. Serve with warm boiled or baked potato on side.

#122
MARAK MISHMISH
Apricot Soup

$^1/_2$ lb. Apricots, quartered
1 pt. Water
1 tsp. Lemon Juice
3 Tbsp. Honey
$^1/_2$ tsp. Vanilla
$^1/_2$ tsp. Cinnamon
1 tsp. Corn Starch

Simmer fruit in water 20 minutes. Add corn starch, simmer 3 minutes. Add lemon juice and honey. Simmer 3 minutes. Stir well. Add vanilla. Remove from fire. Add cinnamon. Serve.

#123
• MARAK SHEUIT
Bean Soup

2 cups Flat White Bean, presoak 8 hours, drain
1 qt. Water
2 Bay leaves
1 tsp. Whole Black Peppercorns
2 Onions, minced
4 Tomatoes, skinned
1 Red Pepper, seeds removed
1 Hot Green Pepper, seeds removed
1 tsp. Salt
1/2 tsp. Pepper
1 bunch Parsley, minced

Place beans in water, bring to boil. Simmer 30 minutes. Add herbs and spices. Simmer 1 hour. Puree onions, tomatoes, peppers. Simmer 20 minutes. Serve with hot Pita bread.

#124
• MARAK FOOL V'SKEDIIN
Bean and Almond Soup

1/4 lb. Haricot Beans, presoaked overnight
1 qt. Chicken stock
1/2 lb. Almonds, raw, skinned, chopped fine
4 Leeks, white only, chopped
3 toes Garlic pressed
1/2 tsp. White Pepper
1/2 cup White Wine
1 tsp. Sugar

Combine beans and stock. Bring to boil and simmer 1 hour. Add almonds. Simmer 20 minutes. Add all remaining ingredients. Simmer 10 minutes. remove from fire and cool. Serve cold.

#125
• MARAK HEMA
Butter Soup

1/2 lb. Butter melted
6 Onions, minced
1 head Celery, minced
1/2 head Cabbage, diced thin
1 bunch Parsley, chopped
1 cup Water
2 qt. Milk
2 Eggs, beaten
1/4 cup Matzo meal

In deep pot. Sauté onions in butter until transparent. Add celery and cabbage. Mix well. Add water and simmer 10 minutes. Add matzo meal and stir well. Pour in milk. Bring to soft boil and simmer 20 minutes. Add parsley. Simmer 5 minutes. Whip in egg. Stir and serve.

#126
• MARAK KERUV
Cabbage Soup

3 qts. Water
1 head Cabbage, cut fine
2 lbs. Brisket, cut in 1 1/2" cubes
2 Onions, chopped
2 tsp. Salt
1/4 tsp. Pepper
1/2 cup Sugar or Honey
1 tsp. Citric acid

In large pot combine water and onion. Boil. Simmer 20 minutes, skim. Add cabbage and brisket. Simmer 30 minutes. Add all other ingredients. Simmer 15 minutes.

#127
CELERY SOUP

4 cups Celery, washed, chopped fine
2 cups Potatoes, peeled, cubed
1 cup Onion, chopped fine
2 Tbsp. Flour
1 tsp. Salt
¹/₆ tsp. Pepper
¹/₄ tsp. Paprika
1 qt. Milk
3 Tbsp. Butter
1 cup Water

Sauté celery and onions in butter minutes. Add water and potatoes. Simmer 12 minutes. Crush with wire mash. Add milk, stir well. Add spice and flour. Blend well. Simmer 10 minutes stirring often.

#128
MARAK TERASS
Corn Soup

1 cup Fresh Corn, cut from cob
4 cups Chicken broth
6 large Tomatoes, peeled, chopped
2 Tbsp. Tomato paste
³/₄ tsp. Salt
¹/₂ tsp. Oregano
¹/₈ tsp. Black Pepper

Place all in pot. Bring to boil. Simmer 15 minutes. Serve.

#129
MARAK SHEUIT SHAMEMET
Creamed Bean Soup

3 Tbsp. Olive Oil
1 lb. Green Beans, cut 1"

$^1/_4$ *lb. Flat Beans, presoaked overnight, washed*
2 Onions
$^1/_4$ *tsp. Caraway seeds*
1 Tbsp. Paprika
2 toes Garlic
2 Tbsp. Flour
1 lb. Potatoes, peeled, diced fine
$^1/_2$ *Bay leaf*
$^1/_6$ *tsp. Pepper*
1 cup Sour Cream
1 bunch Parsley, chopped
1 Parsnip, peeled, chopped fine
2 qt. Water

Sauté onions in oil. Add all spices. Mix well. Add flour and cook roux. Set aside. Place water in pot. Add flat beans and bring to boil. Simmer 35 minutes. Add potatoes and parsnip. Simmer 15 minutes. Add green beans and mixed roux. Simmer 30 minutes. Whip in sour cream. Serve.

#130
CHLODNIK
Cucumber Mustard Soup

3 medium cucumbers, scraped, diced
6 Leeks, chopped
4 cups Water
1 bunch Parsley
$^3/_4$ *tsp. Salt*
$^1/_2$ *tsp. Dry English Mustard (crushed mustard seeds*
  are historic)
$^1/_2$ *tsp. Savory*
$^1/_4$ *tsp. White Pepper*
1 cup Half and Half

Combine cucumbers, leeks, parsley, and water and bring to boil. Simmer 20 minutes. Put vegetables through a ricer, press through sieve into broth. Add spices. Simmer 10 minutes.

Remove from fire and whip in cream. Serve at once.

#131
• "CACIK"
CUCUMBER YOGURT SOUP

6 Cucumbers, peeled, sliced
1 qt. Yogurt
1 Tbsp. Dill
1 Tbsp. Fresh Mint, leaves, chopped
2 Tbsp. Vinegar
1 tsp. Olive Oil
Mix all ingredients together. Chill. Serve with warm Pita.

#132
"FAKI"
Lentil-Tomato Soup

8 Italian Red Plumb Tomatoes
1 lb. Green Lentils, presoaked 8 hours
2 medium Onion, minced
3 toes Garlic, pressed
3 arms Celery, chopped fine
1 bunch Parsley, chopped
1 Tbsp. Mint leaves, chopped
1 tsp. Basil
1 tsp. Salt
$^1/_2$ tsp. Pepper
$^1/_3$ cup Olive Oil
2 quarts Water
2 Tbsp. Red Wine Vinegar
Place water and lentils in pot. Simmer 20 minutes. Add
tomatoes, onions, garlic, and parsley. Simmer 50 minutes. Add
oil, salt, pepper, basil and mint. Cover and simmer 1 hour. Stir
in vinegar. Simmer 5 minutes. Serve with warm Pita bread.

#133
MARAK FOOL
Fava Bean Soup

1 Tbsp. Olive Oil
6 Carrots peeled, $^1/_4$" sliced, pre-blanch 3 minutes
6 arms Celery, $^1/_8$" sliced, pre-blanch 3 minutes
6 medium Tomatoes, peeled
$^1/_2$ cup Broad Beans, pre-soaked 12 hours
$^1/_2$ cup Fava Beans
$^1/_8$ tsp. Hot Pepper sauce
4 cups Veal Bouillon
1 lb. Course Ground Lamb
1 $^1/_2$ cups Riches Coffee White or coconut milk
$^1/_2$ tsp. Salt
$^1/_4$ tsp. Thyme
$^1/_4$ tsp. Celery seed
2 cups Broad egg noodles, cooked

Sauté ground lamb in olive oil. Add carrots and celery, stir and simmer 5 minutes, set aside. In a large pot combine beans, bouillion, spices and herbs. Simmer 1 hour. Add lamb mixture and tomatoes. Simmer 30 minutes. Test for flavor, if not sharp add more hot pepper sauce. Be careful you don't overdo. Add Coffee White. Stir well. Place noodles in soup bowl, ladle soup over. Serve.

#134
• MARAK PEROT
Fruit Soup

3 cups Water
1 qt. Orange Juice
1 cup Prunes, pitted
1 cup Apricots
4 Apples, diced
$^1/_3$ cup Honey

1 tsp. Cinnamon
¹/₆ tsp. Nutmeg
2 Tbsp. Arrowroot
1 tsp. Lemon Juice

Bring orange juice and water to soft boil. Add all fruit. Simmer 15 minutes. Add honey, lemon juice, cinnamon and nutmeg. Simmer 10 minutes. With wire masher squash fruit. Stir well. Soften arrowroot and add. Stir well. Simmer 3 minutes. Chill and serve.

#135
• SHUM MARAK
Garlic Soup

3 Tbsp. Olive Oil
12-15 toes Garlic, sliced thin
5 cups Chicken stock
1 tsp. Salt
¹/₂ tsp. Pepper
¹/₆ tsp. Mace
1 cup Cooked Rice

Sauté garlic in oil for 10 minutes on medium low heat. Add all remaining ingredients. Cover and simmer 15 minutes. Strain soup into rice. Heat rice mixture to soft boil. Serve with Pita bread. This is a very healthy soup: It is reported that garlic clears the blood, aids digestion and makes your Mother-in-law cut her visit short.

#136
• MARAK KURKEVANIM
Giblet Soup

1 lb. Giblets of 1 goose and 2 ducks; heart, gizzard,
*   neck, wing tips. (The head is nice if you are up to it.)*
1 qt. Water
2 Carrots, cleaned, sliced thin

1 *Parsnip, cleaned, sliced thin*
1 *Onion, sliced thin*
2 *arms Celery, chopped*
2 *tsp. Salt*
$^1/_4$ *tsp. White Pepper*
$^1/_4$ *tsp. Cloves*
3 *Tbsp. Flour*
1 *Tbsp. Oil*
2 *Egg yolks*
$^1/_2$ *cup Sherry*

Soak giblets in salt water overnight. Then sauté giblets in margarine. Add water and simmer. Skim twice. Add vegetables. Simmer 20 minutes. Add spices, cover and simmer 15 minutes. Remove giblets and cut them into pieces. Strain stock through sieve. Force vegetables through. Make roux of flour and oil. Whip into stock. Add wine. Simmer as you whisk in the beaten egg. Dish up giblets and pour soup over.

#137
• GOOSE WHITE SOUP

4 *cups Water*
3 *Tbsp. Goose fat*
6 *toes Garlic*
$^1/_2$ *tsp. Thyme*
$^1/_2$ *tsp. Salt*
$^1/_6$ *tsp. White Pepper*
1 *Tbsp. Vinegar*
1 *Egg, separated*
4 *slices French Bread (Burghul is historic)*

Melt goose fat in pan, sauté garlic until brown. Add spice and water. Simmer covered 10-15 minutes, strain and retain stock. Bring to boil. Whip in egg white. Reduce fire to simmer. Whip yolk and vinegar together, add some hot stock and blend well. Blend yolk mixture into hot stock and whisk well. Remove from fire. Place bread in soup bowl. Spoon soup over. Serve hot.

#138
GOULASH SOUP

2 qts. Beef Stock
2 lb. Beef, ground course
6 medium Carrots, peeled, chopped
6 arms Celery, washed, chopped
4 medium Onions, peeled, chopped
$^1/_4$ Cabbage, chopped fine
4 medium Potatoes, peeled, cubed
2 Tbsp. Tomato Paste
4 medium Tomatoes peeled, chopped
$^1/_2$ tsp. Clove
$^1/_2$ tsp. Paprika
$^1/_6$ tsp. Cayenne
$^1/_2$ tsp. Lawry's Season Salt
2 Tbsp. Flour
2 Tbsp. Oil

Mix flour and beef, sauté in oil until nicely browned.
Bring stock to boil, add beef sauté. Simmer 10 minutes. Add
all remaining ingredients and simmer 1 hour. Serve with hot
Black Bread.

#139
• HARIRA
Meat Soup
(Basar)

2 cups Olive Oil
4 Onions, sliced
2 cups Mutton, cut into $^1/_2$" squares
6 Tomatoes, p, chopped
1 bunch Parsley, chopped
1 bunch Purslane, cut above root, chopped

¹/₂ tsp. Ginger
¹/₄ tsp. Saffron powder
¹/₄ tsp. Paprika
¹/₆ tsp. Pepper
¹/₄ tsp. Salt
1 Carrot, chopped
2 quarts Water
¹/₂ lb. Chic-Peas, pre-soaked overnight
¹/₄ lb. Vermicelli
4 Eggs
4 large Soup bones

In large pot heat oil, sauté onions. Brown mutton. Be sure meat is well browned. Add tomatoes and parsley. Stir. Add purslave. Stir; add all other spices. Stir. Add carrot and water. Bring to boil. Add bones. Cover and simmer 30 minutes. Add chic-peas. Simmer 1 hour. Add vermicelli. Cover and simmer 30 minutes. Remove bones, bring to boil. Whip eggs and drizzle into hot soup. Remove from fire and serve.

#140
ISRAELI SOUP
"The Number Soup"

6 Carrots, cleaned, sliced
5 Tomatoes, peeled, chopped
4 arms Celery with tops, chopped
3 Kahlrabi, (yellow turnip) chopped
2 Onions, chopped
1 Squash, peeled and chopped
1 cup Milk
2 Tbsp. Margarine
3 Tbsp. Rolled Oats
4 tsp. Spices 1 tsp. salt, ¹/₂ tsp. pepper,
* 1 tsp. sugar, 1 Tbsp. sorrel, ¹/₂ tsp. curry*
5 medium Potatoes, cubes 1"

6 cups Water

Place vegetables (except potatoes) and water in pot, boil and then let simmer. Cook 1 hour, puree vegetables. Add potatoes. Simmer 20 minutes. Add margarine. Add all spices and oats. Simmer 35 minutes. Add milk. Stir and serve.

"Eat, drink and be merry" Ecclesiastes 8:15

#141
• KADUREY HOUMOUS
Joindee Balls

1 lb. Lamb Shoulder, fatty pieces, ground
1 tsp. Salt
³/₄ tsp. Pepper
2 large Onions, chopped
1 bunch Parsley
2 cups Chic-peas, oven dried 300° for 15 minutes

Grind all ingredients and blend well. Form into ping pong ball's. Drop into lightly boiling soup.

#142
• JOINDEE SOUP STOCK

1 qt. Water
6 Carrots, washed, sliced thick
3 medium Tomatoes, skinned, chopped
³/₄ cup Rice raw, washed
1 Tbsp. Hot Green Peppers, minced
¹/₂ tsp. Cardamon
¹/₄ tsp. Camon (Cumin)
¹/₆ tsp. Cinnamon

Place all ingredients in deep pot. Bring to boil, reduce heat and simmer 1 1/2 hours. Drop joindee balls into boiling soup and simmer 40 minutes. Serve.

#143
• MARAK KEVES
Lamb Soup

6 Bones, cracked, with some meat on
1 qt. Water
1 cup Chick-Peas, pre-soak 8 hours
2 Onions, chopped
1 cup Zucchini, sliced
1 tsp. Salt
1/2 tsp. Pepper
1 bunch Parsley
1 tsp. Cardamon, fresh is best

Place bones in water, bring to boil, skim. Add beans and simmer 2 ½ hours. Remove bones. Add all other ingredients and simmer 45 minutes. Serve in large bowls.

#144
MARAK KELAYOT KEVES
Lamb Kidney Soup

6-8 Lamb Kidneys, trim and slice well, soak in salt
   water
3 pt. Chicken stock
1 Parsnip, cut fine
3 Cucumbers, peeled, seeds removed and chopped
6 Potatoes, peeled, diced
2 Onions, peeled, chopped
3 Tbsp. Olive Oil
2 Tbsp. Flour
1 Bu. Parsley, chopped
1 tsp. Salt
1/2 tsp. Pepper
1/2 tsp. thyme

Sauté drained, washed kidneys in oil until brown. Add onions and simmer until golden. Add flour and make a roux.

Heat stock in deep pot. To roux add 1 cup of stock. Simmer 5 minutes then pour into hot stock. Add all but parsley. Stir. Cover and simmer 3/4 hour. When potatoes are tender add parsley. Stir and serve very hot.

#145
• MARAK ARAVEE
Lamb and Pea Soup

1 lb. Breast of Lamb, cubed 1 $^1/_2$"
1 Tbsp. Margarine or Olive Oil
1 tsp. Salt
$^1/_2$ tsp. White Pepper
3 $^1/_2$ pint Water
2 Carrots, cleaned, sliced
1 Parsnip, cleaned, sliced
2 arms Celery, cleaned, chopped
1 large Onion, peeled, chopped
1 head Cauliflower, cut flowers
1 cup Fresh Peas
1 bunch Parsley, chopped

Brown lamb in margarine. Sauté 5 minutes. Add spices. Add water. Simmer 1 hour. Add vegetables except peas. Bring to boil. Simmer 30 minutes. Add peas. Simmer 10 minutes. Add parsley, stir and serve.

#146
LEEK SOUP

2 qt. Chicken stock
4 Leeks, cleaned, chopped
3 Potatoes, peeled, chopped fine
12 large Mushrooms, washed, chopped
2 Tbsp. Olive Oil
$^1/_4$ tsp. Pepper
1 Egg, beaten

Heat oil, sauté leeks and mushrooms. Add stock and boil 3 minutes. Add potatoes and simmer 35 minutes. Whisk egg into soup. Serve.

#147
MARAK LEMON
Lemon Soup

2 qt. Chicken broth
1/2 cup Rice, brown
2 cups Egg lemon-sauce

Bring broth to boil. Stir in rice. Stir until broth boils again. Simmer 12-14 minutes. Slowly stir in sauce. When soup thickens. Serve at once.

#148
• MARAK ADASHIM HUMIN
Lentil Soup, Brown

2 small Onions, minced
1/2 cup Brown Dry Lentils
8 cups Water
1 tsp. Salt
1/4 tsp. Pepper
1 cup Sorrel leaves, fresh
3 tsp. Olive Oil

Place all ingredients in pot. Bring to boil. simmer 2 hours. Squeeze through sieve or run food mill. Make puree. Reheat and serve very hot with Pita bread.

#149
• MARAK ADASHIM YEROKIM
Lentil Soup, Green

3 small Onions, minced
1/2 cup Green Dry Lentils

8 cups Water
1 ¹/₂ tsp. Cumin
¹/₄ tsp. Pepper
¹/₂ tsp. Salt
2 tsp. Olive Oil

Place all ingredients in pot. Bring to boil. Simmer 2 hours. Squeeze through sieve or run food mill. Make fine puree. Reheat and serve very hot with Pita or sesame toast.

#150
LIMA BEAN SOUP

¹/₄ cup Lima beans, pre-soaked 6 hours
1 cup Yellow peas, pre-soaked 4 hours
2 qt. Water
5 arms Celery, chopped
3 medium Onions
3 medium Carrots, cleaned, chopped
¹/₄ cup Olive Oil
1 Bay Leaf
2 tsp. Salt (retain)
¹/₄ tsp. Pepper

Simmer peas and beans for 1 hour. Add all remaining ingredients and simmer 2 hours. Replace water as required. Add salt. Simmer 10 minutes. Stir and serve.

#151
• MELOHKIA SOUP

10 cups Chicken stock
2 lbs. Melokhid leaves, fresh, chopped very fine, or use
  ¹/₄ cup dried from a Greek grocery store
  (soaked)
1 cup Chicken meat, chopped fine
4 toes Garlic, minced fine

1 tsp. Salt
1 Tbsp. Coriander
¹/₆ tsp. Cayenne
3 Tbsp. Olive Oil

Bring stock to boil, add melokhid leaves, stir. Bring to boil and simmer 30 minutes. While stock is cooking sauté garlic in olive oil and salt. Stir well and crush together. Add coriander and cayenne pepper. Sauté until mixture becomes a paste. Add paste to stock. Stir well. Cover and simmer 3 minutes. Portion meat into bowl. Add soup and serve.

#152
PITRIYOT MARAK
Mushroom Bisque

2 cups Mushrooms, sliced
2 cups Sorrel
2 Scallions, chopped
1 bunch Parsley, chopped fine
1 tsp. Salt
¹/₂ tsp. Pepper
2 Egg yolks
¹/₄ tsp. Celery seed, crushed
¹/₂ cup Dry White Wine
2 Tbsp. Margarine
1 Tbsp. Flour
1 cup Riches Coffee White (Soymilk)
1 qt. Chicken stock

Sauté mushrooms in margarine, add flour, and blend well. In a large sauce pot add chicken stock, sorrel, parsley, scallions, salt, pepper, celery seed. Bring to boil and simmer 15 minutes. Add mushrooms. Simmer 20 minutes. Add wine. Simmer 5 minutes. Whip egg and Coffee White. Whip into the hot soup mix. Serve at once.

#153
• MARAK KEVESS
Mutton Soup

1 Tbsp. Oil
1 lb. Mutton, lean, cubed 2"
2 1/2 pt. Water
1 tsp. Salt
1 Bay Leaf
6 whole White peppercorns
5 whole Allspice
1 large head White cabbage, cored, chopped
3 Carrots, cleaned, chopped
4 large Potatoes, chopped
1 bunch Parsley, chopped

Brown meat in oil. Add water and salt. Bring to boil. Simmer 20 minutes. Skim scum. Add spices and vegetables. Simmer 35 minutes. Add parsley. Simmer 10 minutes. Serve.

#154
OKRA SOUP

1 cup Rice, cooked
1 lb. Beef, cubed 1/2"
1 lb. Okra, washed, sliced
1 large Onion, chopped
1 medium Hot Red Pepper, chopped
3 Tbsp. Olive oil
2 qts. Water
1/2 tsp. Salt
1/4 tsp. Black Pepper

Sauté beef in oil. Brown well, add onion. Stir. Add red pepper. In soup pot boil water and salt with black pepper. Add okra. Boil. Add beef mixture. Simmer 2 hours. Serve over rice.

#155
OXTAIL SOUP

2 qts. Water or Vegetable Stock
2 Oxtails, cut at joints, fat removed, pre-blanched
2 medium Onions
4 Tbsp. Olive Oil
4 medium Carrots, peeled, sliced thin
2 medium Turnips, peeled, chopped
¹/₂ lb. Beef shoulder, cut in strips ¹/₄" x 2"
¹/₂ cup Vermicelli, broken
¹/₂ tsp. Cloves
1 tsp. Salt
¹/₂ tsp. Black Pepper
¹/₆ tsp. Cayenne Pepper
4 arms Celery with tips, minced
1 Tbsp. Flour

Sauté tail joints in oil until well browned. Add onions. Simmer 5 minutes. Pour into soup pot and add water, cloves, salt and pepper. Bring to boil and cover. Simmer 3 hours. Skim scum every 20 minutes. Strain and retain both broth and bones. Cool. Remove meat from bones. Discard bones. Skim fat from broth and discard fat. Add vegetables to broth and bring to boil. Add beef and bone meat. Stir. add cayenne and celery. Simmer 30 minutes. Add vermicelli and flour mixed with broth. Simmer 15 minutes. Serve.

1st Kings 18:21 "He (Elijah) slaughtered the oxen; boiled the meat, — and gave it to the people, and they ate."

#156
PEA SOUP

2 cups Dry Peas
¹/₄ cup Lentils
1 lb. Stew Beef, cubed
2 large Onions, chopped

1 tsp. Salt
$^1/_2$ tsp. Basil
$^1/_4$ tsp. Marjoram
$^1/_8$ tsp. Pepper
$^1/_8$ tsp. Cumin
1 $^1/_2$ cups Sorrel, fresh, chopped
$^3/_4$ tsp. Mint
2 cups Celery, sliced $^1/_2''$

Place all ingredients except sorrel and mint in a dutch oven. Mix well. Bring to boil. Cover and simmer 2 hours. Mash mixture. Add remaining ingredients. Simmer covered 40 minutes.

#157
• MARAK PILPEL
Pepper and Mushroom Soup

6 lbs. Bony chicken parts
1 qt. Water
1 small Green Bell Pepper, chopped
1 stalk Celery, chopped
1 lb. Mushrooms, chopped
1 bunch Parsley, chopped
2 medium Onions, chopped
2 Tbsp. Flour
$^1/_4$ tsp. Cayenne Pepper
1 Tbsp. Curry Powder
$^1/_4$ tsp. Pepper
1 tsp. Salt
$^1/_2$ cup Tahini
1 cup Rice, cooked

In a large pot, combine chicken bones, water, bell pepper, celery, mushrooms, parsley, and onions. Bring to boil and simmer 45 minutes. Remove chicken bones and pick off meat. Discard bones. Place flour and curry in fry pan and lightly brown. Add salt and mix. Add soup. Stir and simmer 20 minutes. Strain and force through sieve. Reheat. Whip in tahini. Stir well. Place minced chicken and 3 tablespoons rice in bowl, ladle soup broth over. Serve.

#158
TYCHE
• Pine Nut (Pignola) Soup

1 lb. Spinach, cut stems and heavy veins. Dip in
    boiling water
1/2 cup Pine Nuts
3 Tbsp. Almonds, minced
1 medium Onion, minced
1/4 tsp. Salt
1/6 tsp. Pepper
1/4 tsp. Nutmeg
1/2 tsp. Cinnamon
3 Tbsp. Butter
2 cups Vegetable stock
1 cup Milk

In deep skillet heat butter and sauté nuts until lightly browned. Add onion and spices. Stir well. When onions are golden add vegetable stock and simmer 3 minutes. Add spinach. Stir well and simmer 10 minutes. Test leafs, they should be al dente. Stir in milk until mixture starts to boil. Remove from fire at once so that it does not scorch. Serve at once. If you like a thicker soup stock, add 2 tablespoons flour with stock and add 2 minutes to cooking time.

#159
MARAK TAPOHEIM
Potato Chowder

4 large Potatoes, peeled, diced
2 medium Onion, sliced thin
5 arms Celery, chopped

2 cups Corn, fresh cut from cob
1 ¹/₂ cups Milk
1 tsp. Salt
¹/₈ tsp. Savory
¹/₄ tsp. Pepper
3 Tbsp. Margarine or Butter
1 quart Cold Water
1 cup Warm Water

Place cold water, vegetables and spices in pot and simmer 25 minutes. Mix milk and warm water. Pour into vegetables, add margarine. Simmer 10 minutes. Serve.

#160
• PULSE SOUP

1 ¹/₂ cups Yellow Split Pea, washed pre-soaked 2 hours
6 cups Chicken Broth
¹/₂ tsp. Pepper
¹/₄ tsp. Cloves
¹/₂ tsp. Tumeric
¹/₂ tsp. Salt
2 Tbsp. Lemon Juice

In large pot bring chicken broth to boil. Add peas and stir well. Simmer 30 minutes. Add spices. Cover and simmer 1 hour. Add lemon juice. Stir and serve in warm bowl over shredded Pita bread.

Daniel 1:12 "— I beseech thee, ten days; and let them give us pulse to eat, and water to drink."

#161
• QUAIL SOUP

3 Quail, cleaned, cut at joints
2 Tbsp. Olive Oil
3 Carrots, peeled and sliced

3 arms Celery chopped
2 medium Onions, chopped
6 Mushrooms
2 Tbsp. Flour
$^1/_2$ bunch Parsley
$^1/_4$ tsp. Salt
$^1/_8$ tsp. Pepper
6 cups Vegetable stock

In large pot. Brown quail in oil. Add vegetables and 1 cup stock. Cover and simmer until water is almost gone. Add flour and spices. Mix well. Add balance of stock. Bring to boil. Then simmer 10 minutes. Serve as main meal with bread.

#162
MARAK NAKNIK
Sausage Soup

10 links Chicken Sausage (see recipe)
4 Tomatoes, peeled, chopped
1 head Cabbage, green, chopped
7 cups Chicken Stock
1 tsp. Salt
$^1/_2$ tsp. Pepper
$^1/_4$ cup Olive Oil
1 head Spinach, cleaned, stems removed, chopped

In deep pot heat oil and sauté onions until golden. Add tomatoes and simmer 3 minutes. Add cabbage and mix well. Add stock. Bring to boil. Add all remaining ingredients. Cover and simmer 2 hours. Portion 1 sausage in each bowl. Fill with broth. Serve Pita on side.

#163
MARAK TERED ESHEL
Spinach Soup Creamed

1 medium Onion, minced

2 cups Spinach, chopped fine
1 cup Sorrel, chopped fine
2 Tbsp. Olive Oil
3 cups Yogurt
1 qt. Water
1 tsp. Salt
4 Tbsp. Flour
1 Egg Yolk
1 tsp. Lemon Juice
1 cup Milk

Place water, spinach and sorrel in pot. Simmer 7 minutes. Drain and mince. Sauté onions in oil until golden. Add flour. Sauté. Add spinach mixture. Mix well. Stir in yogurt and salt. Whip with wire wisk. Whip milk and egg together. Stir into yogurt. Add lemon juice. Simmer 2 minutes. Adjust seasoning. Serve hot.

#164
• TAHINI SOUP

1 cup Rice, pre-cooked
$^1/_2$ cup Tahini
$^1/_2$ cup Cold Water
3 Tbsp. Lemon Juice
1 tsp. Tomato Puree
$^1/_2$ tsp. Salt
$^1/_4$ tsp. Pepper
$^3/_4$ cup Warm Water

In sauce pot combine tahini and cold water. Whip together. Add lemon juice. Blend well. Place on medium fire and stir in warm water. Blend well. Add tomato puree and spices. Stir well. Remove from fire before pot boils. Serve.

#165
MARAK AVOKADO V'AGVANIYOT
Tomato and Avocado Soup

8 medium Tomatoes, peeled, minced, puree
1 cup Sour cream
$^1/_2$ cup Milk
3 Tbsp. Lemon Juice
1 Tbsp. Lime Juice
1 Tbsp. Olive Oil
1 Tbsp. Tomato Paste
1 bunch Parsley, chopped
1 Cucumber, peeled, chopped fine
2 small Avocado, ripe, peeled, pureed
$^1/_4$ tsp. Pepper
$^1/_4$ tsp. Salt
$^1/_8$ tsp. Cayenne Pepper
$^1/_4$ tsp. Dill

Mix tomato, sour cream, milk, and lemon and lime juices. Add oil and blend well. Add tomato paste and blend well. Add parsley and spices. Mix well. Refrigerate. Blend in avocado. Dish up and top with cucumber. Sprinkle dill over. Serve.

#166
MARAK AGVANIYOT V'TERASS
Tomato & Corn Soup

12 Tomatoes, peeled, chopped
2 cups Fresh corn, cut from cob
2 cups Celery, chopped
1 qt. Water
$^1/_2$ cup Pimento chopped
2 Tbsp. Butter
1 cup Milk
2 Tbsp. Flour
1 tsp. Salt

$^1/_4$ tsp. Pepper
$^1/_2$ cup Cheese, grated

In deep pot combine water, tomato, corn and celery. Bring
to boil. Simmer 20 minutes. Sauté flour and butter until lightly
brown. Stir in milk slowly until all is smooth. Pour into tomato
mixture and mix well. Add spice and pimento. Bring to soft boil.
Add cheese. Stir well. Simmer 3 minutes. Serve.

#167
MARAK AGVANIYOT PEKANTE
Tomato Curry Soup

12 medium Red Tomatoes, skinned, chopped fine
3 medium Onions, chopped fine
1 large Apple, chopped
1 Tbsp. Sugar
1 Tbsp. Curry Powder
$^1/_2$ tsp. Salt
$^1/_4$ tsp. Pepper
$^1/_8$ tsp. Cloves
6 cups Beef Stock
1 cup Water
$^1/_2$ cup Tapioca, pre-soaked in 1 cup water 30 minutes

Combine all ingredients except tapioca in sauce pot. Cover
and simmer 1 hour. Rub through sieve. Bring to boil. Add
tapioca. Simmer 15 minutes. Stir often.

#168
"MATIT SOUP"
• Tomato Garlic Soup

$^1/_2$ tsp. Cinnamon
1 tsp. Zhug
5 large Tomatoes, peeled, diced
2 toes Garlic, minced
2 Tbsp. Olive Oil

4 cups Water
2 Tbsp. Flour, soften in water
Sauté garlic and oil. Add tomatoes. Stir. Add water. Cover and simmer 30 minutes. Add flour. Simmer 15 minutes. Add zhug. Simmer 10 minutes. Add cinnamon. Stir. Serve with mint garnish

#169
MARAK YERAKOT
Vegetable Spice Soup
"Schiksuka"

1 Hot Red Pepper, sliced thin
4 Sweet Green Peppers, sliced thin
6 medium Tomatoes, peeled, chopped
1 Eggplant, peeled, sliced
3 medium Onions, peeled, sliced
2 Squash, butternut, peeled, sliced
3 Tbsp. Olive Oil
1 tsp. Salt
$1/2$ tsp. Pepper
1 tsp. Coriander, fresh is best
2 Tbsp. Water
3 Eggs
$1/8$ tsp. Cayenne
Slowly sauté vegetables in oil for 20 minutes. Add water, peppers and spice. Sauté for 12 minutes. Whip eggs, pour over mix and stir until eggs are well set. Serve with hot Pita bread.

#170
WATERCRESS SOUP

6 cups Chicken Stock
1 bunch Watercress, trim off stems, mince fine
2 medium Potatoes, peel, dice
2 cups Half and half cream warm

3/4 tsp. Salt
1/4 tsp. Pepper
1 tsp. Dill
Bring stock to boil. Add potatoes. Simmer 1 hour. Add spice and herbs. Replace water to maintain liquid. Add cress. Blend. Remove from fire. Slowly whip in cream. Serve at once.

#171
MARAK FOOL LAVEN
White Bean Soup

1 lb. White Beans, pre-soaked over night
4 Carrots, cleaned, diced
3 arms Celery, chopped
1 bunch Parsley, chopped
2 Onions, chopped fine
1 Kalrabin, cleaned, chopped
4 Tomatoes, chopped fine
1 Tbsp. Thyme
1 tsp. Salt
1/2 tsp. Pepper
1/3 cup Olive Oil
2 qt. Water
In large pot bring water to boil. Add beans. Stir. Simmer 30 minutes. Skim top. Add all remaining ingredients. Stir. Cover and simmer 2 1/2 hours. Serve.

#172
MARAK OREZ
Wildrice Soup

1/2 cup Wild Rice, cooked al dente
1/4 cup Brown Rice, cooked al dente
1 Onion, minced
8 medium Mushrooms, minced
1/2 cup Flour

4 cups Chicken Stock
$^1/_2$ tsp. Salt
1 cup Sherry Wine
1 bunch Parsley, chopped fine
2 Tbsp. Oil

Sauté onion and mushrooms in oil. add flour and cook roux until golden. Do not scorch. Add stock and cook 5 minutes. Whip all lumps out. Add all remaining ingredients. Bring to boil. Simmer 3 minutes. Serve.

#173
• MARAK TEHMANI
Yeminite Soup

1 $^1/_2$ lb. Beef Ribs
8 cups Water
1 large Onion, chopped
1 toe Garlic, minced
2 Tomatoes, chopped
$^1/_2$ tsp. Salt
$^1/_2$ tsp. Pepper
$^1/_2$ tsp. Curry Powder
$^1/_2$ tsp. Turmeric
1 Tbsp. Tomato Paste
4 Potatoes, peeled, chopped thin

Bring water to boil, add ribs. Boil 4 minutes. skim off fat. Add onions and garlic. Simmer 2 hours. Add tomatoes, salt, pepper, curry, tumeric and tomato paste. Simmer 20 minutes. Add potatoes. Simmer until potatoes are done all dente. Remove from fire and serve with a tossed salad and bread.

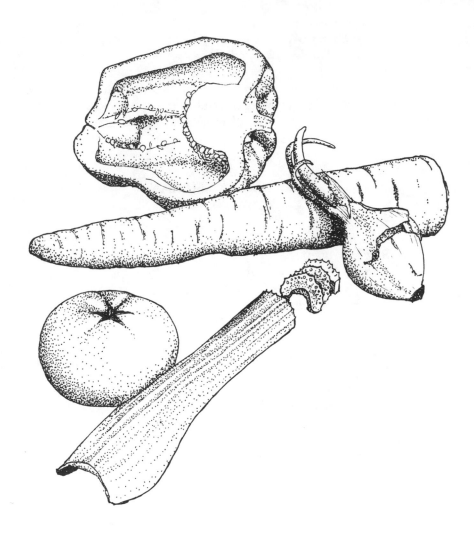

C. SALADS AND VEGETABLES

A Middle Eastern lunch or dinner is not complete unless accompanied by salad and fresh greens, pickled or preserved. A fruit course is also usually served. The fruit course can be fresh, of olives, dates, figs or raisins. In many areas the salad is the full meal and no meat course is served. It is difficult to separate the vegetable from the salad or, for that matter, how an Entree differs from a side dish as they are completely interchangeable from area to area. An example is Kugel. Some cultures eat it as a full meal entree with a small salad, and in other cultures it is a side dish with a heavy entree.

Fungi (Camheen) (Agasi Adame) are eaten in all areas of the "Fertile Crescent." They look like withered potatoes, but taste like mushrooms. This was a vegetable and garnish for the wealthy class since they were not available in large quantities. Cost precluded this item's use by the general populous. See recipe No. 243 for White Truffle.

#174
SALAT KROOV
Apple Cabbage

2 lb. Red Cabbage, sliced fine
2 small Onions, minced
10 Sour apples, peeled, dice
1 cup Chicken Broth
2 Tbsp. Olive Oil
1 Tbsp. Sugar or Honey
2 Tbsp. Flour
1 Tbsp. Lemon Juice
$^1/_6$ tsp. Pepper

Sauté onion in oil. Add sugar and stir carefully. Add cabbage. Stir well. Add 1/2 cup broth. Cover and simmer 30 minutes. add apples. Mix well. Blend flour and chicken broth until smooth. Add lemon and spice. Combine all and simmer

10 minutes. Serve.

#175
ARTISHOK
Artichoke

3 small Artichokes, washed, quartered
1 cup Sugar
1 cup White Vinegar
6 Clove, whole
$^1/_2$ tsp. Nutmeg
$^1/_4$ tsp. Salt
Simmer artichokes in lightly salted water 15 minutes.
Drain. Mix sugar, vinegar, cloves, nutmeg and salt. Pour
over artichokes. Refrigerate 8 hours. Pour off liquid and
serve.

#176
BAKED BEANS

2 lbs. Dry Pea Beans, pre-soak 8 hours
1 lb. Black Eyed Peas, pre-soak 4 hours
1 $^1/_2$ cups Brown Sugar
1 Tbsp. Coleman Dry Mustard
$^1/_2$ tsp. Salt
2 medium Onions, minced
6 qts. Water
$^1/_2$ cup Honey
Place beans and water in large pot. Simmer 1 hour. Pour
off half of water and retain. Add all remaining ingredients.
Stir well. Place in oven and bake 3 hours at 300°. Replace
liquid as required.

#177
TAPUHEY ADAMA METUKA
Baked Sweet Potatoes

6 Potatoes, peeled, washed, cut in half lengthwise
1 cup Honey
1 tsp. Cinnamon
¹/₆ tsp. Clove
3 Tbsp. Butter

Place wet potatoes cut-side up in greased dish. Pour honey over. Sprinkle spice over. Dot with butter. Bake at 325° for 1 hour. Serve.

#178
• BARLEY CASSEROLE

3 cups Chicken Stock
1 cup Barley
4 Tbsp. Olive Oil
¹/₄ cup Almonds, blanched, shredded
¹/₄ cup Pine Nuts, chopped
1 tsp. Salt
¹/₄ tsp. Pepper

Sauté barley and nuts in oil. In a greased casserole, add nut mixture then pour stock over. Cover and bake 45 minutes at 350°. Uncover and check that mixture isn't too dry. If it is, add 1/2 cup water and stir. Bake 25 minutes. Serve.

#179
BEAN STEW

2 medium Onions, sliced thin
1 cup Navy Beans
1 cup Peas
1 ¹/₂ qts. Water
³/₄ tsp. Salt

¹/₄ tsp. Pepper
2 Tbsp. Olive Oil

Place beans and water in pot. Bring to boil. Simmer 2 hours. Add olive oil and onions. Simmer 1/2 hour. Add salt and pepper. Stir well. Serve with vinegar on side.

#180
• BEANS AND BASIL

1 qt. Water
1 cup Fava Beans, shelled
1 cup White Beans, shelled
2 toes Garlic, pressed
3 Tbsp. Olive Oil
¹/₂ tsp. Black Pepper
2 tsp. Basil, chopped fresh
2 tsp. Lemon Juice

Place beans and water in pot. Boil 35 minutes. Drain. Add garlic, oil, pepper and mix well. Add lemon juice and mix well. Allow to cool. Blend in basil. Toss. Serve.

#181
BEERSHEBA SALAD

2 Green Leeks, peeled, chopped
5 large Tomatoes, peeled, chopped
2 toes Garlic, pressed
2 Cucumbers, sliced, salted, washed
1 Green Pepper, chopped
3 arms Celery and tops, chopped
1 Tbsp. Lemon Juice
¹/₂ cup Pickled Lemon, chopped (See recipe)
¹/₂ tsp. Hot Red Peppers, minced
1 Bunch Parsley, chopped
¹/₄ head Lettuce, any kind will work
3 Tbsp. Olive Oil

¹/₄ tsp. Pepper
¹/₂ tsp. Salt

Mix salt, pepper, oil, hot peppers, garlic, and lemon juice. In a separate large bowl mix all other ingredients. Pour dressing over. Toss. Serve.

#182
• BEET GREENS

1 lb. Beet tops, ribs removed, washed
1 qt. Water
¹/₄ tsp. Salt
¹/₈ tsp. Pepper
2 Tbsp. Olive Oil
2 Tbsp. Lemon Juice

Combine all ingredients except lemon juice in pot. Cover and boil 20 minutes. Drain. Sprinkle lemon juice over. Toss. Serve.

#183
•SALAT SELEK
Beet Salad

2 cups Boiled Beets, sliced
2 Tbsp. Lemon Juice
2 Tbsp. Olive Oil
¹/₂ tsp. Salt
1 cup Yogurt
1 small Onion, grated, for garnish

Toss together. Mix well. Garnish with onion. Serve.

The beet of the ancients was the white root beet, called the spinach beet, Beta Vulgaris, Tered. The leaves were the major food source. Pliney wrote that the leaf of the beet was good for the heart and a cure for the ills of the bowels. History shows that the servants of Solomon were able to grow beets in the summertime, even though they are usually not available in the hot days of summer.

#184
• BLACK EYED PEAS STEW

1 lb. Black Eyed Peas, pre-soaked overnight
3 medium Onion, chopped
2 toes Garlic, chopped
5 medium Tomatoes, peeled, chopped
1 Carrot, peeled, chopped fine
3 arms Celery, washed, chopped
1 bunch Parsley, chopped
$^1/_2$ cup Olive Oil
1 tsp. Thyme
1 Tbsp. Basil, fresh, chopped
1 tsp. Salt
$^1/_4$ tsp. Pepper
2 qts. Water

Bring salted water to a boil in dutch oven. Pour in beans. Stir. simmer 45 minutes. Sauté onions in oil until golden. Add tomatoes, carrot, garlic, celery and parsley. Stir and simmer 5 minutes. Pour into beans. Mix well, add spices and herbs. Stir. cover and bake at 300° for 2 hours. All liquid should be absorbed. Cool slightly and serve.

God admonishes man to feed his animals before himself. (Deuteronomy 11:15). How often we have forgotten to feed our pets and then sit down to eat a full meal, and get angry at the animal who begs for food!

#185
• CABBAGE AND BEANS

$^1/_2$ lb. Dried Beans, pre-soaked
1 qt. Water
1 head Cabbage, chopped fine
1 Tbsp. Flour

2 small Onions, minced
1 toe Garlic, crushed
2 Tbsp. Vinegar
2 Tbsp. Honey
1 Tbsp. Sugar
¹/₂ tsp. Salt
³/₄ cup Sour Cream or Buttermilk

Place beans and water in a pot. Bring to boil. Simmer 55 minutes. Add cabbage, onion, garlic. Stir and simmer 15 minutes. Add vinegar, honey, flour, sugar and salt. Stir. Simmer 5 minutes. Blend in sour cream. Simmer 5 minutes. Water should be mostly absorbed. Serve.

"He shall not want for food." Isaiah 51:14

#186
CARAWAY CARROTS

12 medium Carrots, cleaned, diced
2 Tbsp. butter
3 Tbsp. Flour
1 tsp. Caraway seeds
¹/₈ tsp. Pepper
¹/₂ bunch Parsley, chopped fine, retain half for garnish
3 cups Water

In deep pot combine carrots, water, and salt. Bring to boil and simmer 30 minutes. In separate pan melt butter, add flour and sauté to make a medium roux. Add caraway seeds. Blend well. combine with carrots. Stir and simmer for 10 minutes. Should be slightly thick. Dish out and add pinch of parsley. Serve.

#187
CARROT, APPLE, PRUNE PUDDING

6 large Potatoes, peeled, sliced
2 cups Carrots, sliced thin

1/2 cup Apple, peeled, sliced thin
8 Prunes, pitted
1/2 tsp. Salt
1 tsp. Paprika
1 Tbsp. Lemon Juice
1/4 cup Brown Sugar of Honey
2 cups Water
2 Tbsp. Fine Barley

Mix all together in greased casserole pan. Bake at 350° for 1 hour. A variation is to mix 2 lbs. of beef brisket (sliced 1" thick) and 1 extra cup water. Bake for 1 1/2 hours.

#188
• TZIMMES
Carrot Stew

1 large Onion, minced
6 large Carrots, sliced
8 small Potatoes, peeled, cubed 1 1/2"
4 medium Sweet Potatoes, peeled and cubed 1"
2 lbs. Short ribs
1 tsp. Salt
1/2 tsp. Pepper
1/2 tsp. Cinnamon
1/2 cup Honey
2 Tbsp. Schmaltz (chicken fat)
3 tsp. Flour
1 qt. Water

In a dutch oven, braze meat in schmaltz. Add vegetables and water. Simmer 30 minutes. Skim scum off top. Add spices and honey. Simmer slowly 3 hours. Add water if pot begins to run dry. Mix flour and water to form a very loose paste. Add pan juices and blend. Pour into dutch oven. Cover and bake at 350° for 30-35 minutes. Serve.

#189
GEZER MATOK
Carrots Glazed

8 medium Carrots, cleaned, chopped, par boiled
   10 minutes
$^2/_3$ cup Brown Sugar
$^1/_2$ cup Water
2 Tbsp. Margarine
1 tsp. Lemon Juice
In sauté pan combine all ingredients and simmer 20 minutes. Baste often.

#190
• CELERY MARINADE

1 head Pascal Celery, sliced Jullian
$^1/_2$ cup Olive Oil
2 Tbsp. Fennel, chopped
$^1/_2$ bunch Parsley, chopped
2 sprigs Thyme, fresh, chopped
3 Tbsp. Lemon Juice
$^1/_2$ tsp. Salt
$^1/_4$ tsp. Pepper
1 cup Water
In large pot combine oil and all spices and herbs. Add water and lemon juice. Bring to boil. Add celery. Cover and simmer for 15 minutes. Remove from heat and let cool. Serve cold.

#191
CORN PUDDING

5 ears Corn, cut from cob
2 Tbsp. Margarine, melted
3 Eggs, separated, whip each

2 Tbsp. Sugar
$^1/_2$ tsp. Salt
$^1/_2$ tsp. Nutmeg
2 cups Leben

Beat yolks and fold in corn, add margarine, sugar and salt. Stir well. Add nutmeg. Beat in leben, and add egg white. Pour into greased 8 x 8 glass baking dish. Bake at 350° for 50 minutes.

#192
CORN STEW

1 cup Corn, cut fresh from 3 ears
1 medium Onion, minced
1 toe Garlic, minced
1 Tbsp. Olive Oil
1 lb. Zucchini, sliced
4 medium Tomatoes, skinned, chopped
1 tsp. Salt
1 tsp. Oregano
$^1/_8$ tsp. Pepper
$^1/_8$ tsp. Rosemary

Sauté onions in olive oil until golden. Add garlic. Stir. Add all other ingredients. Cover. Simmer 20 minutes. Serve.

#193
• CUCUMBER & GARLIC SALAD

3 medium Cucumbers, sliced thin
4 toes Garlic, peel, slice very thin
2 Scallions, slice white, very thin
$^1/_4$ cup Vinegar
$^1/_2$ cup Olive Oil
$^1/_2$ tsp. Salt
$^1/_4$ tsp. Pepper
$^1/_2$ tsp. Thyme

Toss all together. Refrigerate 2 hours. Toss. Serve.

#194
MELAFEFON TEHMANI
Cucumbers Yemen

2 large Cucumbers, peeled, sliced
1 tsp. Salt
1 Tbsp. Olive Oil
1 bunch Scallions, peeled, chopped
$^1/_4$ tsp. Pepper
1 Tbsp. Fennel
5 Tbsp. Yogurt
$^1/_6$ tsp. Cayenne Pepper

Place cucumbers in colander. Sprinkle salt over. Let sit 30 minutes. Shake dry. Place in greased casserole dish. Add scallions, pepper, fennel, and oil. Cover and bake at 350° for 40 minutes. Pour yogurt over. Sprinkle cayenne over. Cover and bake 10 minutes. Serve.

"He (the Lord) set him atop the highlands, to feast on the yield of the earth;" Deuteronomy 32:13.

#195
• GVENAT SHAMIR
Dill Cheese

1 cup Labni
$^1/_2$ tsp. Salt
$^1/_4$ tsp. Pepper
1 Tbsp. Dill
1 Pimento roasted, chopped fine
$^1/_6$ tsp. Paprika

Mix all ingredients. Spread on Pita. Cut Pita into bite size slices as hors d'oeuvres or side dish. Tap paprika lightly over top.

#196
DILLED BEANS

2 lb. String Beans, ends off, string pulled
$^1/_2$ tsp. Mustard Seed
1 tsp. Celery Seed
3 toes Garlic, chopped
$^1/_8$ tsp. Cayenne Pepper
$^1/_4$ cup Course Salt
2 $^1/_2$ cups White Vinegar
1 $^1/_2$ cups Water
10 heads Dill (or 4 Tbsp. dried)

Place beans in large crock. Pack in standing on ends. Place seeds and garlic in crock. In a separate pot boil: cayenne, vinegar, water, and salt. Place dill in crock. Pour in vinegar, water, salt. Place wood plug on top with clean rock on top. Let sit 5 days. Serve. Can be bottled in 4 pint jars using boiling water bath for 10 minutes with jar sealed.

#197
EGGPLANT AND NOODLES

2 lbs. Eggplant, sliced
2 lbs. Broad Egg Noodles
2 large Onions, chopped fine
2 toes Garlic, pressed
4 Tbsp. Olive Oil
4 medium Tomatoes, skinned, chopped
2 Tbsp. Tomato Paste
$^1/_2$ tsp. Cinnamon
$^1/_4$ tsp. Nutmeg
$^1/_4$ tsp. Paprika
$^1/_6$ tsp. Pepper
$^1/_4$ cup Parmesan Cheese, grated
$^1/_4$ cup Gruyere cheese grated
$^1/_4$ cup Milk

¹/₂ cup Water

Salt eggplant and let sit 20 minutes. Rinse and dry. Sauté onions in olive oil until golden. Add eggplant and sauté until nicely colored. Add tomatoes, tomato paste, and all spices. Stir gently. Add water and simmer 20 minutes. Add more water if required. Boil noodles in salted water until al dente. In a large well-greased baking dish alternate eggplant, noodles, eggplant, noodles. Add cheeses to top. Pour pan juice over top and add milk. Bake at 375° for 30 minutes.

#198
• HATZILIM V'PETROZILIA
Eggplant and Parsley

3 large Eggplants, cut in half
3 large Onions, chopped fine
2 toes Garlic, minced
3 large Tomatoes, skinned, chopped fine
1 bunch Parsley, chopped
1 tsp. Salt
¹/₂ tsp. Pepper
2 ¹/₂ cups Water
3 Tbsp. Olive Oil

Mix parsley, tomatoes, garlic, onions and oil together. Score flesh of eggplant, stuff center of eggplant with mixture. Sprinkle seasoning over. Place eggplants in large baking dish. Add water to dish. Bake at 375° for 1 1/2 hours. Serve.

#199
SALAT HATZILIM
Eggplant Salad

2 large Eggplants, cut and peeled, seeds removed, baked
*   45 minutes at 375°*
3 toes Garlic, pressed
3 Tomatoes, peeled, chopped fine

¹/₂ bunch Parsley, chopped
¹/₄ tsp. Basil
¹/₂ tsp. Salt
¹/₄ tsp. Pepper
³/₄ tsp. Oregano, crushed
¹/₂ cup Olive Oil
¹/₄ cup Dry Red Wine

Chop eggplant and beat in garlic. Beat well as you add tomatoes. Beat and add parsley and basil. Add salt and oregano. Beat in olive oil. Slowly beat in red wine. Check flavor. Serve.

#200
• ETHIOPIAN BEANS

1 ¹/₃ cups White Beans, pre-soak in water 12 hours
³/₄ cup Olive Oil
1 medium Onion, minced
1 tsp. Thyme
3 toes Garlic, pressed
2 Tbsp. Tomato Paste
1 Lemon, juiced
1 bunch Parsley, minced
¹/₆ tsp. Cayenne
¹/₂ tsp. Salt
¹/₄ tsp. Pepper
3 cups Water

Sauté onion in oil until golden. Add garlic and stir. Add beans and stir well. Add spices and tomato. Sauté 2 minutes. Add water. Simmer 2 hours. Add lemon. Beans should be fairly dry. Pour into bowl, sprinkle parsley over. Serve.

#201
• SALAT FOOL
Fava Bean Salad

BEANS
1 cup Fava Beans, pre-soaked 12 hours, drained
2 large Onions, chopped
$^1/_2$ cup Olive Oil
1 Tbsp. Lemon Juice
1 tsp. Salt
$^1/_2$ tsp. Pepper
3 cups Water
Sauté onions in oil until golden. Add water. Boil. Add beans. Simmer 1 ½ hours. Mash. Add all remaining ingredients. Blend well. Refrigerate 2 hours.

SAUCE
2 Tbsp. Olive Oil
1 Tbsp. Lemon Juice
1 bunch Parsley, chopped fine
1 tsp. Paprika
$^1/_8$ tsp. Cayenne
Mix all together. Blend well. Turn chilled beans out on lettuce bed on serving plate. Pour sauce over. Serve.

#202
• "PALUDEH"
Fruit Salad

1 medium Melon, cut into melon balls
3 ripe Peaches, sliced thin, peeled
6 ripe Apricots, peeled, sliced thin
$^1/_3$ cup Sugar
2 Tbsp. Lemon Juice
$^1/_4$ tsp. Salt
1 Tbsp. Pomegranate Juice

2 Tbsp. Rose Water
1 cup Crushed Ice

Combine fruit and mix well. Sprinkle sugar, lemon juice, salt, and pomegranate juice over. Tumble and mix well. Refrigerate 1 hour. Sprinkle rose water over. Refrigerate 30 minutes. Dish up. Sprinkle 2 tablespoons ice over each serving. Serve at once.

Isaiah 61:9 "Those that harvest it shall eat it —"

#203
• FAVA YOGURT

1 qt. Water
4 cups Fava Bean, soak 12 hours
1 tsp. Salt
³/₄ cup Yogurt
1 Tbsp. Savory, chopped
¹/₄ tsp. Thyme
¹/₄ tsp. Pepper
¹/₂ cup Water

Place beans, salt, and water in pot, and boil 20 minutes. Drain beans. Add yogurt, herbs, pepper and 1/2 cup water. Lightly simmer 10 minutes. Caution, do not allow to scorch. Add water. Check seasoning. Serving.

#204
• GREEN BEANS, SPICED

1 lb. Green Beans, trimmed
4 Tbsp. Margarine or Olive Oil
2 tsp. Thyme, fresh is best, chopped
¹/₂ tsp. Basil
1 toe Garlic, pressed
¹/₆ tsp. Pepper
¹/₂ tsp. Salt

1 qt. Water

Place beans in boiling salt water. Cook 4 minutes. Place all other ingredients in second pan, heat and stir. Drain beans, retain water, and add to oil, tumble and fully coat beans. Add 3/4 cup retained water. Cover pan and simmer 5 minutes. Serve.

#205
JAFFA ORANGE SALAD

3 large Oranges (sour Jaffa), peeled, sliced
2 small Avocados, peeled sliced
1 Tbsp. Lemon Juice
2 Tbsp. Olive Oil
³/₄ tsp. Salt
¹/₂ tsp. Sugar
¹/₂ tsp. Dill

Combine all ingredients. Toss and blend well. Serve with pita pocket bread. This is a hot weather lunch.

#206
KIDNEY BEAN SALAD

¹/₂ lb. Kidney Beans, pre-soaked 12 hours
1 qt. Water
2 Onions, chopped fine
1 cup Olive Oil
2 Tbsp. Lemon Juice
¹/₂ tsp. Salt
¹/₄ tsp. Pepper
1 tsp. Basil
3 arms Celery, diced
1 bunch Parsley, chopped

Bring water to boil, add salt and beans. Simmer 35 minutes. Drain and add all remaining ingredients. Mix well. Let sit 4 hours. Toss. Serve.

#207
KUGEL
(Chininun)

1 lb. Egg Noodles, pre-boiled, drained
8 Eggs, beaten
$^1/_4$ cup Brown Sugar
1 cup Cottage Cheese
$^1/_4$ cup Oil
$^1/_2$ cup Raisins, pre-soaked
3 Sour apples, chopped
$^1/_2$ cup Walnuts, chopped
1 Tbsp. Lemon Juice
1 tsp. Cinnamon

In large S.S. bowl mix noodles, cottage cheese and eggs. Blend in raisins, pour into well-greased casserole dish. Sprinkle nuts evenly over noodles. Add apples. Sprinkle lemon juice over. Sprinkle oil over. Sugar and cinnamon top the layers. Bake at 350° for 1 hour. Remove from oven, let cool slightly. Serve.

#208
• "LABNI"
Fresh Cheese

4 cups Yogurt
1 tsp. Salt
Lightly whip mixture. Let sit 10 minutes.

Make bag of 3 layers of cheese cloth. Pour mixture into bag. Hang over catch bowl. Let drip 24 hours in cool room. Discard drip water. Cheese is ready to eat as spread on bread. Serve with "Greek" olives.

#209
LEMON SPROUTS

4 cups Brussel Sprouts, fresh, soaked 10 minutes
3 cups Chicken Bouillon
¹/₄ tsp. Salt
¹/₈ tsp. Pepper
¹/₈ tsp. Dill
¹/₄ cup Margarine
1 Tbsp. Lemon Juice, fresh
1 wedge Lemon, retain

Drain sprouts and place them in a sauce pan with bouillon and simmer 10 minutes. Add all remaining ingredients. Cover pan and simmer 15 minutes. Shake pan occasionally to keep sprouts from scorching. Portion out and serve. Squeeze lemon wedge over.

#210
• SALAT ADASHIM
Lentil Salad

¹/₄ tsp. Black Pepper
¹/₂ cup Brown Lentils, soaked 12 hours
1 qt. Water
2 Tbsp. Parsley, chopped
3 tsp. Lemon Juice
4 Tbsp. Olive Oil
Pinch Cumen

Drain Lentils. Combine all ingredients. Mix well. Refrigerate 2 hours. Serve.

#211
LENTILS & NOODLES

1 ¹/₂ cup Brown Lentils, pre-soaked 6 hours
3 large Onions, peeled, chopped fine

3 toes Garlic, minced
1 tsp. Salt
¹/₄ tsp. Pepper
3 Tbsp. Olive Oil
1 qt. Water
1 tsp. Coriander
¹/₂ lb. Broad Egg Noodles
4 Tbsp. Butter

Boil lentils in salted water 1 hour, drain. Fry onions and garlic in olive oil until golden. Add coriander. Stir well. Pour into lentils and stir. Boil noodles 7-10 minutes, drain. Add butter and coat noodles. Pour lentils into noodles. Mix well on medium heat and serve hot.

#212
MAMALIGA
Corn Mush

1 cup Corn meal
1 tsp. Salt
¹/₄ tsp. Pepper
1 Tbsp. Sugar
2 Tbsp. Margarine or Olive Oil
4 cups Water

Boil water and add spices. Pour in corn meal and margarine. Stir until thick. Serve in bowl with milk and honey on side. Some people add 1 tsp. cinnamon with the spices.

#213
MESHWIYA
Israeli Salad

3 Tomatoes
2 Sweet Red Peppers
2 medium Onions
1 tsp. Hot Chili Peppers

1 small can Tuna, water packed, drained
3 Tbsp. Parsley, chopped
2 Eggs, hard cooked, sliced
1 Tbsp. Lemon Juice
3 Tbsp. Olive Oil
$^3/_4$ tsp. Salt
$^1/_2$ tsp. Pepper
1 toe Garlic, pressed

Mix lemon juice. Oil, salt, pepper, and garlic. In large bowl mix other ingredients, pour oil mixture over. Toss. Serve.

#214
MICHOTETA
Cheese Salad

$^1/_4$ lb. Semi dry cottage cheese
$^1/_2$ lb. Feta cheese, flaked
1 $^1/_2$ Lemon, freshly juiced
1 large Onion, sliced thin, thin
2 $^1/_2$ Tbsp. Olive Oil
1 Cucumber, peeled, diced
1 tsp. Salt
$^1/_4$ tsp. Pepper

Toss all together. Refrigerate 1 hour. Toss and serve

#215
MIXED VEGETABLES

3 cups Water
$^1/_2$ lb. White Beans, pre-soaked overnight
1 large Onion, peeled, sliced
3 medium Potatoes, peeled, sliced
1 head Celery, sliced
2 medium Carrots, peeled, sliced
6 Green onions, chopped

3 toes Garlic, minced
1 Turnip, peeled, sliced
1 tsp. Salt
$^1/_2$ tsp. Pepper
1 Bunch Parsley, chopped
2 Tbsp. Honey
$^3/_4$ cup Olive Oil

In large pot sauté onions in olive oil. Add beans and water. Simmer 2 hours. Add vegetables. Simmer 1 hour. Add all remaining ingredients and stir well. Simmer 30 minutes. Serve.

#216
• MOROCCO CARROTS

$^1/_4$ cup Water
2 $^1/_2$ lbs. Carrots, washed, peeled, sliced $^1/_4$" thick
$^1/_2$ cup Butter
1 small Onion, sliced thin, separated
$^1/_2$ tsp. Nutmeg
$^1/_4$ cup White Wine
$^1/_4$ cup White Raisins, pre-soaked
3 Tbsp. Brown Sugar

Combine butter, carrots, onion, and water in covered sauce pan. Simmer 20 minutes. Add spice, wine and sugar. Cover. simmer 10 minutes. Add raisins. Stir. Simmer 3 minutes. Serve.

#217
MOUNTAIN SALAD

$^1/_2$ tsp. Salt
$^1/_4$ tsp. Pepper
$^1/_2$ lb. Peas, shelled
$^1/_2$ lb. Green Snap Beans, cut
1 Turnip, thinly sliced

2 Potatoes, sliced
2 Carrots, shaved
2 Cucumbers, chopped
1 Celery root, sliced thin
$^1/_2$ lb. Mushrooms, cut $^1/_4$"
1 Truffle, minced
1 Tbsp. Capers
1 Dill pickle, minced
2 cups Mayonnaise (or 1 cup olive oil)
$^1/_2$ cup Cooked Tongue, diced

Par boil each vegetable to be sure it is al-dente (just under done). Rinse each in cold water. Mix all together. Chill. Serve with bread.

#218
MUSHROOM SAUTE

1 pint Large Mushrooms, washed, cut in half
2 Eggs, beaten
$^1/_4$ cup Cream
1 cup Fine Cracker Crumbs
$^1/_2$ tsp. Pepper
$^1/_2$ tsp. Salt
$^1/_4$ tsp. Paprika
3 Tbsp. Butter

Mix crumbs and spice. Blend well. Lay out on flat surface. Dip mushrooms in cream, press into crumbs. Saute in butter until golden brown.

#219
NOODLE PUDDING

8 oz. pkg. Medium noodles, pre-blanch 4 minutes cool
$^1/_4$ lb. Butter, melted
1 cup Sugar
2 Tbsp. Water

1 cup Sour Cream
6 oz. Cream Cheese
$^1/_2$ cup Raisins, pre-soaked
1 Tbsp. Vanilla
5 Eggs, beaten
1 cup Pineapple crushed, drained
1 Apple, grated course
8 oz pk Cottage Cheese
$^1/_2$ tsp. Cinnamon
$^1/_8$ tsp. Nutmeg
$^1/_8$ tsp. Ginger
8 Dried Apricots
$^1/_2$ cup Special K or corn flakes
3 Tbsp. Butter
3 Tbsp. Brown Sugar

Cream sour cream, cream cheese and water. Mix everything except last 4 ingredients, and pour into greased dish. Top with Special K. Sprinkle butter and brown sugar over. Lay apricots over. Bake at 350° for 45 minutes.

#220
OILED BEANS

4 Mushrooms, sliced
1 cup Wax Beans, drained
1 cup Green Beans, drained
1 cup Green Beans, drained
1 cup Kidney Beans, drained
1 medium Bermuda Red Onion, chopped
$^3/_4$ cup Oil
$^1/_2$ cup Vinegar
$^3/_4$ cup Brown Sugar
1 tsp. Salt
$^1/_4$ tsp. Pepper
$^1/_4$ tsp. Thyme

Mix sugar and vinegar. Stir until dissolved. Add herbs

and spices. Mix. Add oil and mix. Add beans. Mix. Chill 2 hours. Toss well. Cover and refrigerate overnight. Toss. Serve.

#221
BAMIA
Okra and Beans

1 lb. Okra, sliced
1 tsp. Tumeric
1 cup Tomato Puree
1 cup Green Beans (Lubia) chopped
3 cups Water
Combine all ingredients.   Simmer 20 minutes.

#222
OKRA AND TOMATOES CURRY

1 lb. Okra, washed, sliced thin
8 medium Tomatoes, peeled, sliced.
$^1/_2$ cup Bread Crumbs
$^1/_2$ tsp. Salt
$^1/_4$ tsp. Pepper
1 tsp. Curry Powder
3 Tbsp. Olive Oil
Sauté tomatoes and onion in oil. In greased casserole dish layer okra and bread crumbs and pour tomatoes over crumbs. Bake covered at 375° for 30 minutes.   Uncover and bake 5 minutes to brown.

#223
• ONION CASSEROLE

8 large Onions, peeled, sliced thin
1 pt. Buttermilk or leben
$^1/_2$ tsp. Salt
$^1/_2$ tsp. White Pepper

241

¹/₄ tsp. Paprika
2 cups Flour
1 Egg, beaten
Beat together flour and milk. Add spices. Blend in egg. Add onion. Mix well. Pour into greased casserole dish. Bake at 350° for 45 minutes.

#224
• ONIONS, BAKED

12 small Onions, peeled
2 Tbsp. Margarine
3 Tbsp. Flour
³/₄ cup Cream
¹/₂ cup Bread Crumbs
¹/₄ cup Cheese, grated course
¹/₂ tsp. Salt
¹/₂ tsp. Pepper
¹/₂ tsp. Paprika
²/₃ cup Water
Par boil onions in water and 1/2 tsp. salt. remove onions to greased casserole dish. Retain broth. Mix flour and 1 tablespoon of broth. Blend well. Add flour to broth and blend. Add spices. Remove from fire and blend in cream. Sprinkle bread crumbs over onions. Pour cream mixture over. Sprinkle cheese over. Dot top with margarine. Bake at 350° for 30 minutes.

#225
ORANGE SALAD

4 large Oranges, sectioned
4 large Carrots, grated
¹/₂ cup Coconut Meat, flaked
¹/₂ cup Orange Juice
1 Tbsp. Lemon Juice

1 Tbsp. Sugar
3 Tbsp. Raisins, pre-soaked in orange juice.
Mix all together. Refrigerate. Serve.

#226
PAN POTATOES

3 large Potatoes, boiled, peeled
1 large Onion, minced
2 Eggs
$^1/_2$ tsp. Salt
$^1/_6$ tsp. Pepper
1 Tbsp. Olive Oil

Mix all together and puree. Warm oil in sauté pan. Pour mixture into pan and slowly brown on each side. Cooking time 15 minutes. Serve steaming hot.

#227
PARSNIPS WITH MUSTARD

10 Parsnip, peeled, cut $^1/_4$"
3 Tbsp. Margarine
3 Tbsp. Brown Sugar
$^1/_2$ tsp. Coleman Dry Mustard
1 Tbsp. Water

Place parsnips in well-greased casserole. Sprinkle with sugar, water over top. Sprinkle mustard over. Dot with margarine. Bake at 400° for 25 minutes. Remove from oven when nicely browned.

#228
• PISTACHIO PILAF

$^1/_4$ cup Pistachio Nuts, chopped
$^1/_2$ cup Pine Nuts
1 cup Rice

2 cups Warm water
$^1/_6$ cup Olive Oil
1 tsp. Mace
1 tsp. Salt
$^1/_4$ tsp. cinnamon

In covered sauce pot mix rice, water and salt. Bring to boil. Reduce heat and simmer 15 minutes. remove from heat and let sit 7-10 minutes. Remove cover and add all remaining ingredients, fluff and stir. Serve.

#229
TAPUHEY ADAMA MELAFEFON
Potato and Cauliflower Casserole

1 head Cauliflower, cut into flowers
2 Eggs, beaten
$^1/_4$ cup Sour Cream
$^1/_4$ cup Cream
1 Tbsp. Lemon
$^2/_3$ cup Bread Crumbs
1 lb. Potatoes, par boiled 3 minutes sliced
$^1/_4$ tsp. Sugar
$^1/_6$ tsp. White Pepper
$^1/_4$ tsp. Salt
$^1/_4$ cup Milk
1 Tbsp. Flour

Mix eggs and cauliflower. Mix milk, salt, flour, pepper, cream, lemon, and sour cream. Layer potato and cauliflower. Pour any egg mix left over for last layer. Pour milk over. Cover. Bake at 350° for 45 minutes.

#230
PRUNES, BAKED

24 Prunes, pitted, pre-soaked
1 Tbsp. Lemon Juice

¹/₄ cup Bread Crumbs
1 tsp. flour
¹/₂ cup Sour Cream
¹/₂ tsp. Cinnamon
1 tsp. Powder Sugar

Combine flour, sour cream, lemon juice and cinnamon. Place prunes in greased baking dish. Pour liquid over. Sprinkle bread crumbs over. Bake at 325° for 30 minutes. Dust top with powder sugar. Serve with fish dish.

#231
• PULSE AND SPINACH

1 lb. Chic-peas (Garbanzos) pre-soaked overnight
2 qt. Water
2 tsp. Salt
2 Tbsp. Olive Oil
2 toes Garlic, minced
1 bunch Parsley, chopped
5 small Tomatoes, peeled, chopped
¹/₄ cup Almonds
¹/₄ cup Hazelnuts
¹/₈ tsp. Saffron
¹/₈ tsp. Cinnamon
2 Eggs, hard cooked, chopped fine
1 lb. Spinach, par boiled

Boil peas in water and salt for 2 hours. Drain and retain liquid. Sauté garlic in olive oil. Add parsley and tomatoes. Simmer 5 minutes. Add nuts and spice. Stir. Add egg. Stir. Add chic-peas. Stir well. Add water the peas were cooked in. Bring to boil. Add spinach. Simmer 10 minutes. When liquid becomes "creamy," serve.

Song of Songs 2:4 "He hath brought me to the banqueting house,—"

#232
RED BEANS AND BUTTER

1 lb. Red Beans, pre-soaked 24 hours
2 Onions, chopped
2 toes Garlic, minced
$^1/_2$ cup Butter
$^1/_2$ tsp. Salt
$^1/_4$ tsp. Pepper
$^1/_4$ tsp. Paprika
$^1/_8$ tsp. Cayenne
2 qt. Water
$^1/_2$ bunch Parsley, chopped

Bring water to boil. Add beans. Simmer 1 hour. Pour off 1/2 of the water. In sauté pan heat 1/2 butter and sauté onions 2 minutes. Add garlic. Sauté 2 minutes. Add sauté to beans. Bring to boil. Add spices. Stir. Simmer 10 minutes. Most of water should be absorbed. Stir in parsley. Serve warm with yogurt on side.

#233
• RED LENTILS POTTAGE

1 Qt. Water
2 cups Lentils
1 $^1/_2$ Tbsp. Semneh
1 Tbsp. Cumin
1 toe Garlic, crushed
$^1/_4$ tsp. Salt
$^1/_6$ tsp. Pepper

Put lentils, semneh, cumin and water into pot. Simmer 1 hour. Add garlic and salt and pepper. Stir well. Simmer till thick. Serve with leben on side. This is the famous dish of the Bible. Esau sold his birthright for a bowl of this pottage.

#234
• RICE AND NUTS

1 qt. Water
2 cups Rice
$^1/_3$ cup Pine Nuts, chopped
$^1/_3$ cup Almonds, peeled, chopped fine
$^1/_2$ cup Raisins, pre-soaked
3 Tbsp. Oil
$^1/_2$ Tbsp. Salt
$^1/_4$ tsp. Pepper
$^1/_2$ tsp. Cinnamon
$^1/_6$ tsp. Allspice

Boil rice al dente. Sauté nuts in oil 2 minutes. Add raisins and stir well. Add spices. Blend well. Mix with cooked rice. Place in lightly greased dish and place in 325° oven for 10 minutes. Serve with meat dish.

"Suddenly an angel touched him and said to him, 'arise and eat'" 1st Kings 18:5.

#235
• RICE, FRIED/BAKED

1 $^1/_2$ cups Rice, precooked
5 Tbsp. Olive Oil
1 tsp. Salt
$^1/_4$ tsp. Pepper
3 $^1/_2$ cups Chicken Stock, hot

In skillet fry rice in oil on medium heat. Do not brown. Stir and simmer 10 minutes. Pour into well greased covered casserole. Sprinkle salt and pepper over. Add stock. Bake at 350° for 45 minutes. Serve.

#236
• RICE STEW

6 cups Milk
1 cup Rice
$^1/_3$ cup Raisins
6 Date, sliced
$^1/_4$ tsp. Salt
$^1/_2$ cup Sugar
$^1/_4$ tsp. Cinnamon
$^1/_8$ tsp. Nutmeg

In heavy pot bring milk to soft boil. Add rice and stir well. Add raisins, stir. Cover and cook 20 minutes. Add all other ingredients, stir well. cover and cook 10 minutes. Stir. Serve with side of yogurt.

#237
BORANI
Rice with Tomatoes

1 $^1/_2$ cups Rice
1 bunch Parsley, chopped
10 Tomatoes, chopped
1 cup Tomato Juice or V8
1 tsp. Salt
$^1/_2$ tsp. Pepper
2 toes Garlic, pressed
3 sprigs (tsp.) Mint, chopped
$^1/_4$ tsp. Cinnamon
2 $^1/_2$ cups Water or Chicken Stock
$^1/_4$ cup Olive Oil

In a dutch oven combine tomatoes, parsley, tomato juice, salt, pepper and garlic. Pour 1/2 of olive oil over. Sauté 5 minutes. Stir well. Add mint and cinnamon. Stir. Pour rice over. Add stock. Cover and bake at 350° for 40-45 minutes. Remove lid, check for moisture. If too dry add 1/4 cup water.

Stir and let sit in oven for 10 minutes. Serve.

#238
RUTABAGA CASSEROLE

1 qt. Water
2 lbs. Rutabaga, peeled, sliced thin
3 Tbsp. Flour
3 cups Beef Stock
1/2 tsp. Sage
1/8 tsp. Pepper
3 Tbsp. Margarine, soften
1 cup Soft Bread Crumbs
1/2 tsp. sugar
1 tsp. Salt

Combine salt, water and rutabaga. Bring to boil, simmer 25 minutes. Drain. Pour into well-greased casserole. Soften flour in 3 tablespoons beef stock.   Mix beef stock, flour mixture, sage, pepper and simmer 5 minutes. Pour over rutabaga. Add bread crumbs mixed with margarine. Bake at 350° for 30 minutes. Serve.

#239
SQUASH, FRIED

3 - 3 1/2 lbs. Summer Squash or Yellow Squash
4 medium Onions
1 bunch Parsley, chopped
3 Tomatoes, peeled, sliced
1/2 cup Olive Oil
1/2 tsp. Salt
1/4 tsp. Pepper
1 cup Water

Sauté onions in oil until golden. Add parsley, tomato, salt and pepper. Stir. Sauté 3 minutes. Add water. Lay squash in pan. Turn heat up and simmer 10 minutes. With spatula

turn over squash. Simmer 10 minutes. Check for tenderness.
Serve.

#240
STRING BEAN SALAD

1 lb. French Beans
1 Tbsp. Lemon Juice
1 large Onion, peeled, sliced thin
1/4 cup Olive Oil
1/2 tsp. Salt
1/4 tsp. Pepper
1 tsp. Dill
1 qt. Water

Combine bean, water, and salt. Simmer 20 minutes, then
drain. Add all remaining ingredients. Toss. Cool. Serve.

#241
SUCCOTASH

2 Cups Lima Beans, pre-soaked 8 hours
2 Cups Corn
1/3 cup Milk
1/8 tsp. Cayenne
1/4 tsp. Salt
1/2 tsp. Sugar
1/2 tsp. Cinnamon
1/2 cup Water
2 Tbsp. Olive Oil
1 Tbsp. Flour

Drain beans, wash, place in pot with water, olive oil, and
spices. Simmer 45 minutes. Add corn. Simmer 20 minutes.
Blend flour and milk. Mix into beans. Simmer 20 minutes.

#242
• TCHEKCHOVKA
Zucchini and Peppers

3 medium Onions, sliced
2 small Capsicum
4 Tbsp. Olive Oil
6 medium Tomatoes
6 medium Courgettes (Zucchini)
1 medium Aubergines (Eggplant), sliced
1 medium Red Pepper
2 toes Garlic, chopped
3 Eggs, beaten

Sauté all vegetables in oil, add spices and herbs, stew all together. Pour in beaten eggs and scramble all together. When eggs are well set serve.

#243
TERFEZIA
White Truffle

1 lb. Truffles, washed, sliced
¹/₄ lb. Butter

Sauté truffles in butter. Do not let butter scorch. Serve as a potato.

#244
TOMATO CURRY

8 large Tomatoes, peeled, sliced
2 Tbsp. Marjoram or Olive Oil
1 large Onion, chopped fine
1 ¹/₂ tsp. Curry powder
1 tsp. Flour
¹/₂ tsp. Pepper
¹/₄ tsp. Salt

Sauté onion in margarine until golden. Add curry. Blend flour, add marjoram, tomatoes and fry in pan with onion, salt and pepper. Mix well. Place tomatoes in serving dish. Pour oil mixture over.

#245
TOMATOES AND PEAS

4 large Onions, chopped fine
2 lb. Chic-peas, pre-soak overnight, drain
5 medium Tomatoes, peeled, chopped
3 qts. Water
2 toes Garlic, pressed
1/2 bunch Parsley, chopped
4 sprig Fresh Mint
1 tsp. Salt
1/2 tsp. Pepper
3 Tbsp. Butter

In dutch oven add water and chic-peas. Bring to boil. Cover. Simmer 3 hours. Add all ingredients. Simmer 1 hour. Uncover and simmer 15-20 minutes. Mixture should be almost dry. Add butter. Stir. Serve.

#246
TOMATO SALAD

8 large Tomatoes skinned, sliced
2 large Bermuda onion, diced
1/2 bunch Parsley
1/2 tsp. Cumin
1/2 cup Olive Oil
1/4 cup Lemon Juice
1 toe Garlic, crushed
1/6 tsp. Pepper

Toss all together. Serve.

#247
TUNA PUREE

2 *Ripe Avocados, peeled, mashed fine*
2 *small cans Water Pack Tuna, drained*
6 *Tbsp. Mayonnaise*
1 *tsp. Dill*
$^1/_6$ *tsp. Thyme*
$^1/_4$ *tsp. Salt*
Mix all together. Spread on small Pita, cut in quarters.

#248
TURKISH MUSHROOMS

2 *cups Mushrooms, cut* $^1/_4$ *long*
$^1/_2$ *cup Olive Oil*
1 *toe Garlic, pressed*
1 *tsp. Hyssop*
$^1/_2$ *tsp. Salt*
$^1/_4$ *tsp. Pepper*
2 *tsp. Lemon Juice*
Mix oil, garlic, hyssop, salt and pepper. Blend well. Add mushrooms, mix well. Allow to set two hours. Pour into fry pan and sauté on medium high. Heat one minutes. Add lemon juice and stir. Pour off oil. Serve.

#249
TURNIP AND CARROT PUREE

5 *medium Turnips, pared, diced*
5 *medium Carrots, peel and slice* $^1/_4''$
$^1/_2$ *cup Warm Milk*
1 *Tbsp. Butter*
$^1/_2$ *tsp. Salt*
$^1/_4$ *tsp. Nutmeg*
$^1/_4$ *tsp. Cinnamon*

1 qt. Water

Combine water and vegetables in pot. Boil. Reduce heat and simmer 13 minutes. With ricer or electrical mixer, reduce to puree. Add butter and spices. Whip 2 minutes. Add milk, and whip 1 minute. Reheat and stir. Serve.

#250
• VEGETABLE PUREE

1 toe Garlic, mashed
2 medium Onions, chopped fine
2 small Eggplants, peeled, chopped
3 small Zucchini, stems removed, chopped
2 large Tomatoes, skinned, chopped
³/₄ cup Olive Oil
2 tsp. Thyme
¹/₆ tsp. Cayenne Pepper
¹/₆ tsp. Black Pepper
¹/₄ tsp. Salt

Sauté onions in oil until golden. Add eggplant. Sauté 3 minutes. Add zucchini and stir. Add all remaining ingredients. Simmer 30 minutes. Mash all vegetables into rough puree. Sauté 5 minutes. Chill. Serve at room temperature.

Numbers 11:15 "The Israelites ate vegetables"

#251
• WHEAT STEW (VARVARA)
Burghul Stew

¹/₂ lb. Wheat, course ground, par boiled 2 minutes
    (Burghul — Burgul)
3 qts. Water
1 cup Raisins
1 ¹/₂ cups Flour
2 tsp. Cinnamon
¹/₂ tsp. Nutmeg

¹/₂ cup Pine Nuts, chopped
¹/₂ cup Pomegranate Seeds
1 cup Honey

Combine wheat and water. Bring to boil. As soon as wheat puffs add raisins and honey. Stir well. Brown flour in fry pan. When golden — caution, do not scorch — pour into wheat mixture and stir until fully combined. Stir in all remaining ingredients. Remove from heat and spoon into bowls. Garnish with extra cinnamon and pomegranate seeds. Allow to cool. Serve.

#252
• YIACHNI

2 lbs. Zucchini, stems removed, sliced in half
1 cup Olive Oil
4 large Tomatoes, skinned, chopped fine
3 medium Onions, chopped
1 cup Water
1 tsp. Mint, chopped
2 tsp. Dill Weed
³/₄ tsp. Salt
¹/₂ tsp. Pepper

Sauté onions in oil until golden. Add tomatoes. Sauté 5 minutes. Add water and zucchini. Simmer 5 minutes. add all remaining ingredients. Stir, cover and simmer 35 minutes.

#253
ZUCCHINI AND CHEESE

2 lbs. Zucchini, washed, sliced, ends removed
2 medium Onions, peeled, sliced thin
3 Tbsp. Olive Oil
1 tsp. Salt
3 Eggs
2 cups Gruyére cheese, grated

$^1/_2$ *tsp. White Pepper*

Sauté onions in oil until golden brown. Lightly poach zucchini in salted water for 3 minutes. Drain and layer into greased casserole dish. Beat eggs, add cheese, salt and pepper. Blend well. Pour over zucchini. Bake at 375° for 25 minutes.

#254
• ZUCCHINI FRIED

5 large Zucchini, sliced
1/2 cup Olive Oil
1/2 cup Flour
1 tsp. Basil
1/2 tsp. Thyme
1/4 tsp. Pepper

Mix flour, basil, thyme, and pepper. Heat oil in fry pan. Press zucchini into flour. Fry in hot oil, brown each side. Serve hot.

#255
ZUCCHINI, SWEET BAKED

5 Zucchini, peeled, sliced
1 large Onion, sliced
1 bunch Parsley, chopped
1/2 tsp. Salt
1/4 tsp. Pepper
1/2 cup Honey
1/2 cup Olive Oil
1 cup Water
1 Tbsp. Flour
1/2 tsp. Paprika

In a baking dish pour in water, alternate layers of zucchini and onion. Pour honey into pan. Sprinkle parsley over. Add spices. Sprinkle flour over top. Bake at 350° for 45 minutes.

Deuteronomy 8:10 "When you have eaten your fill, give Thanks to the Lord your God — We must remember to say Thank You for the gift we have enjoyed!"

#256
ZUCCHINI & THYME

1 1/4 Lbs. Zucchini, cleaned and sliced in 1" pieces
4 Tbsp. Olive Oil
1 tsp. Thyme
1/2 tsp. Dill
1/2 tsp. Salt
1/2 tsp. Pepper

Combine all ingredients in covered fry pan. Sauté 10 minutes or until zucchini is al dente. Shake pan often so zucchini does not stick and burn.

#257
COUR GETTES
Zucchini And Tomatoes

6 medium Zucchinis, trimmed, sliced
1 tsp. Salt
2 Tbsp. Olive Oil
2 Yellow Sweet Peppers, chopped fine
8 large Tomatoes, chopped
1 toe Garlic, minced
1/2 tsp. Basil
1/4 tsp. Thyme
1 qt. Water

Simmer zucchini in salt water 1 minute. Drain and flush with cold water. Set aside. Sauté peppers in olive oil 3 minutes. Add garlic, basil, and thyme. Stir well. Add tomatoes and sauté 5 minutes. Stir often. Add zucchini. Stir. Sauté 2 minutes. Stir. Serve.

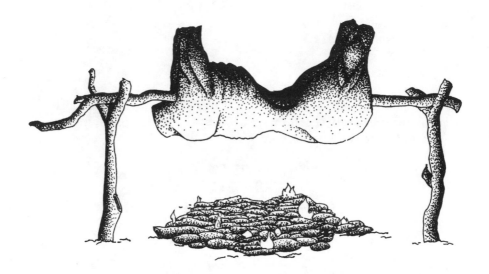

Broiling with Spit

D. MAIN DISHES

#257
AVOCADO OMELETTE

1 Avocado, peeled, cut in half, half minced, half sliced
8 Eggs, beaten
¹/₂ tsp. Salt
¹/₆ tsp. Pepper
1 tsp. Olive Oil
2 Tbsp. Butter

Melt butter and oil in large sauté pan. Combine egg and minced avocado. Whisk together with salt and pepper. Pour into hot pan and make a flat omelette. Turn over and cook second side. Lay sliced avocado over to heat. Pour our onto warm serving dish. Arrange slices. Serve with rice.

#258
BEEF AND BEANS BURGUNDY

1 lb. Ground Beef
1 cup Navy Beans, pre-soaked overnight, drained
1 large Onion, peeled, chopped
2 toes Garlic, minced
¹/₂ cup Dried Bread Crumbs
2 Tbsp. Oil
1 Egg
1 tsp. Salt
2 Tbsp. Margarine
12 Tomatoes, washed, chopped
1 tsp. Basil
³/₄ cup Dry Red Wine
5 cups Water

In a dutch oven boil water, add beans. Stir. Add oil, onion, garlic, and salt. Cover and simmer 1 1/2 hours. Mix beef, bread crumbs and egg together. Form into ping pong size balls. Brown in heated margarine. To beans, add tomatoes, wine and all spices. Place meat balls over top. Cover and bake at 325° for 50 minutes. Remove. Cover and brown for 10 minutes.

"You may eat meat whenever you wish" Deuteronomy 12:20.

#259
• BEEF AND OLIVE CASSEROLE

2 1/2 lbs. Beef, chuck, cubed
12 Pearl Onions
1/4 cup Flour
1/4 tsp. Salt
1/8 tsp. Pepper
3 Tbsp. Margarine or Olive Oil
6 Tomatoes, peeled, chopped
1/2 tsp. Rosemarie
1/2 tsp. Paprika
1 cup Water
1 cup Green, pimento olives, chopped
1 bunch Parsley, chopped

Mix flour, salt, pepper and tumble beef cubes to coat well. In 2 qt. casserole heat margarine and brown meat. Add onions and brown all over. Stir often. Add all but olives and parsley. Mix. Cover, simmer 1 hour 20 minutes. Add olives and parsley. cover and simmer 30 minutes. Serve with potatoes or rice.

Numbers 32:4 "The land that the Lord has conquered for the community of Israel is cattle country, and your servants have cattle." (to eat)

#260
BERRY PANCAKE

1/4 cup 10x Sugar

1 cup Milk
1 cup Ap. Flour
$^1/_2$ cup Wheat Flour
2 tsp. Baking Powder
2 Tbsp. Sugar
$^1/_2$ tsp. Salt
3 Tbsp. Oil
$^1/_2$ cup Blackberries
$^1/_2$ cup Blueberry
4 large Eggs, separated

Beat egg yolks, add milk, flour, baking powder, sugar and salt. Mix smooth. Pour in and blend oil. Beat egg whites stiff. Fold into pancake mixture. Toss berries with sugar. Mix into batter. Pour onto hot griddle. Serve with sliced fresh fruit. This is a main dish for lunch.

#261
• BIBLE STEW

$^3/_4$ cup Broad Beans (phul), soaked 6 hours, drained
$^1/_2$ cup Lentils, soaked 1 hour, drained
$^1/_4$ cup Peas, soaked 2 hours, drained
4 medium Onions, peeled, chopped
4 Leeks, chopped
4 toes Garlic, crushed
$^1/_2$ tsp. Pepper
2 tsp. Cardamon
1 bunch Parsley, chopped
1 qt. Water

Simmer beans in water 1 hour, add all remaining ingredients, simmer 2 hours. Add water as necessary. Stir well. Dish into pottery bowl. Serve with warm flat bread and vegetable.

On the side serve Fresh Figs • Fresh Dates
With a cup of Milk/leben
a piece of flat bread

and a dish of cucumber and yogurt
or boiled beets and dill

#262
• BUCK STEW, VENISON

2 lbs. Venison shoulder clod, cut in 1" cube
2 cups Dry red wine
1 large Onion, chopped
2 arms Celery
1/2 Green Pepper
2 toes Garlic
1 Carrot
1 bunch Parsley
1/2 stalk Celery tops
1/2 tsp. Pepper
1 tsp. Salt
1/2 tsp. Rosemarie
2 Tbsp. Flour
4 Tbsp. Oil

Mix venison, wine, onion and let sit 4-6 hours. In separate pan sauté 4 tablespoons oil and flour. Then add vegetables and mix well. Add all venison meat and 1/2 juice. Blend well. Simmer 1 1/2 hours. Add remaining juice. Mix well. Simmer 2 hours. Serve with broad noodles.

Genesis 9:4 says "eat meat but do not show gluttony," as does Deuteronomy 12:15.

#263
• CARAWAY FISH CASSEROLE

2 lbs. Fish fillets, cubed 2"
2 medium Onions, sliced
4 medium Potatoes, sliced thin
1 tsp. Salt
1 tsp. Caraway Seeds

1 Tbsp. Lemon Juice
1 cup Water
1 bunch Parsley, chopped

Layer fish and potatoes. Cover with onions. Season with salt and caraway. Carefully pour in water. Sprinkle lemon juice over. Cover. Simmer 25 minutes. Sprinkle parsley over. Serve.

#264
• CARROTS, FLAVORED

8 large Carrots, peeled, sliced, pre-blanched in salt
*   water*
1 Tbsp. Ap Flour
1/2 tsp. Pepper
3 Tbsp. Olive Oil
2 cups Yogurt, hot — do not boil
1 tsp. Caraway Seeds

Coat carrots in flour and pepper. Sauté in olive oil for 7 minutes. Remove with slotted spoon to a casserole dish. Mix yogurt and caraway seeds. Pour over hot carrots. Serve at once.

#265
CHICKEN AND BARLEY CASSEROLE

1 5 lb. Roasting chicken, cut at joints
1 Parsnip, peeled and chopped
3 arms Celery, chopped
2 medium Carrots, peeled, sliced thin
2 medium Onions, chopped
1/2 lb. Pearl Barley, washed in warm water
3 Tbsp. Olive Oil
1 Tbsp. Paprika
$^1/_6$ tsp. White pepper
2 qts. Vegetable Stock or Chicken Stock

Place stock in large pot. Add chicken. Bring to boil. Simmer 45 minutes. Remove chicken. Pick off meat. Discard bones. Add barley and vegetables, simmer 10 minutes. Add barley mixture. In oiled casserole add spice and oil. Mix well. Top with chicken meat. Bake covered 30 minutes at 375°. Serve. "So she gleaned in the field and she beat out that which she gleaned, and it was an ephah of Barley." Ruth 3:17

#266
• KALSOHNEHS
Cheese Knish

DOUGH
2/3 cup Flour
1 large Egg, beaten
1/4 tsp. Salt
1/6 tsp. Sugar
Blend well. Roll out thin like blintz skin. Cut into 2" squares. Allow to slightly air dry.

STUFFING
1 1/2 cups Dry Cottage Cheese
5 Tbsp. Sour Cream
1/4 tsp. Salt
2 medium Eggs
1 tsp. Lemon Juice
Beat all together to make a paste. Drop a teaspoon of filling into each dough square. Fold into triangles, crimp edges. Drop into boiling water for 2 minutes. Remove with slotted spoon and fry in margarine or oil until golden brown. Serve with fruit compote and sour cream.
"Go thy way, eat thy bread with joy, and drink you wine with a merry heart;" Ecclesiastes 9:7

#267
• CHICKEN CORIANDER

3 lbs. Roasting Chicken
1/4 tsp. Cumin
1/4 cup Coriander, fresh, (whole leaves)
1/4 tsp. Saffron Powder
2 tsp. Paprika
3 toes Garlic, pressed
2 Tbsp. Olive Oil
2 tsp. Salt
1/6 tsp. Pepper
4 medium Onions, chopped
1/2 bunch Parsley, chopped
1 cup Water
1/4 cup Mint, fresh

In a large Mortar with pestle crush and combine mint, garlic, paprika, saffron, coriander and cumin with 1 tablespoon olive oil. Should be the consistency of prepared mustard, add more oil if required. Wash chicken and blot off excessive water. Sprinkle salt and pepper inside and outside. Rub on the coriander paste. Cover all the skin. In a dutch oven heat water. Place chicken carefully in, back side down. Add onions and parsley. Cover and simmer for 45 minutes. Sprinkle remaining oil over breast. Place under broiler to brown the breast 4-5 minutes. Take care not to burn the chicken. Serve with rice and pan juices.

#268
CHICKEN IN HONEY

1 large Roasting chicken, cleaned
3 Tbsp. Olive Oil
3 Tbsp. Honey
1/2 cup Almonds, ground
1/4 cup Basil, chopped

¹/₂ tsp. Pepper
1 Egg, beaten
¹/₂ cup Fresh Bread Crumbs
¹/₄ cup Water

Make a stuffing of water, bread crumbs, egg, pepper, basil and almonds. Mix well and stuff bird. Coat outside of bird with all of olive oil-honey mixture. Place in roast pan and bake at 350° for 1 ½ hours. Baste often with pan drippings. Serve.

#269
• HAVETAT KAVED
Chicken Liver Omelet
Kaved of Beytzim

¹/₃ lb. Chicken livers
4 Tbsp. Olive Oil
¹/₄ tsp. Pepper
1 sprig Thyme
¹/₄ tsp. Salt
¹/₆ tsp. Basil
1 Tbsp. Onion, minced
8 Eggs, beaten
1 tsp. Port wine

Soak livers in salt water 3 hours, drain. Sauté livers in hot oil. Add thyme, salt, pepper, basil, onion, port wine. Mix well and cook until golden brown. Remove from heat and mince livers. Blend into spice mixture. Pour eggs into pan with oil. Let bottom set. Spoon in livers, fold, turn. Eggs should be nicely set.

Exodus 24:11 says when making a pledge, or sealing a bargain or contract you must share a meal or drink a toast!

#270
CHICKEN AND PRUNES

1 $^3/_4$ lbs. Roast Chicken, cut into pieces
$^1/_2$ cup Raisins
$^1/_2$ cup Prunes, pitted
$^1/_3$ cup Dry Red Wine
$^1/_2$ tsp. Salt
$^1/_4$ tsp. Pepper
1 cup Pearl Onions, peeled
2 Tbsp. Flour
2 cups Water
$^1/_4$ tsp. Thyme
$^1/_8$ tsp. Basil
2 Tbsp. Oil

In a stainless steel or glass bowl combine raisins, prunes and wine. Mix well. Set aside. In dutch oven sauté chicken in oil. Nicely brown. Remove chicken and set aside. To sauté pan add flour, salt, pepper and make a brown roux. Add water and blend well. Add thyme and basil. Stir and simmer 2 minutes. Return chicken to dutch oven. Cover and simmer 30 minutes. Add prune mixture and onions. Cover and simmer 30 minutes. Remove cover, check liquid add 1/4 cup water if gravy is overly tight. Simmer 5 minutes. Serve.

#271
CHICKEN SAUSAGE

2 cups Water
2 lbs. Boneless chicken with skin. Heavy fat removed.
   4" chunks, par boiled 4 minutes. Retain broth.
4 Egg whites
1 large Onion, minced
1 tsp. Sea Salt
$^1/_4$ tsp. White Pepper
$^1/_4$ tsp. Mace

3 Tbsp. Parsley, chopped
¹/₄ tsp. Thyme
¹/₄ cup Dried Apples
¹/₄ cup Dried Apricots
¹/₃ cup Matzo Meal

Grind all solids together, through medium plate. Mix and blend all. Refrigerate for 2 hours. Mix broth and matzo meal. Let sit 30 minutes. Combine first grind and matzo meal, blend. Add all remaining ingredients and mix well. Grind through fine plate. Wash medium sheep casings. Blot dry. Stuff second grinding into sheep casing. Tie off at 4" cut. refrigerate. When ready to cook grill on medium fire, turn often. Cooking time: 7 minutes.

#272
• CHICKEN WITH KUMQUATS

3 lbs. Roasting Chicken, cut
1 cup Orange Juice
2 Tbsp. Lemon Juice
¹/₄ cup Honey
2 Tbsp. Hot Chili Peppers, chopped
12 Kumquats, sugar cured
1 tsp. Salt
1 cup Cooked Rice

In a deep baking dish make a layer of all chicken. Sprinkle sugar over. Pour honey over. Mix lemon and orange juice and pour over. Sprinkle peppers over. Bake at 375° for 15 minutes. Stir chicken. Rearrange pieces skin side up. Add kumquats and bake 35 minutes. Place rice on serving plate. Arrange chicken on rice. Place kumquats along top of chicken. Reduce pan juice in half. Pour over kumquats. Serve.

"The seed of Peace, the vine shall give her fruit, and the ground shall give her increase," (Zacharia 8:12)

#273
• CHOLENT
Hamin; Bahsh

2 qts. Water
1 lb. Beef or Lamb Breast, cubed 1"
$^1/_2$ lb. Small Dried White Beans, pre-soaked
$^1/_2$ lb. Chic-peas, pre-soaked
3 Tbsp. Schmaltz or Goose Fat
2 medium Onions, minced
2 toes Garlic, minced
1 Tbsp. Paprika
$^1/_8$ tsp. Salt
1/2 lb. Chicken or Goose Pieces
4 Eggs
2 Tbsp. Flour
2 cups Water

Sauté onions and garlic in schmaltz.   Add flour and paprika and blend well. Add 2 cups cold water. Simmer 5 minutes. In a large dutch oven, combine beans and peas. Add water. Bring to boil. Add meat. Stir. Add eggs in shell (carefully). Add all remaining ingredients. Cover. Slowly simmer for 2 hours. Check for liquid. Add some if required. Check for spice. Cook 10 minutes to slightly dry. Remove eggs, peel and serve as garnish. Dish up. Serve compote on side.

Stew (Nazid) II Kings 4:38, was slow cooked for a long period of time and most of the liquid was cooked off. Cholent is such a dish.

#274
CINNAMON CHICKEN

3 lbs. Chicken, cut at joints
8 Tomatoes, peeled, chopped
6 Tbsp. Olive Oil
$^1/_2$ cup Dry White Wine

1 Tbsp. Lemon Juice
¹/₂ tsp. Cinnamon
¹/₄ tsp. Cloves
¹/₄ tsp. Salt
¹/₈ tsp. Pepper
¹/₂ bunch Parsley, chopped
¹/₂ cup Water

Rub chicken with lemon juice. Set aside. In heavy fry pan or dutch oven, heat oil and sauté chicken. Turn often to brown all sides. Pour wine over, tumble well to coat chicken. Add tomatoes. Sprinkle all spices and herbs over. Cover and slowly simmer 45 minutes. Add water, cover and simmer 25 minutes. Remove cover and simmer 10 minutes. Check for doneness. Serve with bulgur grain.

#275
GRIBENES, GRIVN, GANZEBORD
Cracklings

¹/₂ lb. Goose or chicken trimmings, fat and skin
1 Carrot, sliced
1 small Onion, sliced
2 Tbsp. Water

Combine all ingredients and sauté 3/4 hour on medium low fire. Stir often. Strain through 3 layers cheese cloth. Save the fat for Schmaltz. Use the crisp pieces as a snack. Lightly salt and serve.

#276
• DAG SHAMIR
Dill Fish

1 3 lb. Dressed fish, head off
4 Tbsp. Olive Oil
1 tsp. Salt
1 Tbsp. Dill

¹/₃ tsp. Pepper

Rinse and dry fish. Rub inside and outside with olive oil. Dust well with spices and herbs. Place in greased baking dish. Cover. Bake at 350° for 1 hour. Serve.

#277
DUCK IN WINE

¹/₂ cup Red Wine
1 5 lb. Duck
1 cup Sour Pie Cherries
¹/₂ cup Prunes, soaked and pitted
1 medium Onion, minced, sautéd
1 cup Bread Crumbs
¹/₂ tsp. Cinnamon
1 tsp. Lemon Peel, grated
¹/₄ cup Sugar
3 Tbsp. Light Salad Oil

Mix salad oil and sugar in pan, heat until sugar is melted. Add bread crumbs and lemon peel. Stir well. Add cherries. Remove from heat and let cool. Add all other ingredients. Mix well. Stuff bird. Place on rack breast side down. Roast at 300° for 2 hours 25 minutes. Baste every 30 minutes with 2 tablespoons red wine.

#278
DUMPLINGS

1 cup Flour
¹/₂ tsp. Salt
¹/₂ tsp. Baking Powder
¹/₈ tsp. Pepper
1 Egg, beaten
¹/₄ cup Milk
¹/₄ bunch Parsley, minced

Mix flour, salt, pepper, and baking powder. In separate

bowl whip egg, milk and parsley. Combine and mix well. Make ping-pong size balls and drop into boiling water. Serve as main dish or soup extender.

#279
EGGS WITH ROE

$^1/_2$ tsp. 10 x sugar
$^2/_3$ cup Heavy Cream
3 Tbsp. Onion, minced
3 Tbsp. Caviar (Roe)
2 Eggs, hard cooked, sliced
4 pieces Toast

Whip sugar and cream until stiff. Beat in onions and caviar. Pour into serving dish. Garnish edges with egg. Dish over toast.

#280
• FALAFEL BALLS

2 cans Chic-peas, drained, mashed
$^1/_2$ tsp. Salt
$^1/_4$ tsp. Tabasco/Hot Pepper Sauce
$^1/_6$ tsp. Pepper
2 cups Dry Bread Crumbs, crushed fine
2 Tbsp. Shortening
2 Eggs, beaten

In bowl mix peas, salt, tabasco, pepper and bread crumbs until mashed. Add eggs. Mix. Add shortening. Mix. Shape into balls 3/4" in diameter. Fry in deep shortening until nicely browned. Lift with slotted spoon and place on paper to dry. Serve with tehina sauce, in a pita bread or with bread on side.

#281
• ABGUSHT
Family Stew

1 lb. Beef, cubed 1"
1 lb. Lamb or Mutton, cubed 1"
4 medium Onions, chopped
8 Tomatoes, peeled, chopped
8 Carrots, scraped, sliced
1 stalk Celery, chopped
5 large Potatoes, peeled, cubed
2 toes Garlic
4 Turnips, peeled, chopped
1/2 cup Flour
2 Tbsp. Oil
1/2 tsp. Salt
1/4 tsp. Pepper
1/2 tsp. Paprika
1/6 tsp. Clove
2 qts. Water

Brown meat in oil, add spices and stir. Add garlic, onions and turnip. Stir and simmer 3 minutes. In deep pot bring water to boil. Add all vegetables. Simmer 10 minutes. Add meat mixture. Simmer 1 hours. Make roux of flour and add to pot. Simmer 30 minutes. Serve over noodles.

"You may eat meat whenever you wish." Deuteronomy 12:20

#282
• KADUREY DAGIM
Fish Balls Boiled

1 lb. Fish, assorted 2 kinds, chopped fine
2 medium Onions, minced
1 slice Bread, white, chopped fine
1 Egg

¹/₂ tsp. Salt
¹/₂ tsp. Pepper
¹/₄ tsp. Marjoram
2 Tbsp. Parsley
3 arms Celery with tops, chopped
1 qt. Water
2 Tbsp. Olive Oil
Combine fish, onions, bread, egg, salt, pepper, marjoram and parsley. Mix very well and form into golf ball sized balls. Boil water, add celery and oil. Boil softly. Drop balls carefully into water and cook 15 minutes. Serve balls with some of celery and stock. Retain left over stock for boiling rice.

#283
• FISH BAKE

1 3 lb. Fish, cleaned, head off
3 tsp. Semneh
1 Tbsp. Zhug
1 tsp. Mint
2 small Onions, minced
1 cup Water
Place fish in casserole dish with water. Cover with onion. Sprinkle zhug and mint over. Add semneh. Cover dish and bake for 1 hour 20 minutes. Serve.

#284
• FISH CAKES

¹/₂ lb. Fish Fillets, diced fine
3 cups Potatoes, diced fine
2 Eggs, beaten
2 Tbsp. Olive Oil
¹/₈ tsp. Pepper
¹/₈ tsp. Salt
³/₄ cup Matzo Meal

1 cup Water

Simmer fish and potatoes in water for 15 minutes. Mash and blend well. Add eggs and olive oil. Whip together. Add spices. Add 2 tablespoons Matzo Meal. Form into 3" x 1/2" patties. Press into remaining Matzo Meal. Fry in deep fat until brown on both sides. 4-5 minutes. Try to keep temperature at 375°.

"We remember the fish we used to eat free — " Numbers 10:5

#285
• FISH CASSEROLE

2 lbs. Fish Fillet, cut 1" cubes (a white meat is best)
¹/₃ cup Dried Bread Crumbs
¹/₄ cup Onion, chopped
1 cup Mushrooms, sliced
2 ¹/₂ cups Milk
¹/₄ cup Flour
³/₄ tsp. Salt
¹/₆ tsp. Pepper
¹/₈ tsp. Cayenne Pepper
2 Tbsp. Butter
2 Tbsp. Grated Parmesan Cheese

Melt butter, add onions and mushrooms. Sauté until light brown. Add flour and spices. Cook roux. Stir in milk until thick. Add sherry and blend. Remove from fire. Place noodles in greased baking dish. Add fish. Pour sauce over. Sprinkle in bread crumbs. Dust cheese over. Bake at 375° for 45 minutes. Serve.

#286
FISH KABOB FOR SIX

6 slices Swordfish cut filets into four equal pieces
(Any firm flesh fish will do)

4 Tbsp. Olive Oil
2 Tbsp. Apple Vinegar
1 tsp. Salt
¹/₄ tsp. Pepper
12 Pearl Onions
12 Cherry Tomatoes
1 tsp. Coriander
¹/₄ tsp. Cumin

Mix olive oil, vinegar, salt, pepper, coriander and cumin. Let sit 20 minutes. Place fish in flat pan, pour marinade over. Let sit 20 minutes. Take skewer and thread piece of fish, onion, fish, tomato, fish, onion, fish, tomato. Baste with marinade. Broil on medium heat. Turn and baste, turn and baste until done.

#287
TIBERIAS FRIED FISH

6 1" Fish Fillets (steaks) use any local fish that has a
*   fairly dense texture, or use halibut*
1 ¹/₂ cups Parsley, chopped fine
2 tsp. garlic, minced
¹/₂ cup Onion, chopped fine
3 Tbsp. Pepper Grass (cilantro) chopped fine
2 tsp. Green Olives, minced
³/₄ cup Virgin Olive Oil
¹/₄ cup Sifted Flour
3 tsp. Lemon Juice
1 tsp. Pepper

Using a mortar and pestle combine and pulp parsley, garlic, pepper grass, 1 teaspoon water and 1 teaspoon oil, and work till the mixture is smooth. Add the lemon juice and blend. This will take a little time. If you are having a large party, say for 12 or so people, increase the portion 3 times and run it through a food processor to make smooth. Place in a glass bowl and set aside.

Combine the flour and pepper on a glass plate. Take a heavy fry pan and heat the oil. Press the fish steaks into the flour, turn and repeat. Shake the loose flour off of the fish and fry for 2 minutes on each side, remove to a warm plate. When all the fish is fried place the plate in a warm oven until time to serve.

Pour off 1/2 of the oil from the pan, and to the remaining oil add the onions and olives and sauté for 3 minutes (do not let the onions burn). Now add the flour pepper dip and blend as you would a roux until just tight. Add the parsley mixture and blend well. If the sauce becomes too tight add a table-spoon warm water at a time until you have a slightly loose pea soup consistency. Pour the sauce over the fish and serve at once with a nice tossed green salad and crisp crust warm bread.

#288
• FISH PEPPER STEW

2 lbs. Fish, assorted kinds, at least 3
$^1/_4$ cup Olive Oil
2 large Onions, chopped course
$^1/_2$ tsp. Salt
$^1/_4$ tsp. Pepper
$^1/_4$ tsp. Paprika
$^1/_8$ tsp. Cayenne
$^1/_2$ Green Bell Pepper, cleaned, sliced thin
$^1/_4$ cup Water

In a dutch oven, combine all except fish. Blend well. Simmer 5 minutes. Layer fish over top. Sprinkle water over. Cover and simmer for 20-25 minutes. Place fish on deep serving platter. Pour pan contents over and serve. Sprinkle paprika lightly over.

#289
FISH RICE

2 medium Onions, minced
3 cups Water or fish bouillon
1 cup Rice
2 Tbsp. Olive Oil
1 Red Pepper, seeds and stem removed, diced
1 Green Pepper, seeds and stem removed, diced
1 lb. Fish, cubed $^3/_4$"
$^1/_4$ tsp. Saffron
1 tsp. Salt
$^1/_2$ tsp. White Pepper

In large pot heat oil and add onion. Sauté until golden.
Add rice and sauté 5 minutes. Add water and spices. Simmer
10 minutes. Add peppers and fish. Stir. Cover and simmer
30 minutes. Stir and serve.

#290
• ZISE - ZOYRE
Fish, Sweet and Sour

1 lb. Fillets of your favorite fish
1 cup Sugar
1 cup Lemon Juice, fresh squeezed
1 Tbsp. Ginger
1 Tbsp. Pimento, diced
$^1/_4$ cup Almonds, blanched
2 cups Water

Wrap fish in a flat envelope of cheese cloth. Place in a
shallow pan with water, slowly simmer — do not boil — 6-7
minutes. In separate pan boil sugar, lemon juice, ginger and
pimento. Lay fish out on platter. Pour sweet and sour sauce
over. Garnish with almonds. Serve.

Nebuchadnezzar was at rest (and saw) — Daniel 4:9 "the
leaves thereof fair, and the fruit thereof much, and in it was

food for all;—"

#291
• "BACKHENDL" OF METUGAN
Fried Chicken

1 cup Bread Crumbs
2 Fryers, cut up
2 Eggs, beaten with water
$^1/_2$ cup Flour
1 Tbsp. Water
1 tsp. Salt
$^1/_2$ tsp. Pepper
$^1/_4$ tsp. Paprika
$^1/_8$ tsp. Cayenne
2 Tbsp. Lemon Juice
2 cups Oil

Blend flour and all spices. Blend egg, lemon and water. Wash chicken, shake dry. Press into flour mixture and coat well. Dip into egg wash. Press into bread crumbs. Fry in hot oil until golden on both sides. Place in baking dish and bake at 350° for 35 minutes.

#292
• GOAT GOULASH

1 $^1/_2$ lbs. Fresh goat, cubed 1 $^1/_2$"
2 medium Onions, chopped
2 Tbsp. Oil
$^1/_4$ tsp. Paprika
$^1/_2$ tsp. Caraway Seeds
$^1/_2$ tsp. Salt
1 cup Water
3 Tbsp. Flour
1 cup Riches Coffee White, (Soymilk) Coconut milk
    may also be used

1 cup Sauerkraut

Sauté onions in oil. Add meat, herbs and spices. Sauté 3 minutes. Add half of the water. Cover and simmer 1 hour. Add flour and water. Simmer 10 minutes. Add sauerkraut. Simmer 5 minutes. Add all remaining ingredients. Bring to boil. Stir. Serve.

"Rebeccah prepared a dish of kid for (Isaac) him, such as he likes." Genesis 27:9.

#293
• "PIPIKLACH"
Gizzards

1 Tbsp. Oil
2 lbs. mixed Gizzards, hearts, livers
1 qt. Water
1 tsp. Salt
^{1}/$_2$ tsp. Pepper
^{1}/$_4$ tsp. Paprika
2 medium Onions, chopped
6 Tbsp. Schmaltz (chicken fat)
1 cup Flour

Bring water and salt to boil. Add gizzards, heart and livers. Simmer 45 minutes. Drain and shake dry. Tumble in flour. Sauté onions in schmaltz and oil until transparent. Add spices and mix well. Add gizzard mix and slowly sauté until all are golden brown. Serve with rice.

#294
• GOOSE, FRUITED

1 cup Orange Juice, set aside for basting
1 10-12 lb. Goose
3 Tbsp. Water
24 Prunes, pitted, soaked 6 hours, chopped
3 Apples, tart, minced

1 Orange, sectioned, chopped
4 arms Celery, minced
3 Tbsp. Brown Sugar
1 cup Bread Crumbs
2 Eggs, whipped easy
1 tsp. Lemon Juice
$^1/_2$ cup Flour
1 tsp. Salt
$^1/_2$ tsp. Garlic Powder

Mix flour, salt, and garlic. Dust bird inside and out. Mix all remaining ingredients together and stuff bird. Roast breast down on V rack for 4 hours at 325°. Baste every 20-30 minutes with 2 tablespoons orange juice. Test for doneness.

Genesis 25:27 "— and Esau was a cunning hunter, a man of the field;—"

#295
• HAMINDAS MEVUSHAL
Hard Cooked Eggs

12 Eggs — chicken or goose
$^1/_2$ cup Onion skins
1 tsp. Salt
$^1/_2$ tsp. Pepper
2 Tbsp. Olive Oil
1 qt. Water

Place all ingredients in pot of cold water, bring to boil. Cover and simmer for 1 hour.

#296
• HELZEL
Stuffed Goose Neck

1 Skin of Goose Neck
2 medium Onions chopped
$^1/_4$ lb. Beef, ground

1 cup Flour
3 Tbsp. Olive Oil
¹/₂ tsp. Salt
¹/₄ tsp. Pepper
1 bunch Parsley
1 Apple or orange

Sauté onions in oil. Add meat. Brown well. Add flour and spices. Blend fully. Add parsley and mix. Stuff neck and sew both ends. Slice apple in 4 slices. Lay apple in pan. Pour ½ cup water in pan. Lay neck over apple. Bake at 350° for 1 hour. Serve.

#297
• ICRE

1 lb. Fresh Fish Roe
1 Tbsp. Salt
¹/₂ cup Fresh Lemon Juice
¹/₂ cup Olive Oil
¹/₈ tsp. Garlic, pressed
3 Tbsp. Parsley, minced

Place roe in glass bowl, sprinkle salt over. Cover and place in refrigerator 12 hours. Wash roe and remove membrane. In your electric mixer, beat roe, add lemon juice and olive oil. Alternating each as you beat. Add garlic powder, beat. Spread on Demi Rye bread. Sprinkle parsley over.

#298
• KAUFTA
Meat Balls

4 cups Water
1 ¹/₂ cups Bulgar, course grind
2 Onions, chopped fine
1 ¹/₂ lbs. Lamb or Veal, ground fine
1 tsp. Salt

$^1/_2$ *tsp. Mint Powder*
$^1/_2$ *tsp. Tarragon*
$^1/_2$ *tsp. Paprika*
2 *Tbsp. Oil*
3 *Tbsp. Oil*

Simmer water and bulgar for 40 minutes. Sauté onions and lamb grind in 3 tablespoons oil and spices. Mix well with 1/3 bulgar. Mash any lumps. Form into large ping pong balls. Sauté in 2 tablespoons oil. When nicely browned add to bulgar soup mixture. Bring to boil, simmer 15 minutes. Add water if necessary.

#299
• MACCABEE FISH

2 *lbs. Fish Fillets (Karpion or Hake are the usual*
  fish to use if fresh)
1 *Tbsp. Water*
2 *Eggs, beaten with water*
2 *Tbsp. Lemon Juice*
2 *Tbsp. Prepared Mustard*
$^1/_6$ *tsp. Lemon Rind, grated*
2 *Tbsp. Corn Meal*
$^1/_4$ *cup Oil*
$^1/_6$ *tsp. Pepper*

Pepper fillets. Blend lemon juice, lemon rind and mustard into paste. Coat both sides of fillets and let sit for 20-25 minutes. Dip fish into eggs then coat with corn meal. Fry golden on both sides. Place in hot oven for 10 minutes. Serve.

#300
• KUFTEH GUSHT
Meat Loaf

1 *lb. Lamb, ground medium*
$^1/_2$ *lb. Beef, ground medium*

2 medium Onions, ground medium
1 bunch Parsley, minced
4 arms Celery with tops, chopped fine
3 medium Tomatoes, minced
3 Tbsp. Bread, chopped fine
$^1/_2$ tsp. Salt
$^1/_4$ tsp. Pepper
$^1/_4$ tsp. Cinnamon
$^1/_6$ tsp. Ginger
1 Tbsp. Lemon Juice
$^1/_4$ cup Water
2 Eggs, beaten

Mix all together and place in baking dish. Bake 1 hour at 350°.

"When you have eaten your fill, give thanks to the Lord" Deuteronomy 8:10.

#301
• KUFTA HAMOUTZIM
Meat Balls in Tomato Sauce

2 lbs. Ground Beef or Ground Lamb
5 toes Garlic, crushed
$^1/_4$ cup Parsley, minced
5 Tbsp. Matzo Meal
$^1/_2$ tsp. Salt
$^1/_4$ tsp. Pepper

Mix all together and roll into ping pong size balls. Set aside.

6 Tbsp. Tomato Paste
1 toe Garlic, crushed
1 tsp. Salt
$^1/_4$ tsp. Pepper
2 Tbsp. Oil
1 cup Water
1 tsp. Lemon Juice, fresh, retained

284

Mix together. Bring to a soft boil for 30 seconds and set aside. In one cup of oil fry balls at high temperature, 400° Fahrenheit until golden brown, the same as you would fry falafel. Cooking time about 5 minutes. Remove from oil with slotted spoon and place in sauce. Simmer mixture together for 10 minutes. Add lemon juice and simmer 5 minutes. Serve over rice.

#302
• KAWAREH HUMMUS
Chickpeas and Feet

2 Calves feet, washed and scraped
5 Tbsp. Olive Oil
1 tsp. Salt
$^1/_2$ tsp. Pepper
$^1/_2$ tsp. Turmeric
$^1/_6$ tsp. Cayenne
2 cups Chick-peas, pre-soaked overnight
3 Hard cooked eggs
2 qts. Water

Blanch feet in boiling water 3 minutes. Pour off water, wash, rinse. In large fry pan heat oil and sauté feet and brown on all sides. Add chick-peas and all spices. Stir well. Add water and simmer 4 hours. Add water as required. Remove meat from bones. Discard bones. Tumble meat in chick-peas. Stir well. Serve.

"and ye shall eat the fat of the land." Genesis 45:18.

#303
• KEBAB
Grill, Meshwi, Brochette

1 lb. Ground Chuck
1 tsp. Salt
$^1/_2$ tsp. Pepper

$^1/_4$ tsp. Cumin
2 toes Garlic, pressed
2 Tbsp. Parsley, chopped fine
$^1/_8$ tsp. Paprika
$^1/_8$ tsp. Bicarbonate of soda

Mix meat, spices and herbs. Blend well. Let sit 30 minutes in warm room. Blend again. Add bicarbonate of soda. Mix well. Form into golf balls, place on skewer. Broil, turn often. Serve with Pita bread.

#304
• KHORESHE FESENJAN
Duck and Pomegranate

2 large Pomegranates, cut in half, seeds removed and
*   separated*
1 cup Sugar
1 Duck, cleaned, cut into $^1/_4$ pieces
2 Onions, chopped
2 cups Walnuts
2 Tbsp. Olive Oil
1 Tbsp. Lemon Juice
$^1/_2$ tsp. Cinnamon
$^1/_2$ tsp. Salt
$^1/_4$ tsp. Pepper
$^1/_2$ cup Water

In glass bowl, combine pomegranate seeds and sugar. Mix and let sit 12 hours. Stir several times. Rub in a sieve until only bare seeds are left. Mix juice and sugar together. Discard seeds. Set aside.

Sauté duck in oil. Brown all sides. Remove duck and sauté onions and nuts. Add lemon juice and water. Mix well. Place duck in casserole dish. Pour onion mixture over. Pour pomegranate mixture over. Sprinkle spice over. Cover. Bake at 350° for 40-45 minutes. Check for doneness. Serve.

" — you may eat food without stint, — " Deuteronomy 8:9.

#305
• KIBBEH, BAKED

2 cups Burghul, soak in tepid water, 20 minutes
1 lb. Lamb Shoulder, ground
1 tsp. Flour
1 tsp. Mint leaves, dried, crushed
2 medium Onions, sliced fine, sauté
1 medium Onion, minced, raw
1 Tbsp. Pine Nuts, minced
$^1/_3$ Tbsp. Raisins, chopped with a French knife
$^1/_4$ tsp. Cinnamon
$^1/_4$ tsp. Cloves
$^1/_8$ tsp. Pepper
3 Tbsp. Semnek (for kosher use schmaltz)
2 Tbsp. Oil

Mix meat, sautéd onions, spice and semneh and set aside. Drain burghul, stir in flour. Mix well. combine meat mixture and flour mixture. Mix well. Take a well greased square pan. Spread in 1/2 of meat mixture, spread in raisins, top with pine nuts and raw onions. Spread in remaining 1/2 of meat mixture. Pat smooth with your hand. Oil the top. Cut slicing marks in top. Bake at 375° for 50 minutes. Serve.

" — you shall not pick your vineyard bare, — you shall leave them for the poor — " Leviticus 19:10.

#306
• KIBBEH, FRIED

Same recipe as baked, except when mixture is combined, make small balls, ping pong size. Poke hole in center. Stuff with pine nut, raisins and onions. Close hole with lamb mixture plug. Fry in deep oil until golden brown. Serve with rice and zhug or tehina on the side.

#306B
• KISHKA
Stuffed Derma, Nakaitoris

2 12" Beef casings, cleaned and scraped
1 cup Ap flour
$^1/_2$ cup Matzo meal
2 Onions
1 Carrot, grated
$^1/_4$ tsp. Paprika
$^3/_4$ tsp. Salt
$^1/_4$ tsp. Pepper
$^1/_2$ cup Schmaltz (chicken fat)
$^1/_2$ bunch Parsley, chopped

Mix all together. Blend well. Stuff casing. Sew up ends. Place in pan with roast. Cover with water and cook. Or can be baked by itself. Place on thick slice of onion or bell pepper. Cover with water and bake at 350° for 2 hours.

#307
• KLOPS

1 lb. Ground Chuck
2 medium Onion, minced
3 Slices Bread, soaked, shredded
1 Egg, whipped
1 tsp. Salt
$^1/_2$ tsp. Pepper
$^1/_4$ tsp. Cayenne Pepper
1 toe Garlic, pressed
$^1/_2$ bunch Parsley, chopped fine

Mix all together well. Place in loaf pan. Bake at 350° for 1 hour.

#308
• KONDY STEW

1 lb. Lamb Shoulder, cubed
2 medium Onions, chopped
3 medium Carrots, sliced thin
4 arms Celery, sliced 1"
$^1/_2$ lb. Zucchini
2 Tbsp. Olive Oil
$^1/_2$ tsp. Salt
$^1/_2$ tsp. Pepper
$^1/_8$ tsp. Turmeric
1 tsp. Cinnamon
2 cups Rice, pre-boiled 10 minutes, washed, drained
3 Eggs, whipped lightly
1 cup Water

Sauté lamb in oil. Blend 1 cup of rice with eggs. Mix well. In a well greased casserole dish place 1 cup rice (not egged). Lay in meat and oil. Lay in vegetables. Sprinkle on all spices. Cover with egged rice. Pour in water.* Cover tightly. Bake at 350° for 1 hour 20 minutes. Serve.

* Note: Kondy may be used to stuff acorn squash. Cut large squash in half lengthwise. Remove seeds. Place a tennis ball size kondy mixture in squash. Put squash in covered dish and bake at 350° for 1 hour 20 minutes.

#309
KUBANE

1 Tbsp. Warm water
1 lb. Flour
$^1/_4$ cup Semneh
1 tsp. Dry Yeast
2 $^1/_4$ cup Water
1 tsp. Salt
$^1/_4$ tsp. Red Pepper

Dissolve yeast in warm water. Blend into flour and salt. Add semneh and red pepper. Mix well. Add water. Knead. Place in warm spot for 2 hours to rise. Place in well-greased covered pan. Bake at 250° for 8 hours. Serve. This dish is often made on the back of the stove similar to Cholent.

#310
• KURDISH HASH

1 Tbsp. Oil
$^1/_2$ lb. Shoulder of Lamb, sliced thin
1 large Onion, chopped
3 cups Boiled Rice
2 Eggs
$^1/_2$ tsp. Salt
$^1/_4$ tsp. Pepper
$^1/_2$ bunch Parsley, chopped

Brown lamb in oil and sauté 5 minutes. Add onion and stir. Add rice and "stir fry". Beat eggs and pour over. Mix well. When eggs set, sprinkle parsley over and serve with tomato.

#311
LAMB BREAST, STUFFED

1 cup Water
1 Lamb Breast, pocket cut in
$^3/_4$ cup Brown Rice, par boiled 20 minutes, drained
$^1/_2$ tsp. Salt
$^1/_4$ tsp. Pepper
$^1/_4$ cup Pecans, crushed
1 bunch Parsley, minced
1 small Onion, minced
4 Tbsp. Olive Oil
$^1/_2$ cup Flour

Combine rice, salt, pepper, onion, nuts and parsley. Mix

well. Stuff pocket and sew shut. Braise meat in skillet with oil. Pour 1/2 cup of water into skillet and place in 350° oven for 40 minutes. Turn meat. Add balance of water and bake 35 minutes. If meat dries in pan add more water as needed.

Ezra 7:17 "therefore thou shalt with all diligence buy with this money, bullocks, rams, lambs, with their meal-offerings and their drink-offerings, and shalt offer them upon the altar of the house of God —"

#312
LAMB WITH BRUSSEL SPROUTS

2 1/2 lbs. Lamb Shoulder, cut in 2" cubes
3 medium Onions, chopped
3 cups Sprouts, cleaned
3 Tbsp. Olive Oil
1 cup Tomato Sauce
1/4 cup Green Bell Pepper, diced
1 cup Water
1 tsp. Salt
1/2 tsp. Pepper
3 Tbsp. Parsley, chopped

In sauce pan heat oil and sauté lamb. Brown well. Add all remaining ingredients. Cover and simmer 2 hours. Dish and serve.

#313
LAMB CHOPS

6 Shoulder Lamb Chops
1/4 cup Olive Oil
1/4 cup Onion, minced
1/4 cup Parsley, chopped
2 toes Garlic, pressed
1/2 tsp. Salt
1/8 tsp. Pepper

¹/₄ cup Dry White Wine or Apple Vinegar
Mix all oil, spices, herbs, and wine. Blend well. Place
lamb in shallow pan. Pour oil mixture over. Allow to
marinate for 3 hours turning meat over after 1 1/2 hours.
Remove meat and broil. Turn often and baste with marinade
each time.

#314
• LAMB GOULASH

6 Lamb Shanks, cut into pieces
3 Tbsp. Olive Oil
3 toes Garlic, pressed
4 Tbsp. Zhug
2 medium Onions, chopped
1 qt. Water
Sauté lamb in olive oil 5 minutes. Add garlic and zhug.
Stir well. Add onions and saute 3 minutes. Add water, cover
and let simmer for 2 ½ hours. Serve with rice garnish as soup.

#315
• LAMB KIDNEYS IN WINE

2 lbs. Fresh Kidneys
1 qt. Water
2 Tbsp. Vinegar
3 Tbsp. Flour
2 Tbsp. Olive Oil
2 toes Garlic, pressed
1 tsp. Salt
¹/₄ tsp. Pepper
³/₄ tsp. Oregano
¹/₂ tsp. Marjoram
1 bunch Parsley, chopped
12 medium Mushrooms, washed, cleaned
1 cup Dry Red Wine

Soak kidney in water with vinegar for 20 minutes. Remove outer skin and slice. Dust with flour. Heat oil in heavy pan, sear and brown meat. Add all ingredients, cover and simmer for 20-25 minutes. Serve over rice.

#316
• LAMB LEG, ROASTED

2 cups Water
1 Leg of Lamb
4 toes Garlic, cut $^1/_2$
2 tsp. Salt
1 tsp. Pepper
4 Tbsp. Oil
1 Tbsp. Lemon Juice
1 Tbsp. Thyme

With sharp knife make slits into lamb. Push garlic pieces into slits. Rub oil over lamb. Sprinkle with salt, pepper and thyme. Place in roast pan, fat side up. Sprinkle lemon juice over. Add water. Roast at 450° for 20 minutes. Reduce heat to 350° for 3 hours. Serve with juice.

#317
LAMB OREGANO, FRIED

8 Lamb Chops
$^1/_4$ cup Olive Oil
1 Tbsp. Lemon Juice
$^1/_2$ tsp. Oregano
$^1/_2$ tsp. Salt
$^1/_4$ tsp. Pepper
1 Tbsp. Flour

Mix oil and spices together. Place lamb in pan. Pour oil over. Let sit 2 hours. Remove chops. Sprinkle lightly with flour. Pan fry. Baste with oil marinade. Turn and repeat. Serve.

#318
• KAFTA SNOBAR
LAMB PATTIES

2 Tbsp. Tahini
2 Tbsp. Lemon Juice
1 toe Garlic, minced
¹/₂ tsp. Salt
1 lb. Lamb, ground
¹/₂ tsp. Pepper
¹/₂ cup Onion, grated
2 Tbsp. Parsley, chopped
1 tsp. Mint chopped, fresh if possible
2 Tbsp. Margarine
2 Tbsp. Olive Oil
¹/₂ cup Pine Nuts
¹/₃ cup Riches Coffee Whitener (Soymilk)
¹/₈ cup Flour

In bowl combine tahini, Riches Coffee White, lemon juice and garlic. Blend well and set aside. Combine lamb, salt, pepper, onion, parsley and mint. Form into balls. Press down with heel of hand to make patty. Dust with flour and fry in margarine and olive oil mixture. Remove meat from pan. Pour tahini in fry pan and mix well. Add remaining flour. Sauté 1 minute. Add pine nuts. Stir well. Pour over meat. Serve at once.

"the mandrake gives fourth fragrances, and at our doors are all manner of precious fruits, — " Song of Songs 8:14.

#319
LAHM BI AJIM
Lamb Pie
Entree or appetizer

PASTRY
1 pack Dry Active Yeast
3 Tbsp. Warm Water

$^1/_2$ tsp. Sugar

1 tsp. Salt

$^1/_4$ cup Olive Oil, retain 2 Tbsp. until end

1 cup Tepid water

FILLING: Sauté meat in oil 3 minutes. Add onions. Stir for 2 minutes. Add all ingredients and sauté 3 minutes. Cool. Mixture should be fairly damp.

2 Tbsp. Olive Oil

$^1/_2$ cup Onion, chopped fine

1 lb. Lamb Shoulder, minced fine

1 tsp. Salt

$^1/_2$ tsp. Pepper

2 Tbsp. Parsley, chopped

$^1/_8$ tsp. Cloves

$^1/_8$ tsp. Nutmeg

$^1/_6$ tsp. Cinnamon

$^1/_3$ cup Pine Nuts, chopped toasted

$^1/_2$ cup Water or Wine

FOR PASTRY: Dissolve yeast in warm water, add sugar. Let sit 10 minutes, then add all other ingredients. Mix pastry into soft dough. Knead until elastic. Add more flour if needed. Place in warm spot. Cover and let sit approximately 2 hours. Punch down dough on work area. Work in the remaining oil. Knead until smooth. Divide into 20 equal balls. With palm of hand flatten each ball into 1/8" rounds. With your thumbs press out sides into a tart shell with sides higher than center. Fill center with 1 tablespoon of the filling mixture. Place on greased sheet pan. Bake 20 minutes at 450°. Serve with sauce.

#320
• ADEN LAMB MEATBALLS

The Yemenite Jews are a very old people who created a distinct cuisine using the Talmud injunctions as the basis for the new San'a menu. One of the dishes that they brought back to the Holy Land was this meat ball dish.

2 1/2 lbs. Ground Lamb
1 cup Kasha (Burgle Wheat) or Bread Crumbs
1 cup Beef Stock
1/4 cup Dry Red Wine
4 Tbsp. Brandy
1/4 cup Cilantro
3 Tbsp. Garlic, chopped fine
2 Tbsp. Pepper
1/4 cup Parsley, chopped fine
2 medium tomatoes, minced
1 small Bell pepper, cleaned and chopped fine
3 tsp. Olive Oil
1 medium Onion, chopped fine
2 medium Eggs, beaten
1/8 tsp. Salt, if this is on your diet

In a mixing bowl combine kasha and wine and let set 10 minutes. Combine lamb, cilantro, garlic, pepper, parsley, and eggs. Blend all together and mix well. Form into ping pong sized balls, and roll firm but not hard.

In a deep sided iron skillet heat olive oil and brown meat balls on all sides. Add onion and sauté until the onions are transparent, then add brandy and all other ingredients and bring to a boil. Cover and reduce heat. Simmer 30 minutes.

Prepare with rice or pasta. Check flavor of the meat ball mixture. Portion on plate alongside the starch. Serve with a small salad.

"Who fed you in the wilderness with manna, —" Deuteronomy 8:16.

#321
LAMB AND PILAV

1 1/2 lbs. Lamb, cubed 1"
2 large Onions, chopped fine
4 medium Tomatoes, peeled, chopped

4 Tbsp. Tomato Paste
4 cups Cracked Burghul Wheat
1 tsp. Salt
$^1/_2$ tsp. Pepper
$^1/_2$ cup Olive Oil or Butter
2 cups Water

Sauté onions in 1/2 of the olive oil until golden. Add lamb and brown well. Add tomatoes and tomato paste. Stir. Add spices, stir. Add water. Simmer 1 1/2 hours. Add more water if needed. In separate pan fry wheat in balance of olive oil. Add pinch of pepper. When nicely colored pour into lamb mixture and mix well. Cover pan and simmer slowly for 10 minutes. All water should be absorbed. Tumble and mix. Serve hot.

#322
LAMB AND POTATOES

1 Leg of Lamb
3 toes Garlic, minced
1/4 tsp. Pepper
$^1/_2$ tsp. Oregano
$^1/_2$ tsp. Thyme
3 Tbsp. Lemon
2 Tbsp. Olive Oil
10 medium Potatoes peeled
2 cups Tomato Juice
6 medium Tomatoes peeled, chopped
1 cup Water

Rub leg in oil, sprinkle spices and herbs over place in roasting pan fat side up and bake 1 hour at 425°. Add potatoes, tomatoes, tomato juice, water and roast at 350° for 1 hour. Baste and turn leg. Roast for 20 minutes. Place leg on serving tray. Surround with potatoes. Reduce pan juice in half and pour over leg. Serve.

#323
LAMB SAUSAGE

4 1^1/$_2$ lbs. Lamb Shoulder, cubed 2"
1 ^{1}/$_2$ lbs. Beef Chuck, cubed 2"
^{1}/$_2$ cup Buckwheat flour
2 Tbsp. Salt
2 Tbsp. Sage
1 ^{1}/$_2$ Tbsp. Pepper
1 Tbsp. Mustard Seed
1 bunch Parsley, chopped

Grind meat through course plate. Spread meat out on board. Sprinkle flour, spices, and herbs over meat. Blend the meat mixture together. Grind mixture through medium plate. Stuff sheep casings and twist off at 4". Tie and refrigerate. Broil over medium heat. Turn often. Check for doneness.

#324
OF MEMULAH
Lamb Stuffed Chicken

1 4-5 lb. Roasting Chicken, washed
1 lb. Lamb Shoulder, ground
4 Tbsp. Oil
1 medium Onion, chopped fine
^{1}/$_2$ cup Almonds, chopped
^{1}/$_4$ cup Pine Nuts
1 cup Rice, cooked
2 medium Tomatoes, peeled, chopped
^{1}/$_2$ tsp. Salt
^{1}/$_4$ tsp. Pepper
^{1}/$_2$ tsp. Cinnamon
8 small Red Potatoes

Sauté lamb in oil and lightly brown. Add onion and sauté 2 minutes. Add almonds and pine nuts. Sauté 1 minute. Mix rice, tomatoes and spices. Blend well. Remove from fire and cool. Rub outside of chicken with oil. Dust with salt and pepper. Stuff bird with lamb mixture. Sew up bird. Place breast down in a roasting pan. Surround with potatoes. Bake at 450° for 35 minutes. Turn bird breast up. Bake at 350° for 45 minutes. Serve.

#325
• LAMB AND SWEET PEAS

2 ¹/₂ lbs. Lamb Shoulder, cubed 2"
3 medium Onions
3 medium Tomatoes, peeled, chopped
3 lbs. Sweet Peas, soaked 20 minutes, drain
3 Tbsp. Olive Oil
1 ¹/₂ cups Water
2 Tbsp. Honey
1 tsp. Salt
¹/₄ tsp. Pepper

Sauté lamb and oil. Brown. Add tomatoes and onions. Sauté 2 minutes. Add water, honey, salt and pepper. Simmer 1 hour. Add peas. Simmer 25 minutes. Stir. Check peas for doneness. Serve over broad noodles or rice.

"Eat like a human being what is served to you, do not chomp your food, or you will be detested" (The Aphorism of Ben Sira) Ben Sira 31:17.

#326
LUCHUCH PANCAKE

1 lb. Flour
1 pkg. Dry Yeast
1 Tbsp. Warm Water
1 Egg Yolk, whipped
3 cups Water
¹/₂ tsp. Salt

$^1/_2$ tsp. Coriander
$^1/_2$ cup Olive Oil

Mix yeast and warm water. Add flour, water, salt and coriander. Mix well and allow to sit in warm place 1 hour. In separate bowl mix egg and oil. Blend well and warm slightly. Combine all but oil and blend well. Heat oil in pan. Pour 3 oz. of flour mixture into pan and bake as Yorkshire Pudding. Serve with Hilbe.

#327
• LENTIL CAKE

FILLING
$^1/_2$ lb. Lamb, cooked and chopped fine
$^1/_4$ lb. Lentils, cooked, riced
$^1/_2$ tsp. Cumin
$^1/_4$ tsp. Red Pepper, cayenne
3 medium Onions, minced
2 toes Garlic, minced
$^1/_2$ tsp. Salt
$^1/_4$ tsp. Pepper
1 Tbsp. Olive Oil

Sauté onions in oil, add garlic and stir. Add all spices, sauté 1 minute. Add lamb and stir. Add lentils. Stir until lamb is warm. Mix well. Set aside.

DOUGH
1 lb. Flour
1 pkg. Dry Yeast
1 tsp. Warm Water
2 cups Water
1 tsp. Salt

Make dough. Let rise 1 hour, then roll out and cut into 4" squares. Set out on floured surface. Allow to slightly air dry 10 minutes. Then place one tablespoon of filling in the center. Pinch together. Deep fry in boiling oil until golden brown.

Serve.

This dinner in a pastry shell was the forerunner of pasti and the pot pie.

#328
LIMA BEAN CHICKEN

3 cups Water
1 5 lb. Stewing Chicken
1 Carrot, grated
2 arms Celery with tops, minced
2 medium Onions, minced
1 lb. Lima Beans, pre-soaked 12 hours
1 cup Soup Stock or Bouillon
1 tsp. Salt
$^1/_2$ tsp. Pepper
$^1/_2$ cup Honey

In a large pot boil water, add chicken, vegetables, limas, salt and pepper. Boil 5 minutes, cover and simmer 1 hour 20 minutes. Add soup stock and honey. Simmer 20 minutes. Check if limas are tender. Serve in turene.

#329
• LIVER, YEMENI FOR 4

1 $^1/_2$ lbs. Liver, sliced, broiled. When just done, cube
1 cup Hilbe

Pour hilbe over cubed liver. Toss well, return to sauté pan. Stir twice over high heat. Serve with rice and zhug on side, with hot Pita bread.

#330
• MOROCCAN EGGS

1 cup Water
1 $^1/_2$ lbs. Lamb, double ground fine

1 bunch Parsley, chopped
1 tsp. Dried Mint
1/2 tsp. Dried Marjoram
1/2 tsp. Allspice
1/2 tsp. Cumin
1/2 tsp. Salt
3 Tbsp. Olive Oil
8 Eggs

Mix lamb, spices and herbs. Blend well. Roll into tiny balls 1" diameater. Heat olive oil and brown meat balls. Roll around to fully brown all sides. Pour in water. Simmer balls 15 minutes. Water should be cooked out. Break eggs in pan. With wooden spoon scramble eggs around meat balls. When well set remove from fire and serve with boiled rice.

"If you follow My Laws and faithfully observe My Commandments, I will grant your rains in their season, so that the earth shall yield its produce and the trees of the field their fruit." (Leviticus 26:3,4)

#331
MUSHROOM LOAF

2 lbs. Mushrooms, washed, sliced
3/4 cup Bread Crumbs, crushed
3 Eggs, slightly beaten
1/2 cup Carrots, shredded
1/4 cup Onions, minced
1/4 tsp. Salt
1/4 tsp. Pepper
1/4 tsp. Thyme
1/2 cup Heavy Cream
2 Tbsp. Flour

Whip flour, cream and egg together until slightly thick. Pour over bread crumbs. Add all ingredients and blend well. Pour into greased floured loaf pan. Bake at 375° 45 minutes. Check that custard is well set. Cool slightly. Serve.

#332
• MUTTON IN QUINCE

2 lbs. Mutton chops
2 lbs. Quince, sliced
2 Tbsp. Olive Oil
1 Onion, sliced
3 small Tomatoes, peeled, sliced
$^3/_4$ tsp. Salt
$^1/_2$ tsp. Pepper
$^1/_2$ tsp. Marjoram
$^1/_4$ tsp. Thyme
$^1/_2$ cup Water
1 cup Dry Red Wine
3 Tbsp. Brown Sugar

Sauté mutton in olive oil. Brown well. Place in casserole. Sauté onion and tomatoes. Pour over mutton. Add spices and herbs. Layer in quince. Add water and wine. Sprinkle sugar over. Cover and bake at 350° for 1 hour 15 minutes. Serve.

Obadiah the steward of the palace (1st Kings 18:4) provided food and drink to the prophets who were in hiding.

#333
MUTTON RICE

$^1/_2$ lb. Mutton, cut into 1" cubes
2 medium Onions, cleaned, chopped
1 cup Rice
$^1/_2$ cup Pistachio Nuts, chopped
3 cups Hot Water
2 Tbsp. Raisins, pre-soaked
$^1/_4$ tsp. Cinnamon
$^1/_6$ tsp. Cloves
$^1/_4$ tsp. Salt
$^1/_6$ tsp. Pepper
1 Tbsp. Oil

In dutch oven sauté mutton in oil and brown. Add onions.
Sauté 3-5 minutes. Pour all remaining over meat. Cover and
simmer 30 minutes. Water should be fully absorbed.

#334
MUTTON SAUSAGE

1 1/2 lbs. Lean Mutton
1/2 lb. Beef Shoulder
1/4 cup Cold Water
1 Tbsp. Apple Vinegar
6 toes Garlic, minced
1/2 tsp. Dry Hot Red Pepper Flakes
1/2 tsp. Salt
1/2 tsp. Pepper
1/4 tsp. Paprika
1/8 tsp. Cayenne Pepper
1/2 bunch Parsley, chopped

Grind meat through course plate. Spread out on board.
Mix all remaining ingredients together and pour evenly over
meat. Mix well. Cover and refrigerate 2 days. Form into
patties and fry in light olive oil. Serve hot.

#335
• MUTTON AND PEPPERS

1 medium Onion, chopped
2 lbs. Mutton or Beef, cubed 2"
8 medium Tomatoes, peeled, chopped
4 medium Green Peppers, cleaned, chopped
1 Tbsp. Flour
1/2 tsp. Salt
1/4 tsp. Pepper
2 cups Water
3 Tbsp. Oil

Sauté onion in oil until golden. Add meat and brown. Add

spices and 1 cup water. Cover and simmer 1 hour. Blend in flour. Mix well. Add all remaining ingredients. Simmer 20 minutes. Serve with rice.

#336
MUTTON AND CARROTS

1 1/2 lbs. Mutton or Lamb, cubed into 1 1/2" pieces
2 medium Onions, chopped
1 toe Garlic, pressed
12 large Carrots, cleaned, sliced
4 Tbsp. Oil
2 Tbsp. Flour
1 1/2 cups Water

Dredge meat in flour. Sauté in oil. Brown well. Add onions and garlic. Sauté 2 minutes. Mix well. Add 3/4 cup water. Cover and simmer 1 hour. Add all remaining ingredients. Cover and simmer 20 minutes. Serve.

#337
•TADJIN
Mutton Stew

1 1/2 lbs. Mutton, cut 2" cubes
1/2 cup Flour
1/4 cup Olive Oil
3 medium Onions, chopped
2 medium Sweet Peppers, cleaned, cut in strips
1 qt. Water
1/6 tsp. Saffron Powder
12 Apricots, pre-soaked in water
1 tsp. Sugar

Sauté mutton dredged in flour in oilve oil. Brown. Pour into a crock casserole dish. Add onions, peppers, saffron and water. Cover and stew for 1 hour. Add apricots and sugar. Check for water. Simmer 20 minutes. Serve with rice.

#338
OX RAGU

1 ¹/₄ lbs. *Boned sirloin, cut into strips*
2 Tbsp. *Margarine*
³/₄ tsp. *Salt*
¹/₂ tsp. *Pepper*
¹/₂ tsp. *Paprika*
2 medium *Onions*
2 Tbsp. *Flour*
1 ¹/₄ cups *Water*
2 Tbsp. *Tomato Puree*

Brown meat in margarine. Add onions, sauté until golden. Sprinkle flour over. Stir. Add all remaining ingredients and simmer 35 minutes. Serve with boiled green lentils.

#339
OXTAIL STEW

3 lbs. *Oxtails, cut at joint*
¹/₄ cup *Flour*
¹/₄ cup *Oil*
8 *tomatoes*
4 *Rutabaga*
2 *Turnip*
2 qts. *Water*
¹/₂ tsp. *Basil*
¹/₄ tsp. *Thyme*
¹/₆ tsp. *Pepper*
¹/₄ tsp. *Dry English Mustard*
1 cup *Mushrooms, cut* ¹/₄"
8 small *Potatoes, washed*
4 *Carrots, peeled, chopped*
2 cups *Dry White Wine*

Dredge tail in flour. Heat oil and brown nicely on all sides. With slotted spoon remove tail to dutch oven. Take remaining flour and add to oil, make brown flour roux. Set aside. In dutch oven add vegetables except mushrooms and potatoes. Add spices and herbs. Add water. Bring to boil. Cover and simmer 1 ½ hours. Add potatoes and flour roux. Simmer 30 minutes. Add wine and mushrooms. Stir and mix well. Simmer 20 minutes. Serve with hot black bread and fig compote.

#340
• PARTRIDGE ROAST

2 Hens, cleaned
$^1/_2$ tsp. Salt
$^1/_4$ tsp. Pepper
2 Tbsp. Oil
$^1/_4$ cup Red Currant Jelly, melted
$^1/_4$ cup Water

Wash birds well, dry, then oil. Sprinkle salt and pepper over. Place in covered pot. Pour currant jelly over. Add water. Bake at 375° for 35 minutes. Check for doneness. To test twist leg bone and see if it moves freely.

"and it came to pass at evening, that the quails came up, and covered the camp;" Exodus 16:13.

#341
• PCHAI
(Regel Kerushah; Kuri, Drelyes, Fisnoga, Pilsa, Pitcha, Footsnoga, Drelies)

1 Roaster Comb
12 Chicken Feet
2 small Onions
1 Rutabaga, sliced thin
2 Carrots, sliced in $^1/_4$"
3 arms Celery
2 Tbsp. Prepared Mustard

307

1 toe Garlic, pressed
1 tsp. Salt
$^1/_4$ tsp. Pepper
2 Bay Leafs
1 Tbsp. Lemon Juice
2 Eggs, hard cooked
1 qt. Water

Clean and scale feet. Cover feet and cocks comb with water. Add all spices and vegetables. Simmer 2 1/2 hours. Strain juice into mold pan. Allow to begin to jell. Slice carrots in 1/8ths. Slice egg and mince comb. Stir lemon and comb into jell, add carrots and sliced egg. Stir gently to properly place eggs and carrots. Refrigerate. Slice and serve with mustard.

#342
• PEPPER STEW

1 Green Bell Pepper, minced
8 Sweet Red Peppers, minced
8 Sweet Green Peppers, minced
6 large Onions, minced
1 cup Sugar
1 cup Apple Vinegar
2 Tbsp. Olive Oil
1 tsp. Dill
$^1/_2$ tsp. Sesame Seeds
1 qt. Boiling Water
$^2/_3$ cup Cold Water

Place peppers in pot with onions. Mix. Pour boiling water over. Let steep for 10 minutes. Drain. Add all other ingredients. Boil softly for 5 minutes. Pour into 3 canning jars and seal, or serve as side dish to roast of beef or lamb.

#343
•DAG KAVUSH
Pickled Fish

3 lbs. Fish, cleaned, save skin, head, bones. Set
  filets aside
3 cups Vinegar
2 large Onions
3 Bay Leafs
2 Whole Cloves
2 Tbsp. Salt
12 Peppercorns
$^1/_2$ tsp. Pepper
2 Onions
2 Carrots $^1/_2$ sliced, $^1/_2$ grated

In large pot combine fish scraps, peppercorns, vinegar,
bay leafs, cloves, 1/2 salt. Cover and boil for 1/2 hour. Strain
and retain broth. Place fillets in casserole dish. Sprinkle
with salt and pepper. Surround with sliced carrots and
onions. Pour stock over. Bring to boil. Simmer 15 minutes.
Refrigerate 4 hours. Garnish with grated carrot. Serve.

#344
• PIGEON STEW

2 Carrots, peeled, sliced
4 Pigeons, cleaned and washed
2 cups Bread Crumbs
1 bunch Parsley, chopped
$^1/_2$ tsp. Pepper
$^3/_4$ tsp. Salt
2 Tbsp. Oil
1 cup Beef or Chicken Stock
$^1/_2$ cup Dry White Wine
1 Tbsp. Cinnamon

In bowl mix crumbs, parsley, salt, pepper and wine to make dressing. Stuff birds. Place birds in greased baking dish. Rub with oil. Dust with cinnamon. Add carrots. Bake at 350° for 40 minutes. Baste with stock. Serve wtih rice and pan juice.

#345
• PILAU

1 cup Olive Oil
2 medium Onions, minced
1 tsp. Salt
$^1/_2$ tsp. Pepper
10 large Carrots, peeled, sliced
1 lb. Lamb Shoulder, cubed
$^1/_2$ cup Black Raisins
3 cups Cooked rice (10 minutes or until rice is al dente)
2 toes Garlic, pressed
1 tsp. Cinnamon

Sauté onions in oil until golden. Add meat, spices, and garlic and sauté until meat is brown. Add carrots, stir. Cover meat mixture with al dente rice. Pour 2 cups water into pot. Cover with tight fitting lid and steam slowly 1 ½ hours. Add 1/2 cup water, sprinkle cinnamon over. Cover and simmer 30 minutes.

#346
POTATO AND LAMB CASSEROLE

1 lb. Lamb and Beef Leftovers, course ground
2 Eggs, beaten
2 Tbsp. Tomato Puree
$^1/_2$ tsp. Salt
$^1/_4$ tsp. Pepper
2 lbs. Potatoes, peeled, par boiled, sliced
2 Tbsp. Parsley, chopped
2 Tbsp. Oil

3 Tbsp. Water

Blend meat and beaten egg. In a greased casserole dish layer potato and meat. In second layer sprinkle 1/2 salt, pepper and parsley. When complete, sprinkle remaining spices and herbs. Sprinkle oil over. Mix tomato and water and sprinkle over top. Cover and bake at 375° for 15 minutes.

#347
FTUT STEW
Potato Stew

4 large Potatoes, peeled, cubed
1 Tbsp. Fat or Olive Oil
2 lbs. Cubed Chuck
$^1/_2$ tsp. Cardamon
4 toes Garlic, minced
$^1/_2$ tsp. Cumin
8 Green Onions, sliced
2 cups Zucchini, sliced
3 small Pita bread, torn in small pieces
3 cups Water

Sauté meat in fat, add spices, stir well. Add vegetables, stir. Simmer 5 minutes. Add potatoes and water. Simmer 1 hour. Add pita, stir. Simmer 5 minutes. Serve with Hilbe on side.

#348
• QUAIL

4 Quail, cleaned, cut in half
$^1/_2$ cup Olive Oil
1 tsp. Pepper
1 tsp. Salt
1 tsp. Thyme
16 large Grape Leaves

Rub Quail well in olive oil, sprinkle herbs and spices both sides. Wrap in leaves. Place in casserole dish. Bake at 350°

for 20 minutes or broil on a medium grill for 10 minutes each side.

#349
QUINCE STEW

2 Tbsp. Olive Oil
2 cups Rice, pre-boiled 10 minutes, rinsed
3 Quince, peeled, sliced
3 Carrots, sliced thin
2 large Potatoes, peeled, sliced
1 cup Zucchini, sliced
2 large Onions, sliced
1 tsp. Cinnamon
$1/2$ tsp. Salt
$1/2$ tsp. Pepper
$1/8$ tsp. Nutmeg
1 qt. Water

Place all ingredients into a covered stew pot. Slowly simmer 8-10 hours. Replace water if required to keep slightly moist.

#350
RHUBARB STEW

1 lb. Rhubarb, tops removed, chop stem 1"
1 lb. Lamb or Beef, cubed
2 medium Onions, chopped
1 bunch Parsley, chopped
2 cups Water
3 Tbsp. Oil
$1/2$ tsp. Salt
$1/3$ tsp. Pepper
$1/2$ tsp. Cinnamon
$1/4$ tsp. Nutmeg
$1/6$ tsp. Ginger

Sauté meat and onions in oil for 3 minutes. Add spices and parsley. Mix well. Add water. Cover and simmer 45 minutes. Add rhubarb. Cover and simmer 10 minutes. Stir. Serve wtih rice or Pita bread.

#351
• RAYOTS - LUNG STEW

3 small Pita bread, torn into pieces
2 lbs. Rayots, washed, cubed
2 medium Onions, chopped
2 Tbsp. Olive Oil
2 Cardamon Pods
1 bunch Parsley, chopped
2 toes Garlic, sliced
1 Tbsp. Zhug
1 qt. Water

Mix all ingredients except Pita together, cover pot and simmer 3 hours. Add Pita and stir. Simmer 5 minutes. Serve.

#352
• SAMAK
Fish Fried

6 Fish Fillets
2 Tbsp. Flour
1 tsp. Salt
$1/4$ tsp. Pepper
$1/8$ tsp. Cayenne
1 cup Olive Oil
2 Tbsp. Parsley, chopped

Mix flour and spices together. Coat the fish filets in flour mixture. Fry in hot oil. Turn and repeat 3 minutesl each side. Remove to paper blotter. Sprinkle with parsley. Serve.

#353
• SHORBI
Lamb Stew

4 Tomatoes, peeled, chopped
2 lbs. Lamb Shoulder, cubed 2"
2 Onions, sliced thin
2 Tbsp. Oil
1 lb. Potatoes, peeled, cubed 1"
4 Hot, Green Peppers, chopped
1 lb. Green Beans, cut 1"
$^1/_6$ tsp. Cayenne Pepper
$^1/_4$ tsp. Salt
$^1/_6$ tsp. Pepper
$^1/_4$ tsp. Paprika
2 cups Boiling Water

Sauté onions and lamb until nicely browned. Pour into covered pot. Add water. Simmer on low fire for 1 hour. Add all other ingredients. Cover and simmer 1/2 hour. Serve with warm bread.

#354
SHORT RIB CASSEROLE

3 lbs. Short ribs, cut every 2 ribs
2 Tbsp. Oil
1 cup Lima Beans, pre-soaked overnight, drained
2 Onions, chopped fine
2 cups Water
$^1/_2$ cup Brown Sugar or Honey
1 tsp. Salt
$^1/_2$ tsp. Pepper
$^1/_2$ tsp. Paprika
3 Tbsp. Lemon Juice
6 Okra, sliced

Sauté ribs in oil until golden brown. Place ribs in greased casserole. Sprinkle spices over. Cover with lima beans, sauté onions in rib pan. Pour over beans. Sprinkle lemon over, add sugar. Bake at 325° for 30 minutes. Add water. Cover. Bake 1 hour. Lay in okra. Bake uncovered 15 minutes. Serve.

#355
• SPICED FISH

3 lbs. Fish cleaned and scaled
¹/₂ cup Olive Oil
3 Tbsp. Lemon Juice
1 tsp. Salt
¹/₄ tsp. Tarragon
¹/₈ tsp. Pepper
¹/₄ tsp. Thyme
1 bunch Parsley

Mix oil, spices, and herbs together. Let sit 20 minutes. Place fish in glass dish. Pour mixture over. Let sit 30 minutes. Turn fish and let sit 30 minutes. Bake for 30 minutes at 375. Baste often.

#356
STRIPED FISH
Serves 6

2 lbs. Striped Bass or Rock Fish, fillets
2 cups Onions, chopped fine
¹/₂ cup Olive Oil
2 cups Green Bell Peppers, cleaned, chopped fine
1 cup Walnuts, ground
1 tsp. Salt
¹/₂ tsp. Pepper
¹/₂ cup Parsley, minced
¹/₃ cup Pomegranate seeds, fresh
1 cup Tahina
3 toes Garlic, pressed

$^1/_2$ cup Lemon Juice
$^1/_2$ cup White Wine or Water
$^3/_4$ tsp. Salt

Sauté onions in olive oil until golden. Add peppers and walnuts. Sauté 5 minutes. Remove from fire and stir in salt and pepper. Add parsley and half of the pomegranate seeds. Stir well, set aside. Blot fish dry and place in well greased baking dish. Spoon walnut mixture over fish. Bake at 350° for 25 minutes. While fish is baking, mix tahina, garlic, lemon juice, and salt. Slowly add wine until proper consistency is reached. It should be thick. Carefully remove fish to serving platter. Pour 1/2 tahina mixture over. Garnish with pomegranate seeds. Serve with warm Pita and extra tahina sauce on the side.

"— I would cause thee to drink of spiced wine, of the juice of my pomegranate." Song of Songs 8:2

#357
• HOLISHKES
Praakes; Holipce, Galuptzes, Ollipses, Prokkes
Stuffed Cabbage

$^1/_4$ cup Brown Rice, raw
1 lb. Chopped Beef
1 lb. Chopped Lamb
1 Carrot, grated
2 Eggs, beaten
2 medium Onions
$^1/_2$ tsp. Salt
$^1/_4$ tsp. Pepper
1 large Cabbage
$^1/_4$ tsp. Sour Salt (Citric acid crystals)
$^3/_4$ cup Brown Sugar
1 cup Tomato Ketchup
2 cups Water

In a large bowl mix beef, lamb, rice, carrot, eggs, onions,

salt and pepper. Set on counter for 30 minutes. Strip cabbage leafs and drop them into boiling water. Cover pot and remove from fire. When cool enough to handle with your fingers, pour off water, and take a leaf, put a teaspoon of the meat mixture in center. Roll up leaf, tuck in end, place seam side down in a greased baking dish. Repeat and squeeze the roll ups together. Mix sugar, ketchup, sour salt, and water together. Blend well and pour over the roll ups. Cover and bake at 350° for 1 hour. Uncover and bake 20 minutes. Add water if pan becomes dry.

#358
• SWEET BURGHUL

2 tsp. Semneh — butter mix
1 cup Burghul
3 cups Water
1 tsp. Cinnamon
$^1/_6$ tsp. Salt
$^1/_2$ cup Honey

Place water, burghul and salt in pot. Simmer 30 minutes. Add cinnamon and stir well. Add honey and simmer 2 minutes. Serve. Sprinkle cinnamon powder on top.

Deuteronomy 8:7,8 "— God is bringing you into a good land — a land of wheat and barley — "

#359
• KILIC SIS
Swordfish, Broiled

4 Fillets of Swordfish
1 large Onion, sliced thin
4 Tbsp. Lemon Juice
3 Tbsp. Olive Oil
$^1/_2$ tsp. Salt
$^1/_4$ tsp. Pepper

12 Bay Leaves, soaked in warm water
Mix onion, lemon, olive oil, salt and pepper. Place fish in flat dish. Pour seasoning mixture over top of fish. Let marinate 2 hours. Pour water off of bay leaves. Remove fish and cube into 4 pieces each. Place on skewer: bay leaf, fish, bay leaf, fish, bay leaf, fish, bay leaf, fish. Repeat for each skewer. Brush with marinate. Broil 3 minutes. Turn, broil 4 minutes, turn. Broil 2 minutes. Remove and serve with rice.

DARCHAY TSHUVA supports the position that the Israeli swordfish called 'Fish Ispada' is fit. Rabbi Klein is the authority of the position that sword fish is indeed kosher and "fit" under the law even though the fish throws its scales before it becomes an adult.

#360
• UKKHA
Vegetable Puree and Fish

3 lbs. Fish Fillets
1 Onion, cleaned, chopped
2 Tbsp. Butter
3 arms Celery, washed, chopped
1 Parsnip, washed, chopped
1 Carrot, peeled, chopped fine
1 tsp. Marjoram
¹/₄ tsp. Salt
¹/₄ tsp. Pepper
2 cups Vegetable Stock
2 Eggs

Sauté all except fish and eggs. Simmer 30 minutes. Add liquid as required. Force through sieve. Heat. Whip in egg. Pour into casserole dish. Layer fish on top. Bake at 350° until fish is nicely browned. Brush butter over top. Remove from heat. Serve with sour cream.

#361
• TAJEIN JAJA ZITOON
Olived Chicken

2 Stew Chicken
2 toes Garlic, sliced
1 tsp. Salt
$^1/_2$ tsp. Pepper
$^1/_2$ tsp. Paprika
$^1/_4$ tsp. Turmeric
3 Tbsp. Olive Oil
2 Pickled Lemons
1 cup Green Olives, minced
1 qts. Water

Oil chickens inside and out with olive oil then dust with spices. Broil birds on each side for 5 minutes. Place birds in large pot with water. Add garlic. Bring to boil. Add olives, lemons and left over oil. Simmer slowly 2 hours. Serve chicken topped with olives from pot. Strain. Retain juice to boil rice.

#362
SOFRITO
Veal Braised

8 slices Veal Shoulder
1 cup Flour
1 tsp. Thyme
$^1/_2$ tsp. Pepper
$^1/_4$ tsp. Salt
$^1/_8$ tsp. Basil
3 toes Garlic, minced, retain
2 Tbsp. Vinegar
1 bunch Parsley, chopped
$^1/_4$ cup Olive Oil
1 cup Water

Mix flour spices and herbs together. Dip veal in water. Shake off excess. Press into flour mixture, turn and coat second side. In heavy skillet heat oil. Add garlic and parsley. Brown meat on medium fire. Turn and repeat. Pour 1 cup water over. Simmer 40 minutes. Turn meat twice. Do not let pan cook dry. Check for tenderness. Serve with rice.

#363
VEAL IN BEER

3/4 lb. Veal Breast, cut with pocket
1 cup Bread Crumbs
1/2 cup Onion, chopped fine
1 Tbsp. Margarine
2 toes Garlic, pressed
1/4 cup Dry Red Wine
1/2 tsp. Salt
1/6 tsp. Pepper
1/4 tsp. Paprika
3/4 cup Brown Sugar
4 large Tomatoes, peeled, chopped fine
1 Tbsp. Tomato Paste
12 oz. Beer
1 cup Water

Sauté onion in margarine. Mix in bread crumbs. Add wine. Stir well. Stuff pocket and sew up. Place veal in greased baking dish. Add tomatoes and tomato paste. Add spices and herbs. Sprinkle sugar over. Pour in beer. Bake at 325° for 1 hour. Add water. Bake 2 hours.

Proverbs 23:32 says go easy when drinking wine, and don't mix your drinks, because "at the least it biteth like a serpent, and stingeth like a basilisk. And you — shall behold strange things."

#364
• VENISON CURRY

2 lbs. Venison Shoulder, cubed 1"
2 Tbsp. Olive Oil
1 qt. Water
2 Tbsp. Curry
¹/₂ tsp. Pepper
¹/₄ tsp. Cumin
8 Tomatoes, peeled, chopped
¹/₂ cup Raisins, soaked in warm water
3 toes Garlic, minced

Mix spices, herbs and vegetables together. Add 1/2 cup of the water. Simmer 5 minutes. Place lamb and water in pot and bring to boil. Simmer 20 minutes. Skim. Add spice mixture. Simmer 2 hours. Liquid should reduce to 1/2. Serve over rice.

#365
• VENISON GRILLED

Prepare joint of all wild game the same way. Skewer with long rod. Be sure leg is well balanced for the spit. Rub well with olive oil. Sprinkle with salt, pepper, thyme and dill. Grill over fairly hot fire. Should cook 1 ½ hours. Baste often with spice oil. Do not let skin burn.

#366
• VENISON KABOB
Serves 12

1 full rib eye, sliced 1" thick
1 lb. Mushroom caps
24 Bay leaves, pre-soaked 4 hours in warm water
24 Cherry Tomatoes
1 cup Olive Oil

¹/₂ cup Apple Vinegar
¹/₂ tsp. Pepper
1 tsp. Thyme
Mix oil, vinegar, pepper and thyme. Lay venison out in pan. Pour marinate over. Let sit 6 hours. Take skewer and thread rib eye folded in half lengthwise, mushroom, bay leaf, tomato, rib eye, mushroom, bay leaf, tomato. Take next skewer and repeat. Baste with marinate, broil over medium heat. Turn and baste until done.

Mother at Hearth Oven

E. BAKERY

#367
BARLEY BREAD

2 cups Barley Flour
3/4 tsp. Salt
2 tsp. Sugar
2 tsp. Baking Powder
1 cup Heavy cream
2 Tbsp. Butter

In a medium bowl combine flour, sugar, salt and baking powder. Stir in cream and butter to form soft dough. Take large greased baking sheet, spoon the dough in lumps onto the sheet. Dust hands with flour and pat dough into a circle loaf 1/2"-3/4" thick x 14" in diameter. Take fork and mark cuts. Bake at 450° for 12 minutes. Lightly brown. Cut like pie, butter pieces. Serve hot.

Cake is the symbol of victory (Judges 7:13-14) Gideon, son of Joash, The Judge-General spoke of "a cake of barley in the Midianite camp."

#368
• BARLEY, LENTIL BREAD

1 1/2 cups Ap Flour
1 3/4 cups Barley Flour
1/4 cup Green Lentils, crushed
3 pkgs. Dry Yeast
3 Tbsp. Warm Water
1 tsp. Sugar
1 1/4 cups Chicken Broth
2 Tbsp. Honey
1 tsp. Salt
3 Tbsp. Oil

Combine yeast, water, and sugar and let sit 10 minutes.

Mix flours together, pour yeast in and mix. Add all remaining ingredients. Mix and knead on floured surface until smooth and elastic. Cover and let rise 30-40 minutes. Punch down and knead. Divide in two. Place in two greased 9 x 5 pans. Let rise 30 minutes. Bake at 375° for 45 minutes. Top should be nicely brown.

1st Kings 19:6 "and there, beside his head, was a cake baked on hot stones —"

#369
LEHEM SHAHOR
BLACK BREAD

1/4 cup Rolled Oats
1/2 cup Wheat Germ
1/4 cup Millet
1/2 cup Buckwheat Flour
1 cup Rye Flour
2 1/2 cups Whole Wheat Flour
1 cup Ap White Flour
3 pkgs. Dry Yeast
1 1/2 cups Warm Water
1 cup Milk or Leben
1/4 cup Molasses
1 Tbsp. Salt
2 Tbsp. Crisco, soft

In a large bowl add water and dry yeast. Whisk. Let sit 5 minutes then stir in milk, molasses, salt, wheat, rolled oats, germ, buckwheat flour and millet. Blend well. Add shortening. Stir well. Add slowly, alternating, rye flour and whole wheat. Stir until dough pulls away from bowl. It will be stiff. Add Ap flour slowly. Cut in with spoon or hands. Blend well. If wet add a little more Ap flour. Turn out on floured surface, knead and dust, dust and knead until dough is no longer sticky. It will be thick and hard to work with. Knead some more. Place in greased bowl. Cover tightly. Let rise 1 hour 10 minutes. Knock down, cut in half. Flatten out. Fold each piece in half. Pinch seams together. Place in greased 8 x 4 baking pan. Cover let rise 1 hour. Bake at 375° for 50-55 minutes. Test for doneness. Cool on wire rack.

#370
BROWN BREAD

3 cups Ap Flour
1 cup Wheat Flour
$^1/_4$ cup Wheat Germ
1 $^1/_2$ cups Oat Meal — rolled oats
$^3/_4$ cup Cracked Wheat — bulgar
1 cup Rye Flour
2 $^1/_2$ cups Warm Water
2 pkgs. Dry Yeast
3 Tbsp. Unsulfered Molasses
2 Tbsp. Honey
2 tsp. Salt
3 Tbsp. Margarine
2 cups Milk or Leben
1 cup Sharp Cheddar Cheese, chopped

Scald milk and margarine, add salt, molasses and honey. Blend well. Cool. Dissolve yeast in warm water. Let sit 3 minutes. Blend into milk mixture. Add flours and grain, a little of each and mix, repeat. Dough should leave side of pan. Add more Ap flour if required. Knead on floured surface. Dough should be smooth and elastic. Ball and place in greased bowl. Cover and let rise 1 1/2 hour in warm spot. Knead down. Add cheese. Cut in half and place in baking pans. Cover and let rise 1 hour. Bake at 375° for 40 minutes. You will need to test for doneness to establish the exact cooking time for your city. Brush top with butter. Cool. Serve.

"Jacob said, the Lord will give me bread to eat, —" Genesis 28:20.

326

#371
• BUBKA

Use standard challah recipe. Instead of braiding the dough, press out like a dough for jelly roll.
Mix all together:
¹/₄ cup Cinnamon
2 tsp. Nutmeg
¹/₂ tsp. Ginger
¹/₂ cup Raisins, pre-soaked
6 Figs, chopped
¹/₂ cup Sugar
Spread evenly over dough and roll up tight. Pinch ends and place on cookie sheet. Oil top with margarine and lightly dust with 1 tablespoon cinnamon sugar. Let rise 30 minutes. Bake 375° for 40 minutes. Cool. Serve.
Genesis 40:2 says that there were 57 different kinds of bread.

#372
BUCKWHEAT BREAD

2 cups Buckwheat Flour
¹/₂ cup Prunes, chopped
¹/₂ cup Brown Sugar
1 ³/₄ cups Buttermilk or Leben
1 ¹/₂ tsp. Salt
¹/₂ tsp. Baking Powder
2 Tbsp. Raisins, pre-soaked
In a large bowl combine buttermilk, sugar, salt and baking powder. Stir well. Add flour. Mix well. Add prunes and raisins. Blend. Pour into greased wax paper lined 8 x 4 loaf pan. Let rest. Pre-head oven to 325°. Bake at 325° for 45 minutes. Test for doneness with toothpick. Cool upside down on rack. Remove pan. Let age overnight.
Buckwheat is an herb and not a true cereal grain, but has

been used as a bread flour since the earliest times.

#373
CARAWAY RYE BREAD

2 cups Rye Flour
3 cups Stone Ground White Flour
¹/₂ cup Ap Flour
2 Tbsp.Cornmeal
4 pkgs. Dry Yeast
2 cups Warm Water
1 tsp. Sugar
2 tsp. Salt
2 Tbsp. Oil
1 tsp. Caraway Seeds (blend in or put on top)

Dissolve yeast in sugar and water. Let sit 10 minutes. Add 2 cups white flour, salt and oil. Beat smooth. Add rye flour and beat smooth. Add remaining flour and beat smooth, knead until elastic. Cover with damp towel and let rise 20 minutes, pound down and knead smooth. Place in greased bowl, cover and let rise 1 hour. Punch down and let rise a second time. Cut dough in half, form into round loaves. Take an extra teaspoon of corn meal and flour baking sheet. Place loaves on sheet. Sprinkle caraway seeds over. Bake at 375° for 45 minutes. Cool.

#374
• YEMINITE ROLLS
CHAKNUIN

8 ¹/₂ cups Flour
3 ¹/₄ cups Water
¹/₂ tsp. Salt
¹/₃ cup Sugar
8 oz. Margarine

Mix flour, water, salt and sugar. Blend well and let rise

1 hour. cut into 12 equal pieces. Roll out each piece and spread with margarine. Fold in half and spread top with margarine. Fold in half again. Roll up long way, as you would for jelly roll. Place on cookie sheet and bake in warm oven, 150° fahrenheit for 10 hours. Place pan of water on shelf below the roll pan. This is a traditional dish that is a fine yeast roll replacement. In the olden days these rolls were baked in the oven after cooking was complete and the fire was banked for the night.

Genesis 49:20 relates how Asher produced and sold cakes and fancy bread to the Phoenicians.

BARKHOS;HALLAH, TATSHERES, HALLA, CHALLAH

Hallah is the traditional bread of the Sabbath. It is braided and made of the best flour. Making fresh Hollah — Hallah — Challah, is the ultimate pleasure — warm and caring. The taste is without equal. This is the bread of the rich man. So on sabbath all are rich and we eat Hallah. Sprinkle poppyseeds or sesame seeds over the top of the bread to symbolize the manna which fell in the desert. Tradition has us set aside a small piece of the dough as a gift to God. (Numbers 15:17).

#375
HALLAH PEGGY

2 pkgs. Yeast
¹/₄ cup Lukewarm Water
1 tsp. Sugar
6 cups Flour
1 tsp. Salt
3 Eggs
4 Tbsp. Vegetable Oil
2 Tbsp. Sugar

1 ¹/₃ cups Hot Water
¹/₄ cup Honey

Dissolve yeast in warm water. Add sugar. Sift flour and salt in a bowl. Make a well in center of flour and add dissolved yeast. Cover and let stand. Beat eggs in separate bowl. Combine oil, sugar and hot water. Cool. Stir into yeast mixture. Combine all and mix. Knead on a floured board. Knead firmly until ball becomes smooth and elastic. Place in greased bowl. Cover and let rise 1 hour 20 minutes. Knead a second time. Turn and work, turn and work. Divide into 4 parts. Form 3 8" ropes. Braid. Pinch ends. Place on greased baking sheet. Take dough left and divide in 3. Make small braid. Place on top of large loaf. Cover and let rise 1 1/2 hours. Brush top with egg wash. Sprinkle poppy seeds over. Bake at 375° for 40 minutes.

11 Samuel 6.17 "David give a cake of bread to every person in the country as a sign of thanksgiving."

#376
CORN BREAD

1 ¹/₃ cups Corn Meal
1 tsp. Sugar
¹/₃ cup Flour
1 tsp. Baking Powder
¹/₂ tsp. Soda
1 Egg, beaten
1 cup Sour Cream
2 Tbsp. Oil
¹/₂ tsp. Salt
3 Tbsp. Parsley, chopped

Sift together all dry ingredients. Blend egg, sour cream, oil and whip lightly. Combine with flour. Blend well. Add remaining ingredients. Blend. Pour into a greased 8" pan and bake at 400° for 20-25 minutes.

#377
CORN CAKE

1 cup Corn meal
1 cup Boiling Water
1 tsp. Salt
1 tsp. Oil

Mix corn meal and salt. Pour in water and mix well. Spoon onto very hot pan in pancake size. Brown both sides. Cover. Turn heat down and steam 5 minutes.

#378
LEHEM SHAMIR
Dill Bread

2 pkgs. Dry Yeast
$1/4$ cup Warm Water
$1/2$ tsp. Sugar
1 cup Creamed Cottage Cheese, warmed
2 tsp. Brown Sugar
2 Tbsp. Onion, grated
2 tsp. Dill
$3/4$ tsp. Salt
$1/4$ tsp. Baking Soda
1 Egg
$2 1/2$ cups AP Flour
1 tsp. Oil

Mix yeast, water and sugar. Set aside for 8 minutes. In mixing bowl combine cottage cheese, sugar, onion, oil, dill, salt, soda, egg and bubbling yeast. Add flour and beat well. Form into ball, place in greased bowl. Cover and let rise 1 1/2 hours. Knead down. Form into ball and place in greased 2 qt. round baking pan. Cover and let rise 30 minutes. Bake at 350° for 45 minutes. Brush top with butter and sprinkle crystal salt over. Cool.

Numbers 15:19 "and you will eat of the bread of the land."

#379
• FLAT BREAD

¹/₂ cup AP Flour
1 cup Barley Flour
¹/₂ cup Sesame Seeds, crushed into flour
¹/₂ cup Onion, minced
1 cup Water
¹/₆ tsp. Salt
¹/₂ cup Leben

Mix all together and make a damp pancake. Place on flour dusted baking sheet and bake at 350° for 20 minutes. Turn twice. Eat hot.

The prophet Elijah (Eliyahu Ka-Navi) asked a widow woman for water and a piece of bread. Kings 17:7-16. Bread has become the symbol of faith and hope.

#380
GINGERBREAD MEN

4 cups White Flour
2 tsp. Cinnamon
1 tsp. Nutmeg
¹/₂ tsp. Cloves
¹/₄ tsp. Baking Soda
2 cups Brown Sugar
1 ¹/₂ cups Soft Butter
1 Egg
¹/₄ cup 10 x Sugar for dusting

Cream butter and eggs. Mix flour and all spices. Add soda. Blend with creamed butter. Mix well. Chill dough in refrigerator at least 2 hours. Roll out on floured board. Cut with gingerman cutter or with sharp knife, cut into 3" triangles. Place on dry cookie sheet. Place in 350° oven for 8-9 minutes. Cool slightly. Dust with 10 x sugar.

Gingerbread and cookies are a historic Egyptian food and were brought back to Israel from the Exodus. Both countries still enjoy the cakes and cookies. Dry gingerbread is good as the base for stuffing of goose.

Lamentations 1:11 "all her people sigh, they seek bread; they have given their pleasant things for food —"

#381
• OOGAT "HAWEIJ"
Ginger Cake

2 1/4 cups AP Flour
2/3 cup Butter
3/4 cup Brown Sugar
2 Tbsp. Molasses
3 Tbsp. Warm Water
1 tsp. Lemon Rind, grated
1 tsp. Soda
1/2 tsp. Salt
1 tsp. Cinnamon
1 tsp. Cloves
1/2 tsp. Nutmeg
3/4 tsp. Cardamon
1/2 tsp. Ginger

Cream butter and sugar, add spices, mix. Add water, molasses and lemon rind. Whip together. Add dry ingredients and mix well. Knead until smooth. Ball. Place in refrigerator for 2 hours, on floured surface. Roll out 1/4" thin. Cut into diamond shapes. Place on greased cookie sheet. Bake at 350° for 8-10 minutes. Cool.

"If thine enemy be hungry, give him bread to eat, if he be thirsty give him water to drink," Proverbs 26:21.

#382
• HALKE

3 cups Flour
2 tsp. Baking Powder
3 Eggs
3 Tbsp. Brown Sugar
$^1/_4$ cup Schmaltz — rendered chicken fat
1 Tbsp. Onion, grated
$^1/_2$ cup Warm Water
1 tsp. Salt
$^1/_6$ tsp. Pepper
$^1/_4$ tsp. Cinnamon

Beat eggs, add sugar, water, schmaltz, onion, salt, pepper, cinnamon and mix well. Mix flour and baking powder. Knead into egg mixture and work until moist bisquit dough. Add flour if needed. Use as topping for any meat casserole in balls or dumplings.

Exodus 2:20 "ask him in to break bread" the priest of Midian asked Moses to eat with him as a sign of "Thanks" for his "friendship."

#383
HAMISH COOKIES

3 Eggs
1 cup Sugar
1 cup Oil
1 tsp. Baking Powder
$^1/_6$ tsp. Salt
2 tsp. Cinnamon
$^1/_4$ tsp. Nutmeg
3 cups Flour
1 tsp. Vanilla
1 cup Nuts, chopped fine
$^1/_4$ cup Coconut

Cream eggs, sugar and oil. Add all other ingredients. Mix well. Divide into 4 equal balls. Roll out into long narrow strips. Bake at 325° for 30 minutes. Slice every 1/2". Return to oven to dry.

#384
• HONEY SOURDOUGH BREAD

4 Tbsp. Corn Meal
2 cups Sourdough Starter
3 cups AP Flour
1 cup Whole Wheat Flour
2 cups Buttermilk

Mix all together and blend well in a crock or glass bowl. Cover with damp towel and set in a warm spot overnight. Then add:

2 Tbsp. Butter
2 Tbsp. Brown Sugar
1 1/2 tsp. Salt
1/4 cup Honey
1 cup Whole Wheat Flour
2 Tbsp. Bran

Knead well until smooth and satiny. Add AP flour if needed, 1 Tbsp. at a time. Better a little under than a little over. Form into ball and let rest 20 minutes. Cut in half and place in well greased loaf pans. Cover with damp towel and let rise 1 hour 20 minutes. Bake at 375° for 25 minutes. Reduce heat to 325° and bake 20 minutes. Check for doneness with toothpick in center. Cool on wire rack. Serve warm.

Two loaves of bread are used on the Sabbath and holy days as a reminder of the double portion of manna which was gathered on "the sixth day" in preparation for "The Sabbath." (Exodus 16:5)

#385
KAMISH ROLL

3 *Eggs*
³/₄ cup Oil
1 tsp. Cinnamon
¹/₆ tsp. Nutmeg
¹/₈ tsp. Ginger
¹/₂ tsp. Salt
³/₄ cup Oil
2 Tbsp. Potato Starch
³/₄ cup Matzo Cake Meal
³/₄ cup Nuts
1 Tbsp. Lemon Juice

Cream eggs, sugar and oil. Add all dry ingredients and allow to sit 20 minutes. Moisten hands with oil and shape mixture into 4 long rolls. Bake at 350° for 30 minutes. Remove, cut into 1/2" slices. Return to oven for 10 minutes of drying.

"you shall make a gift to the Lord from your first yield of your baking,—" Numbers 15:21.

#386
KASHA BREAD

2 cups Whole Wheat Flour
1 cup Buckwheat Flour
1 cup Kasha (Buckwheat groats)
2 pkgs. Dry Yeast
2 cups Water
¹/₂ tsp. Salt
¹/₄ cup Butter
¹/₃ cup Molasses
1 Tbsp. Salt
¹/₂ tsp. Clove
¹/₂ tsp. Cinnamon

¹/₆ tsp. Nutmeg
3 Tbsp. Warm Water
1 Tbsp. Brown Sugar
³/₄ cup Warm Water

Soak kasha in 2 cups of water for 8 hours. Drain off water. Place damp Kasha in top of double boiler with 1/2 tsp. salt, mix. Simmer 20 minutes. Measure 1¼ cups kasha and place in mixing bowl. Add butter, molasses, salt and spices. In separate bowl mix yeast, sugar and 3 Tbsp. warm water. Let sit 3 minutes add to kasha mixture. Stir. Add flours and 3/4 cup warm water. Make a stiff dough, beat. Add more flour if wet. Beat. Place in bowl, cover and let rise 1 hour. Pound down, knead. Roll into ball. Place in greased loaf pan, cover and let rise 1 hour. Place in cold oven. Set at 400°, bake for 15 minutes. Turn down to 350° and bake 50 minutes. Turn off oven and let bread coast 10 minutes more. Serve warm.

"as for Asher, his bread shall be fat, and he shall yield royal dainties." Genesis 49:26.

#387
• KHOUBZ
Arab Bread

4 cups AP Flour
1 pkg. Dry Yeast
2 tsp. Salt
2 Tbsp. Oil
1 cup Hot Water, <u>not</u> boiling, put your finger in
1 Egg, whipped with 1 tsp. water

Mix 1/2 of flour, yeast, salt, oil and hot water and beat well for 3 minutes. Stir in balance of flour a little at a time. Be sure dough is not sticky. Add more flour if needed. Knead on floured surface for 5 minutes. You must really work the dough hard. Take out all your hostilities and smack it around. Cut into 8 equal pieces. Cover and let rise 30 minutes. Roll out in pancake shape very, very, very thin.

Place on floured baking sheet. Brush egg wash over pancake. Cover and let rise 20 minutes. Bake in very hot — 500° oven for 10 minutes. The pancake should be nicely puffed and light brown.

"A man came from Baal-Shalishah and he brought the man of God some bread of the first reaping —" 2nd Kings 4:42

#388
• MACHSHEE

1 cup Farina
3 cups Water
1 tsp. Salt
1 bunch Parsley, chopped
2 medium Onions, minced
2 Tbsp. Olive Oil
2 cups Ground Lamb, lightly sautéd in 1 Tbsp. oil.

Simmer farina in salt water for 15 minutes. Remove from fire and stir in parsley, onion, and 1 Tbsp. oil. Blend well. Cool. Form into balls. Press thumb into center of ball. Fill cavity with meat. Plug hole with dollop of farina. Place on greased sheet and bake at 425° for 25-30 minutes. Should be golden brown. This is very similar to the Chinese BAN described by Marco Polo. Sweet meat bun.

"— I also baked bread on the coals, I roasted meat and ate it —" Isaiah 44:19.

#389
• MATZO FOR PASSOVER

The rules:
1. Protect the ingredients from moisture
2. Prepare the dough rapidly
3. Cook at high temperatures

Shemurah flour is the only flour to be used if pre-prepared. You may grind you own wheat. The water must be spring water and allowed to sit overnight in a dark place, cool and still.   When you are ready to start, wash your hands in cold water.

In a new bowl mix:
3 ¹/₄ cups Flour
1 cup Water

Mix and knead. Break into small balls. Knead and flatten balls into a pancake shape 6-7 inches in diameter. Prick with fork.   Place in extra hot oven 500° and bake for 3 minutes. Remove before the Matzo burns.   Total time from start of preparation to removing baked Matzo should not exceed 18 minutes.   Under strict Jewish law this matzoah may not be used at the seder table.

(Exodus 12:17) "And you shall observe the feast of the unleavened bread, — ye shall eat unleavened bread, — Seven days shall there be no leaven found in your houses;—"

Lot fed the two angels (Genesis 19:1,3) "a feast for them and baked unleavened bread, and they ate."

#390
OAT BREAD

5 ¹/₂ cups AP Flour
2 cups Quick Oatmeal
3 pkgs. Dry Yeast
1 Tbsp. Salt
1 ³/₄ cups Boiling Water
¹/₂ cup Molasses
¹/₃ cup Crisco Oil
2 Eggs, beaten
2 Tbsp. Rolled Oats
1 Egg
1 Tbsp. Water

Mix 2 ¹/₂ cups flour, yeast and salt. Blend. In saucepan combine boiling water, oatmeal, molasses and Crisco. Blend well.   Pour into flour mixture and blend with slow electric mixer for 1 minute. Whip on medium high for 2 minutes. Blend in eggs and 2 cups flour. Add remaining flour slowly until dough is soft and free from bowl. Turn out on floured surface and knead well. Place in greased bowl. Cover and let rise 1 hour. Cut dough in half. Press flat and fold in half to fit into 2 well-greased 8 x 4 pans. Sprinkle rolled oats in pans. Place folded loaf in each pan. Let rise 1 hour. Make egg wash. Brush top. Sprinkle rolled oats over. Bake at 375° for 40-45 minutes. Test for doneness.

Ecclesiastes 11:11 "cast thy bread upon the waters, —"

#391
• PAN BREAD

3/4 cup Barley Flour
3 Eggs
1/2 tsp. Salt
3/4 cup Leben or Milk
4 Tbsp. Honey
4 Tbsp. Butter (retain for pan)
1 tsp. Cinnamon/Sugar

Mix all together. In a heavy iron skillet melt butter. Pour dough in pan. Place in pre-heated 425° oven. Bake 15 minutes. Sprinkle cinnamon on top. Bake 10 minutes. Top should be golden brown.

Numbers 15:19 "And you eat of the bread of the land, you shall set some aside as a gift to the Lord" The bread of the land was of the five species — wheat, barley, spelt, oats and rye. As the grain ripened in its season, bread was baked, and a pinch (1/48) was set aside as a gift to the Lord. It was the opinion of the early Rabbis that setting aside a "portion" was a repudiation of idolatry.

#392
• PEDA BREAD

6 cups AP Flour
3 Tbsp. Olive Oil
2 Tbsp. Sugar
1 tsp. Salt
1 cup Milk
2 cups Warm Water
2 pkgs. Dry Yeast
1 Egg, beaten
¹/₄ cup Sesame Seeds

Mix yeast and water. Let rest 5 minutes, beat in 1 cup flour, milk, sugar, salt and oil. Add 2 cups flour and mix well. Add 2 cups flour and mix well. Take last cup of flour and cover work surface. Turn dough out and knead until smooth and elastic. Most of flour will be used up. Cover and let rest 30 minutes. Knead 2 minutes. Cut in half. Place second piece of dough in covered dish and refrigerate. Cut out a ½ cup chunk of dough and set aside. Work dough into a flat round cake. Cut an X in center of cake and work the cut into a hole, smooth and round about 4"-4 ½". Keep working the cake so that it is flattened to 10" or 11" in diameter. Then take the ½ cup chunk of dough set aside and plop it into the hole. Brush the top of the cake with olive oil. Cover and heat oven to 350°. Brush top of cake with beaten egg. Sprinkle sesame seeds over. Bake for 35-40 minutes. Crust is a nice rich brown. Test center with toothpick for doneness. You will need to experiment with this bread to fit your local altitude and humidity. Cool on wire rack. Make second loaf next day. Warm dough in air 10-15 minutes before baking.

Unleavened Bread (Exodus 12:34) "So the people took their dough before it was leavened, their kneading bowls wrapped in their cloaks upon their shoulders, and they left."

#393
PIE CRUST

2 cups AP Flour
1 tsp. Salt
$^1/_6$ tsp. Nutmeg
$^3/_4$ cup Crisco
5 Tbsp. Ice Water

Mix flour, salt and nutmeg. Blend well. Add Crisco and cut in until all shortening is balled the size of a pea. Sprinkle 4 Tbsp. water over. Toss flour well using a stainless steel fork. If dough does not hold together, work in last tablespoon water. Shape dough into ball. Cut ball in half and refrigerate, covered. Roll out the unrefrigerated half on a floured surface. Start from center and fan out. Do not over work, do not squash. When proper size for pan, fold dough in half and lift into pan. Press gently into place. Trim. If a two-crust pie, place first crust in pan into refrigerator. Remove second ball of dough and repeat rolling process. To fill pie, remove pan from refrigerator. Moisten edge of dough with water. Fill with desired filling. Lay second crust over top. With fork press tip into top and cut a V vent, then press tines of fork against edge of pie pan and crimp the two crusts together. Moisten dough edge with water. Bake at prescribed temperature.

Note: to keep edges from over browning, wrap aluminum foil over crimp edge for first 30 minutes of baking. Then remove foil.

#394
MON CAKES
POPPY SEED CAKES

$^1/_2$ cup Oil
3 Eggs
$^1/_2$ cup Honey

3 cups Flour
$^1/_6$ tsp. Salt
$^1/_2$ cup Poppy seeds, washed and soaked 1 hour
2 tsp. Baking powder

Mix all together. Roll out thin. Cut with 3" glass. Place on greased cookie sheet. Bake 375° for 12 minutes. Should be nicely brown.

"The meal offering with them — (shall be) — of choice flour with oil mixed in —" Numbers 29:3.

#395
POTATO BREAD

3 medium Potatoes, peeled, cut in halves boiled, save water
2 $^1/_2$ cups Water
1 pkg. Dried Yeast
$^1/_4$ cup Warm Water
$^1/_4$ cup Butter
2 Tbsp. Brown Sugar
1 tsp. Salt
1 cup Mashed Potato
6 cups AP Flour
1 Tbsp. Wheat Germ
1 $^1/_2$ cups Potato Water, very warm

Dissolve yeast in warm water. Add sugar and mix well. Set to rest. In bowl blend potato water, butter and salt until butter is melted. Add potato and yeast mixture. blend well. Stir in flour and wheat germ, a little at a time. Turn dough out on floured work surface. Knead well. Add flour if needed to produce a smooth and elastic dough. Place in greased bowl. Roll around to coat. cover and let rise 1 1/2 hours. Turn out on floured surface. Punch down. Cut in half. Cover and let rest 15 minutes. Flatten each section into an oblong piece, 3 fold and pinch edges. Place in baking pan. Cover and let rise 30 minutes. Preheat oven to 400°. Bake for 20 minutes.

Reduce heat and bake at 350° for 20-25 minutes. Cool on wire rack.

#396
RICE CUSTARD

1 tsp. Salt
³/₄ cup White Rice
1 qt. Milk
2 cups Water
6 Egg Yolks
1 cup Honey
2 tsp. Cinnamon
¹/₂ tsp. Nutmeg

Combine rice, milk and 1 cup of water and simmer for 50 minutes. Stir often. Add honey and blend well, add salt. Whip egg yolk and water. Pour into rice and stir. Simmer 5 minutes. Pour into serving bowl. Refrigerate 2 hours. Serve.

#397
RICE PUDDING

4 oz Long grain rice, cooked with milk in double boiler
1 pt. Milk
3 cups Cream
5 oz Sugar
¹/₈ tsp. Salt
¹/₂ tsp. Vanilla Extract
6 Egg Yolks, beaten
6 Egg Whites, set aside
¹/₂ cup Raisins, pre-soaked
1 tsp. Cinnamon
4 Tbsp. Sugar

Mix all in same pan except raisins. Bring to soft boil. Stir until sauce thickens. Stir in raisins. Pour into custard cups. Refrigerate. Whip egg white with sugar and make very thick.

Top pudding and serve.

#398
RYE BREAD

$^3/_4$ cup Rye Flour
2 cups White Flour
$^3/_4$ cup Corn Meal
1 pkg. Dry Yeast
1 tsp. Sugar
1 cup Milk
$^1/_4$ cup Molasses
1 tsp. Carraway seeds
$^1/_2$ cup Water
1 tsp. Salt

Soften yeast and sugar in 1 Tbsp. warm water. Combine ½ of the white flour, corn meal and yeast mixture. In sauce pan combine milk, molasses, water and salt. Warm to just below boiling. Pour into flour mixture and mix with electric mixer until well blended. Pour in rye flour and carraway seeds. Mix well. Add remaining white flour. Knead 2 minutes. Cover and let rise 1 hour. Punch down. Place in greased casserole, cover and let rise 40 minutes. Place in 325° oven and bake for 35 minutes. Cover top of bread with aluminum foil. Bake 15 minutes. Serve hot.

"and Joseph sustained his father, — with bread, according to the want of his little ones." Genesis 47:12

#399
SEMOLINA BREAD

7 cups Semolina Flour
2 cups Warm Water
4 pkgs. Dry Yeast
3 Tbsp. Sugar
1 $^1/_2$ tsp. Salt

345

5 Tbsp. Olive Oil
2 Tbsp. Butter
2 Tbsp. Sesame Seeds, roasted
1 tsp. Anise Seed
1 Egg, beaten

Mix yeast, ½ of the warm water, 1 Tbsp. sugar. Let sit 10 minutes. Mix in semolina flour. Blend well. Let sit 5 minutes. Add salt, oil, and butter and knead well. Add remaining water, mix and knead well. cover with damp cloth and let rise 1 hour. Punch down and add sesame and anise seeds. Knead well for 5 minutes. Cut into 4 equal pieces. Roll each into soft ball, place on large greased sheet pan. Cover and allow to rise 1 hour. Wash with beaten egg. Bake in 450° oven for 15 minutes. Reduce heat to 350° and continue baking for 22 minutes. Thump bread with thumb, if hollow sound remove and cool. If not bake 5 minutes longer.

Ruth 3:14 "and Boaz said unto her at meal time: Come hither, and eat of the bread, and dip thy morsel in the vinegar,—"

#400
• SESAME SQUARES

1 cup Sesame seeds
½ cup Honey
½ cup Brown Sugar
¼ cup Boiling Water
⅙ tsp. Salt
½ cup Walnuts, chopped

In a double boiler combine sugar, honey, water, and salt. Bring to boil. Cook until mixture forms a soft ball when dropped into cold water. Add sesame seeds and nuts. Stir well for 4-5 minutes. Pour out on wet board. Mark deep with wet knife. Let relax 10 minutes. Cut through and serve.

Jeremiah 2:17 "I brought you to this country of farm land to enjoy its first fruit and its bounty; — "

#401
SOUR DOUGH BREAD

8 cups Dough Starter, bubbly and light
4 cups White Flour
1 tsp. Salt
3 Tbsp. Sugar
¹/₂ tsp. Baking Soda
3 Tbsp. Oil

On floured work surface mix all together to form stiff dough ball. Knead well until smooth. Place in greased bowl. Cover with damp cloth. Let rise 1 hour 20 minutes. Knead down. Cut into two balls. Place in greased pans, cover. Let rise 1 hour. Bake at 375° for 1 hour. You will need to experiment with this bread to get the right consistency for your particular city. Altitude and moisture play a big part in good sour dough bread. Be sure you do not over fill the baking pans. Do not over knead the dough. Do not work in metal pans, only use glass or crockery. Note: if using potato starter reduce amount to 6 cups.

Lamentations 5:9 "we get our bread with the peril of our lives."

#402
SOUR DOUGH STARTER
Potato

1 medium Potato, grated, raw
1 ¹/₂ cups White Flour, unbleached
1 cup Warm Water
1 tsp. Salt
1 Tbsp. Sugar

Mix water and flour. Blend in slat and sugar. Mix well. Add potato. Blend. Pour into wide mouth glass jar. do not use metal or plastic. Use only wood, glass or crockery. Cover jar with cheese cloth and allow to sit in a warm room for 24 hours.

Stir well. Cover with plastic wrap. Let sit 3 days at 75° to 84°. Do not let heat go over 85° or the yeast will die. Stir well. Refrigerate. When you see 1/2" to 3/4" of clear liquid on top of jar the starter is ready to use.

#403
SOUR DOUGH BREAD DOUGH STARTER
Wheat

3 cups High Glutin Flour
1 pkg. Wine Yeast
1 Tbsp. Warm Water
2 ¹/₂ cups Warm Water
1 tsp. Mineral Salts (yeast food)

Soften yeast with 1 tbsp. water. Mix all together. Beat well. Form into balls. Dust outside of ball with extra flour. Place in covered crock. Keep warm (15 hours) overnight. You will have a nice sharp sour milk flavor the next day.

#404
SPINACH MUSHROOM PIE

1 cup Spinach, boiled, chopped
3 Eggs, beaten
2 Tbsp. Butter
1 ¹/₂ cups Cream
¹/₄ tsp. Pepper
¹/₈ tsp. Cayenne Pepper
¹/₄ tsp. Salt
¹/₈ tsp. Nutmeg
1 cup Swiss Cheese, grated
¹/₂ cup Gruyere Cheese, grated
¹/₂ cup Mushrooms, chopped

Beat eggs and cream together until slightly thick. Sauté spinach and mushrooms in 2 Tbsp. butter. Mix all together. Pour into pie crust. Bake at 375° for 35 minutes.

348

#405
STRAWBERRY PIE FILLING
MOMOSSA; FRUIT PIE

20 oz. Whole Strawberries
1/2 cup Sugar
3 Tbsp. Quick Cook Tapioca
1 tsp. Lemon Juice
1 Egg Yolk, beaten
1 Tbsp. Milk
1/8 tsp. Cinnamon

Mix strawberries, sugar, cinnamon, tapioca and lemon juice in large bowl. Mix well. Add milk and egg yolk. Blend. Pour into 8" pie shell. Cover and bake at 400° for 45 minutes. Note: for parve pie eliminate milk and substitute water. The same filling will work for any soft fruit or berry.

#406
TOMATO-ZUCCHINI PIE

2 cups Zucchini, sliced thin
3 Tomatoes, peeled, chopped fine
2 Tbsp. Butter
1 tsp. Basil
2 Tbsp. Parmesan Cheese
4 Eggs, beaten
1 small Onion, chopped fine
1 1/2 cups Cream
1 cup Grugere Cheese, grated
1/2 cup Swiss Cheese
1/4 tsp. Cayenne Pepper
1/4 tsp. Paprika
1/4 tsp. Salt

Beat eggs and cream together until slightly thick. Sauté butter, onions, tomato and zucchini. When onions are transparent, let cool. Mix all ingredients together and pour into pie shell. Bake 375° for 35 minutes.

#407
SWEET BREAD

2 ¹/₂ cups AP Flour
1 ³/₄ cups Brown Sugar
¹/₂ cup Pine Nuts
¹/₂ cup Raisins
¹/₄ cup Figs, chopped
1 tsp. Cinnamon
¹/₄ tsp. Nutmeg
¹/₂ tsp. Salt
¹/₂ cup Margarine
1 tsp. Baking Soda
1 cup Leben or Buttermilk
2 Eggs, beaten

Mix flour, brown sugar and spices. Add margarine. Cut until crumbly. Stir in nuts. Add soda and mix. In separate bowl mix leben, eggs, raisins and figs. Stir into flour mixture. Blend. Cut in half. Grease and flour 2 round pans. Bake at 350° for 35 minutes. Dust with 10x sugar and cinnamon mixture.

David gave bread to all the men and women of Israel — "to each a loaf of bread, a cake made in a pan, and a raisin cake." (2nd Samuel 6:19)

#408
CHOREK
Sweet Bun

2 lbs. Flour
4 pkgs. Dried Yeast (1 oz.)
4 Tbsp. Sugar
3 Tbsp. Olive Oil
¹/₂ cup Warm Water

4 Tbsp. Butter
¹/₈ tsp. Vanilla Extract
4 Eggs
³/₄ cup 10 x Sugar (you can crush regular sugar)
¹/₄ cup Milk
¹/₂ cup Raisins
1 tsp. Cinnamon

Dissolve yeast in half of the warm water and sugar. Let sit 10 minutes. Stir in 1 ½ cups flour. Blend well. Add balance of warm water. Knead well for 5 minutes. Roll into ball. Grease with 1 Tbsp. olive oil. Place in bowl. Cover with towel. Set aside to rise for 35 minutes.

In separate bowl mix remaining flour and remaining oil, butter, vanilla, and cinnamon. Mix well. Set aside.

In separate bowl beat eggs and 10x sugar, add to yeast dough. Mix well. Add all remaining ingredients together. Knead well. cover and let rise 45 minutes. Cut golf ball size lumps. Roll gently and place on greased cookie sheet. Let rise 30 minutes. Brush tops with egg wash. Bake in 350° preheated oven for 23 minutes.

Psalms 104:14 It is asked, who " — brings forth bread out of the earth, — and bread that stayeth man's heart."

#409
WHEAT BREAD

4 cups Whole Wheat Flour
2 pkgs. Dry Yeast
1 tsp. Sugar
1 ³/₄ cups Milk or Leben
¹/₃ cup Honey
2 Tbsp. Olive Oil
2 tsp. Salt
1 tsp. Cinnamon

Combine 1/2 the flour, dry yeast, and sugar. Mix. In sauce pan, heat milk, honey, olive oil, salt and cinnamon until warm. Pour into flour and mix with electric mixer at high speed for 3 minutes. Stir in remaining flour to make a stiff dough. Turn out on floured board and knead until smooth and elastic. Form ball and place in greased bowl. Cover and let rise 1 hour. Punch down. Shape and place in greased loaf pan. Cover and let rise 35 minutes. Bake at 375° for 35 minutes. Cool on wire rack.

"Make the wave offering of choice wheat flour and lift it high as an offering to the Lord —" Then it was to be eaten by Aaron and his sons. (Numbers 8:11) (Exodus 29:2,3).

#410
• WHEAT BREAD, FRIED

1 cup Whole Wheat Flour
6 Tbsp. Semneh (Butter, clarified)
³/₄ cup Cold Water

Combine flour and 1/2 of the semneh. Cut together and wash with your fingers to produce tiny flakes. Add 1/2 of the water and knead all together. Knead hard. Ball dough. If it does not hold together nicely add more water. Knead for 8 - 9 minutes. Place in bowl, cover and let rest 30 minutes. Cut into 4 equal pieces. Ball. Roll out on floured surface into a thin pancake. Brush top with semneh. Fold in half. Brush top with semneh. Fold in half. Roll out into pancake shape. Repeat with other 3 pieces. When complete cover with slightly damp towel. Let rest 2-2 1/2 hours. Place on dry griddle or fry pan. At medium heat fry until lightly browned. Turn and repeat. Brush top with semneh and cook 2-3 minutes. Turn and repeat. Set aside and cover. Repeat and fry other pancakes. Keep warm until served.

Sarah, at the direction of Abraham, made cakes for "The three strangers." Abraham, as a modest host offered "a morsel of bread."

#411
WHITE CORN BREAD

2 cups AP Flour
1 cup White Corn Meal
¹/₄ cup Brown Sugar
2 Tbsp. Butter
2 pkgs. Dry Yeast
2 Eggs, beaten
1 cup Milk, scalded
1 tsp. Salt
¹/₄ tsp. Cinnamon

Pour milk over corn meal. Stir out lumps. Add butter and sugar. Stir well. Add cinnamon. Stir in yeast. Blend well. Blend in eggs. Stir in salt and AP flour. Beat together 4-5 minutes. Put dough in greased pan. cover, set in warm place. Let rise 1 1/2 hours. Beat down. Ball. Place in greased loaf pan. Cover and let set 1 hour in warm place. Set in cold oven. Bake for 25 minutes at 375°. Set heat at 350° and bake for 25 minutes. Brush top with butter. Serve warm.

Joseph gave to his father "ten she-asses loaded with corn and bread —" Genesis 45:23.

Index

RECIPES INDEX

Leviticus 19:35 "You shall not falsify length,weight, measure —"

Weights

Biblical Weights and Measures

The general weight and measure system was not consistent, nor was it accurate. All weights were approximate. Shekel is the Hebrew word for weight. Silver and gold were weighed against the Shekel.

1 Pim - 2/3 Shekel

1 Shekel - 2/5 Oz. - 11.5 Grammes (Genesis 24:22) (16 grams is the second

    choice)

50 Shekel - 1 Mina - 20 Oz. - 571 Grammes

60 Minas - 1 Talent - 75 lbs. - 3400 Grammes

1 Heqat - 1 Bushel

16 Heqat - 1 Khar - 1 Bag

Barter was the major trade method, but some metal was used as a system of exchange, Abraham paid 400 shekels of silver for the cave of Machpelah. Exodus 30:13 speaks of a 1/2 Shekel tax as "tribute unto the Lord."

Liquid and dry measures were more exact. The most common measure was the Omer. Exodus 16: Omer is the tenth part of an Ephah. An Omer of Manna, placed in a jar by Aaron was put before the Lord, as a reminder to be kept for the generations.

Dry Measure

1 Omer - 1/2 Gallon - 2.3 Litres

10 Omer - 1 Ephah - 5 Gallons (1 1/10 Bushels)

Liquid Measure

1 Hin - 5/6 Gallon - 3.8 Litres (Exodus 29:40)

6 Hin - 1 Bath - 5 Gallons (Bat, Bath) (II Chronicles 2:9)

10 Bath - 1 Kor - 50 Gallons.

Linear Measure
1 Finger — 3/4 Inch
4 Fingers — 1 Palm - 3 Inches
3 Palms — 1 Span - 9 Inches
1 Cubit — 1.5 feet (Genesis 7:20)
2 Spans — 1 Cubit - 18 Inches

Acre — 2 oxen in yolk and the amount of land that they can plow in one day from sun up to sun down.

Some of these measurements are in use today in various parts of the world.

Cost of Foods in the Bible
1 oxen 100 denarii
1 calf 20 denarii
1 ram 8 denarii
1 lamb 4 denarii

According to Matthew 10:29 1 Seah of fine flour or two Seah of barley was 1 shekel. Most payment was in kind, barter, where you traded a crop or cow, or something else you did not need for something your neighbor had that you did need.

30 measures of flour was 335 bushels (1 Kings 5:2)

David bought the threshing floor of Arannah the Jebusite (On Mount Maria) for 50 shekels of silver (600 grams). This was the site of Solomon's Temple.

"A false balance (weight) is an abomination to the Lord; But a perfect weight is His delight." (Proverb 11:1)

Unit Measurement • Metric Measurement • European
Length

1 inch (")	=	2.5 centimeters
1 foot (')	=	30 centimeters
1 meter	=	39 inches
1 kilometer	=	0.6 mile

Volume

1 fluid oz.	=	30 c.c. or milliliters
1 qt.	=	1.056 liters
1 gal.	=	4.224 liters
1 tsp.	=	5 milliliters
1 Tbsp.	=	15 milliliters
1 cup	=	1/4 liter
2 cups = 1 pt.	=	1/2 liter
4 cups = 1qt.	=	1 liter

Weight

1 oz.	=	28 grams
1 lb.	=	450 grams
2.2 lbs.	=	1 kilogram

Temperature

Fahrenheit	Celsius
32	0
100.4	38
257	125
302	150
347	175
392	200
450	232
500	260

U.S. Can Sizes

8 oz. Can	1 Cup
# 1 Can	1 1/3 Cups
# 2 Can	2 1/2 Cups
# 2 1/2 Can	3 1/2 Cups
# 3 Can	4 Cups
# 10 Can	13 Cups

Oven Temperature

Slow Oven	275° - 325° F.

Moderate Oven	350° - 375° F.
Moderate Hot	400° - 425° F.
Hot	450° - 475° F.
Very Hot	475° + F.

Abbreviations

pkg.	Package
tsp.	Teaspoon
Tbsp.	Tablespoon
pt.	Pint
qt.	Quart
C.	Cup
BP	Baking Powder
BS	Baking Soda

USA, Weights and Measures

Liquid Conversion

Unit

	Gills	Pints	Quarts	Gallon	Barrel	Liter
1 Gill	1	1/4	1/8	1/32	1/1008	0.12
1 Pint	4	1	1/4	1/8	1/252	0.47
1 Quart	8	2	1	1/4	1/128	0.95
1 Gal.	32	8	4	1	1/32	3.79
1 Brl.	1008	252	126	31.5	1	119.24

Household Conversion

Unit

	Dram	Tsp.	Tbsp.	Ounce	Gill	Cup	Pint	Qt.
1 Dram	1	3/4	1/4	1/8	1/32	1/64	1/128	1/256
1 Tsp.	1/13	1	1/3	1/6	1/24	1/48	1/96	1/196
1 Tbsp.	4	3	1	1/2	1/8	1/16	1/32	1/64
1 Oz.	8	6	2	1	1/4	1/8	1/16	1/32
1 Gill	32	24	8	4	1	1/2	1/4	1/8
1 Cup	64	48	16	4	2	1	1/2	1/4
1 Pint	128	96	32	16	4	2	1	1/2
1 Qt.	256	192	64	32	8	4	2	1

Bottle Comparison

U.S. Bottle Unit =	Ounces		Ounces	=	Metric
Sixteenth	1				
Tenth	1.6		1.7		50 ML
Half Pint	8		6.8		200 ML
Pint	16		16.9		500 ML
Fifth 4/5	25.6		25.4		750 ML
Quart	32		33.8		1 L
Magnum	50		50.7		1.51 L
1/2 Gal	64		59.2		1.75 L
Jeroboam	102.4		101.4		3 L
Gallon	128				

Cooking Utensils

- Cooking Stone, Kirayim (Leviticus 11:35)
- Fire tongs, Melkahayim (Isaiah 6:6).
- Shovels, Ya'im (1 Kings 7:40).
- Hand-mills, Quarn.
- Jugs, Kad for storing water, meal, corn
- Goat skins, Hemet and Nod, for transporting liquids
- Metal jugs, Zappahat.
- Goat skins, Hemet and Nod, for transporting liquids
- Metal jugs, Zappahat
- Baskets of reeds, palm, clay, for serving of dry fruits and pastry.
- Assorted vessels, Dud, Kiyyor, Kallahat, Parvr, Sir, Zelahah, were use for cooking and sometimes serving. These were vessels of various sizes and shapes.
- Bowls of bronze, silver, gold, iron, copper and clay were used for the serving of foods, hot and cold.
- Three prong fork (1 Samuel 2:13) was used for lifting and turning.
- Knives, Ma'Akelet, for cutting. Knives of flint (stone) survived into the Iron Age due to religious conservatism, and were used in ceremonies whereas iron, brass and copper were for home use.

SUPPLIES

The herbs, spices and unusual ingredients listed in the text, if not easily found in you local supermarket, can be found in any Greek, Armenian or Italian grocery store. Some major metropolitan cities, such as Chicago, San Francisco and New York, now have Arab markets where you can find all the Middle East condiments, flours, herbs, and spice.

I suggest you look in your telephone directory under

Grocers-retail, or Grocers — specialty.
     Here are a few for your consideration:
     Spartan Grocery, 2604 W. Lawrence Ave., Chicago
     Greek Import Company, 2801 W. Pico, Los Angeles
     Morgan's Grocery, 736 S. Roberts St., St. Paul
     Middle East Imports, 223 Valencia St., San Francisco
     Mediterranian Market, 36th & McArthur, Oklahoma City
     Paprikas Weiss, 1546 Second Avenue, NY, NY
     Columbus Food Market, 5534 W. Harrison Street, Chicago
     Nosher's Heaven, 437 Pennington Street, Elizabeth, N.J.
     Malko Importing Co., 185 Atlantic Avenue, Brooklyn,
N.Y.
     Sidney's European Market, 710 Collins Avenue, Miami
Beach
     Syrian Grocery Co., 270 Shawmut Avenue, Boston
     Mourag Grocery, 2419 Market Street, Detroit
     Lekas & Drivers, 98 Fulton Street, Broooklyn
     Olympic Grocery, 4303 W. Vliet Street, Milwaukee
     Should you not be able to find a grocery in your area that
can supply the special needs of this book, a telephone call to
the ladies aid society at the Greek Orthodox Church, The
Armenian or Serbian Church, the Maronite Catholic (Lebanon) will help to locate you needs. I have always found the
ladies to be most helpful and usually I get invited to the
fantastic church suppers.
     Some of the recipes in this book have been modernized for
ease of preparation. The taste has remained true to the
original, and some of the cooking methods have been changed
to fit the needs of today's cooks.

The Artist

Bruce Siegel developed a love for art at an early age. As a son of a fourth generation Cantor and artist, his interest in art was sparked by watching and imitating his father.

Bruce studied art at the Milwaukee Area Technical College, the University of Wisconsin, Pima College and the University of Arizona. He worked as staff artist and instructor in art education for the Milwaukee Board of Jewish Education, during which time he designed their Teacher Creative Center.

The Artist has taught classes in Hebrew Calligraphy, and has designed many covers and pamphlets for the Jewish Community Center as well as the general community.

Bruce currently has his own graphic arts company and is involved in projects ranging from illustrations to teaching, to designing corporate logos and specialized art.

The Prophesy

Amos 9:13,14,15

Behold, the days come, saith the Lord, that the plowman shall overtake the reaper, and the treader of grapes him that soweth seeds; and the mountains shall drop sweet wine, and all the hills shall melt. And I will bring again the captivity of my people of Israel, and they shall build the waste cities, and inhabit them: and they shall plant vineyards, and drink the wine thereof; they shall also make gardens, and eat the fruit of them. And I will plant them upon their land, and they shall no more be pulled up out of their land which I have given them, saith the Lord their God.

Bibliography

Note: In order to keep the bibliography in proper scope and within manageable limits, only those works of direct relevance have been included in the listing. It should be noted that the assistance in locating references for this effort were many and the people directly involved far too numerous to mention by name, however I should like to thank the staff of the Reading Rooms of the University of Missouri, Kansas City; the University of Illinois, Circle Campus, Chicago; Public Library Crown Point, Indiana; Public Library Merriville, Indiana; University of Chicago, Chicago; Wayne State University, Detroit.

Daily Life in Ancient Rome - J. Carcopino, Yale University Press: New Haven 1941.

Encyclopaedia Britannica, vol: 1, 3, 5, 6, 9, 19, 22 — William Benton: Chicago, 1974.

Encyclopaedia Judaica, vol: 1, 3, 4, 8, 9, 10, 11 — Keter Publishing House: Jerusalem, 1972.

"Everyday Life in Bible Times" — National Geographic Society, 1967. Story of Man Library, Melvin M. Payne, Pres.

Farming & Gardening in the Bible — A. I. MacKay. Rodale Press: Emnaus, PA, 1950.

Garden Party on a Rug — Sunset. May 1973. Pages 204-205

Harpers Bible Dictionary — M.S. Miller. Harper and Row: New York, 1973.

Harpers Encyclopaedia of Bible Life — M.S. & J.L. Miller. Harper and Row: New York, 1971.

Hering's Dictionary of Classical Cookery, Fachbuchverlag. W. Bickel. Dr. Pfanneberg Co.: Germany, 1974.

Jews in Their Land — David Ben-Gurion. Doubleday & Co., Inc.: Garden City, New York, 1966.

Jewish Holidays and Festivals, B.M. Edidin. Hebrew Publishing Co.: New York, 1940.

Larousse Gastronomique, P. Montagne. Crown Publishers: New York, 1961

Living with the Bible, M. Dayan. William Morrow Co.: New York, 1978.

Loaves & Fishes: Foods from Bible Times, M. Kinard. Keats Publishing, Inc.: New Canaan, CT, 1975.

Art of Lebanese Cooking, G. N. Rayess, Librairie Du Liban: Beirut, 1966.

Hazor, Y. Yadin Random House: New York, 1975.

Jesus of Nazareth, J. Klausner, Macmillan: New York, 1926.

Herod, J. S. Minkin, Macmillian: New York, 1936.

Middle Eastern Cooking, P. Smouha. Andre Deutsch: London, England, 1955.

Our Oriental heritage, W. Durant. Simon & Chuster: New York, 1954.

Plants of the Bible, L. Untermeyer. Golden Press: New York, 1970.

The Holy Scriptures. Jewish Publication Society: Philadelphia, PA, 1955.

Biblical Archaeology. W. G. Dever and S.M. Paul. Quadrangle, New York Times Books: New York, 1974.

The Way It Was in Bible Times. M. T. Gilbertson. Lutterworth Press: London, 1961.

Lebanon. McKays Guide to the Middle East. E. C. Gellhorn. David McKay Co.: New York, 1965.

How the Early Hebrews Lived and Learned. E. Bonser. Macmillian: New York, 1965.

Archaeology and the Religion of Israel. W. F. Albright. Johns Hopkins Press: Baltimore, 1941.

Foods in Antiquity. A survey of the Diet of Early Peoples. Don and Patricia Brothwell: London, 1969.

Fish Saving: A History of Fish Processing. Chas L. Cutting. New York 1956.

The Oxford Book of Food Plants. S. G. Harrison; G. B. Mansfield: Oxford, 1969.

The Economic Life of the Ancient World. Jean Philippe Levy: Chicago, 1967.

Grain-Mills and Flour in Classical Antiquity. L. A. Moritz. Oxford, 1958.

A History of Domesticated Animals. F. E. Zeuner. London, 1963.

Ancient Egypt: A Cultural Topography. Hermann Kees. London, 1961.

The Holy Bible, King James version. World Publishing Co.: Cleveland, 1940.

Trade Routes and Commerce of the Roman Empire. M.P. Charlesworth. Cambridge University Press: 1924.

The Fruits of the Holy Land. M. Nurock, A Good. Israel University Press: Jerusalem, 1968.

Great People of the Bible. Readers Digest Association: Pleasantville, NY 1974.

Masada. Y. Yadin. Random House: New York, 1966.

Food in History. R. Tannahill, Stein and Day: New York, 1973.

The Book of Legends. H. E. Goldin. Jordan Publishing Co.: New York, 1937.

Jerusalem: City Holy and Eternal. S. W. Baron. Hemisphere Publications: New York 1954.

Ancient Israel. H.M. Orlinsky. Cornell University: Ithaca, 1954.

Jewish Customs and Ceremonies. B. M. Edidin. Hebrew Publishing Company: New York, 1941.

Jewish Holidays and Festivals. B. M. Edidin. Hebrew Publishing Co.: New York, 1940.

Why Be Jewish, M. Kahana. Stein and Day: New York, 1977.

A History of the Jews. S. Grayzel. Jewish Publication Society of America: Philadelphia, 1947.

When a Jew Celebrates. H. Gersh. Behrman House, Inc.:

New York, 1971.

Inside the Synagogue. Freeman and Sugarman: City, 1963.

The Pentateuch & Haftorah. Soncino Press, London, England, J. H. Hertz, C.H. Ed. 1960.

The Way it Was in Bible Times. M. T. Gilbertson. Lutterworth Press: London, 1961.

Epilogue

A Way of Life

From the faith of the descendants of Abraham came the code of the Brotherhood of Man, Hammurabi's code, dealing with the fairness in business relationships. The law of Moses dealt with the heart of man. The Ten Commandments deal with fairness, a guide for peace with self, family, and community, which if followed completely would produce Paradise. One paramount part of the law deals with slavery; no slave could be kept longer than six years, and then had to be set free. No slave could be treated cruelly or be deprived of basic rights. The Hebrews have been the only true Democracy in the history of man.

To understand the Jews, it is necessary for the Christians and the Muslims, to read the Holy Scriptures, the Masoretic text, called the Old Testament, for it is the history of the Jews, and expounds on the soul of the people as they struggled with the "Idea" to create a way of life. This way of life was the basis for the development of Christianity and Islam. Without a full understanding of your past how can you understand your present.

The law of Moses became the model for the French Declaration of the Rights of Man, and the American Declaration of Independence. The summation of the basic law is, "Do not unto another as you would not have him do unto you." Deal justly, love mercy."

If we look at the world today we see immeasurable miseries left by war, we see injustice, slavery, brutality, the threat of war, menace by dictators, the rights of people trampled by despots, we see the "Idea" of the Jews forgotten by Christian and Mohammedan, laughed at by non-believing Russians, we see our world in turmoil. Perhaps if we all redirect our efforts to the Laws of Moses, and the way of life, we can help save the world for our children and our children's children, with freedom for all.

History has written that when the Jew is safe from harm, all the world is safe from harm, and every man may sit under his fig tree and reflect in harmony with those around him. As we eat the foods of the People of Israel, let us all reflect on the total fabric that is all of us.

SHOLOM ALEICHEM

Peace Be With You

Aleichem Sholom